VITALISM

ON THE TRACKS OF LIFE

Gioacchino Leo Séra

Translated from the Italian
by J.M. Kennedy

To the Memory of my Father

CONTENTS

INTRODUCTION

On the Genealogy of Nietzschean Vitalism

The term "vitalism" has become somewhat confused in recent years.

In biology, vitalism refers to a set of ideas going back millennia which hold that living beings are distinct from non-living inanimate objects because they contain some sort of non-material *life energy*, to which different cultures and theorists have given different names.[1] The concept to which vitalism is usually opposed is mechanism. The *Catholic Encyclopedia* of 1913 states that mechanism

> seeks to explain all "vital" phenomena as physical and chemical facts; whether or not these facts are in turn reducible to mass and motion becomes a secondary question, although Mechanists are generally inclined to favour such reduction. The theory opposed to this biological mechanism is no longer Dynamism, but Vitalism or Neo-vitalism, which maintains that vital activities cannot be explained, and never will be explained, by the laws which govern lifeless matter.

Since the distinction between the living and the non-living would *seem* to be self-evident, vitalism was the dominant paradigm in the human sciences, or proto-sciences, for most of their existence, from the ancient Greeks up to the early modern period, though there have always been dissenting voices such as Democritus and Lucretius, who are seen today as forerunners of mechanism. And it is they, and not their vitalist contemporaries, who inspired the scientific thinkers of the Renaissance, who in turn inspired the founders of modern biology and other sciences, such as Descartes, Newton, and later Darwin.

It was against these mechanist thinkers of the early modern period that a new and more nuanced theory of life

---

[1] e.g. Greek *pneuma*, Sanskrit *prana*, Chinese *qi*. More recently psychologist Wilhelm Reich called it *orgone*, and French philosopher Henri Bergson called it the *élan vital*. There are many others—which is not to say that all of these concepts are identical.

energy was asserted in the 18th and 19th centuries. The term "vitalism" was coined by Charles-Louis Dumas in 1800 to refer specifically to the doctrines of Paul Joseph Barthez and the Montpellier School of Medicine. Barthez had developed the concept of the "vital principle" in contradistinction to both the physical body *and* the soul or conscious mind, a third "thing" (though he could never decide if it was material or not) which bears some resemblance to later ideas of the unconscious developed in psychology.

Barthez wrote:

> It seems to me that one cannot help but distinguish the Vital Principle of Man from his thinking Soul. This is an essential distinction, whether one imagines that these two principles exist by themselves and are substances, or whether one supposes that they exist as attributes and modifications of one and the same substance... It makes little difference if one calls the Vital Principle Soul, Arché, Nature, etc., but what is absolutely essential is that no connection is ever drawn between the determination of this principle and the affections that derive from the faculties of prudence or any other faculties attributed to the Soul.[2]

These vitalists—or neo-vitalists, since their ideas were hardly the same as the older and quasi-religious ideas of a mystical life force—made some notable objections to the prevailing mechanist views in science. But ultimately, the existence of vital energy could not be proven to the satisfaction of the scientific method, and today vitalism in the sciences is usually dismissed with Julian Huxley's witty retort that positing a "life energy" no more explains life than positing a "locomotive energy" explains a train.

So what does any of this have to do with philosophy, and more specifically with Nietzsche? Although Nietzsche's

---

[2] cited in "Roots of French Vitalism: Bordeu and Barthez between Paris and Montpellier" by Silvia Waisse, Maria Thereza Cera Galvão do Amaral and Ana M. Alfonso-Goldfarb (*História, Ciências, Saúde – Manguinhos*, Rio de Janeiro, v.18, n.3, jul.-set. 2011.)

philosophy is grounded in biology, he did not put forth any specific theory of biology and science. His overriding position was extreme skepticism towards everything—i.e., the scientific method—and he was heavily influenced by Lange's *History of Materialism* in his early career, as is especially evident in *Human, All-Too Human* and *The Dawn*. Thus to the extent that he takes a side in the mechanism versus vitalism debate, he sides with the mechanists and their skepticism (something which is also true, as we will see, of the author of this book Leo Séra).

The convergence of biological vitalism and Nietzsche comes through Schopenhauer. Schopenhauer, the first great influence on the young Nietzsche, was unquestionably a biological vitalist, as shown by the chapters on "Physiology and Pathology" and "Animal Magnetism and Magic" in *On the Will in Nature*.[3] Although this belief in a *life energy* as such did not carry over into Nietzsche's philosophy, doubtless because it smelled of theology and metaphysics, what did carry over was Schopenhauer's insistence on the *unconscious* nature of the will:

> this *will*, far from being inseparable from, and even a mere result of, *knowledge*, differs radically and entirely from, and is quite independent of, knowledge, which is secondary and of later origin; and can consequently subsist and manifest itself without knowledge: a thing which actually takes place throughout the whole of Nature, from the animal kingdom downwards ...
>
> [K]nowledge with its substratum, the intellect, is a merely secondary phenomenon, differing completely from the will, only accompanying its higher degrees of objectification and not essential to it ... [4]

Thus for Schopenhauer, as for Barthez, neither the conscious volition nor the intellect are the same as the will, or life principle. For Schopenhauer, the will is metaphysical. Barthez could not decide if the life principle was material or

---

[3] "Animal magnetism" is yet another term for the "life energy," from the work of Franz Anton Mesmer.

[4] Schopenhauer, *On the Will in Nature*, Rogue Scholar Press, 2023, p. 24-25

not, immanent or transcendent, but he is in agreement with Schopenhauer that it is not conscious. For Nietzsche, the principle of life was what he later called the *will to power*. Like Schopenhauer's will and Barthez's life principle, it is something other than the conscious mind and reasoning intellect. Unlike Schopenhauer's will, it is entirely immanent in existence.

Nietzsche arguably does leave open the possibility that there is a transcendent element or dimension, insofar as his philosophy, rooted in skepticism and epistemological modesty, does not absolutely deny the transcendent so much as ignore it, since it is not apparent to the senses and is hopelessly mired in abstract concepts and illusions. This insistence on immanence would later be identified as a key characteristic of the school of thought of which Nietzsche would be considered a progenitor, and which would eventually be called "German vitalism"—*lebensphilosophie*.

Lebensphilosophie

Lebensphilosophie is "life philosophy." Its translation as "vitalism" has been somewhat unfortunate, since that term already existed in the sciences and denotes a different set of concepts and ideas, although there is sometimes overlap. Frederick Beiser in his recent study of German *lebensphilosophie* gives the following list of its characteristics:

> a completely immanent philosophy, void of all transcendent entities; individualism and relativism in ethics; opposition to pessimism and an affirmative attitude toward life; historicism and hermeneutics in the study of culture and society; and an individualist and relativist conception of philosophy. *Lebenphilosophie* was the first strictly non-religious philosophy—its first principle was atheist or agnostic—and the first explicitly relativist ethics in the history of Western philosophy.[5]

---

[5] Frederick Beiser, *Philosophy of Life: German Lebensphilosophie 1870-1920* Oxford University Press, 2023 p. vii

Although Nietzsche himself did not use the term *lebensphilosophie* (let alone "vitalism") to describe his ideas and views, that label came to be applied to him and to other, later thinkers who share some or all of these characteristics. Beiser focuses on Wilhelm Dilthey and Georg Simmel, both contemporaries of Nietzsche. Whereas Nietzsche was a right-wing radical—he endorsed Georges Brandes' description of his philosophy as "aristocractic radicalism"—Dilthey and Simmel were both political liberals. Thus, from its inception in these three thinkers, *lebensphilosophie* or German vitalism has been split between its right and left wings.

In his encyclopedic article "Life: Vitalism" for the left-wing *Theory, Culture & Society*, written in 2006, Scott Lash uses "vitalism" and *"lebensphilosophie"* interchangeably and gives the following genealogy of vitalist thinkers:

> There are three important generations of modern vitalists. There is a generation born about 1840–45 including Nietzsche and the sociologist Gabriel Tarde; the generation born about 1860 including the philosopher Bergson and the sociologist Simmel, and the generation born about 1925–33 including Gilles Deleuze, Foucault and Antonio Negri. Contemporary neo-vitalism can in many respects be understood as Deleuzian. There seem to be two vitalist genealogies. One connects Tarde to Bergson and Deleuze, and the other runs from Nietzsche through Simmel to Foucault. The Bergsonian tradition focuses on perception and sensation while the Nietzschean tradition focuses on power.

What we see here is that, as with Nietzsche himself, *lebensphilosophie* underwent a kind of rehabilitation and reorganization after the second World War, with its rightist elements being suppressed or misrepresented. This is largely due to the prominence of Gilles Deleuze, who wrote influential books on Nietzsche and Henri Bergson in the 1960s and who considered himself to be a vitalist, famously declaring, "Everything I've written is vitalistic, at least I hope it is."[6]

The genealogy that Lash establishes for contemporary Deleuzian vitalism is not, however, the only branch that grew from the root of Nietzsche's ideas (or, as followers of Deleuze would prefer to say it, not the only shoot from the Nietzschean rhizome). In his 1932 study *The Vitalism of Count de Gobineau*, Gerald Spring establishes a quite different genealogy of vitalism-*lebensphilosophie*. He sees its antecedent in Romanticism, both in Germany and in France, and the development of Romanticism into *lebensphilosophie* as a result of its fusion with ideas of the active unconscious from the Montpellier vitalists and others.

> The romantic theory of the German poets and philosophers amounts practically to a generalization of the vitalism of biological theorists, they were given to extending the vitalistic formulas to all orders of reality. Depreciating mechanism or cold intelligence these German romantics glorified "vital impulse" which they considered to be the underlying principle of all reality. To intellectual analysis which decomposes the whole into its parts and mechanical construction which builds up by means

---

[6] It's assumed that Deleuze is referring to the tradition of *lebensphilosophie* and not medical vitalism, although there are some intriguing overlaps between Barthez and Deleuze, such that one has to wonder if he read him and was influenced by him. Silvia Waisse writes:

> This is the reason why 'Montpellier vitalists'– Bordeu, Fouquet, and Jean J. Menuret (1733-1815), among others – gave paramount importance to sensitivity, defined as the outcome of the multiplication of specific lives, or little lives, within the organism. In other words, the body should be considered "an infinite assemblage of little bodies, all similar, all equally animated, all equally alive, each with a life, an action, a sensitivity, a functioning, and its own specific movements, and at the same time a general life, sensitivity, etc., common [to all]" (Menuret, 1765, p.240a). ...
> Consequently, the objects proper to the science of man are the forces of the vital principle, the mutual connections between them ("sympathies"), their assemblage into a 'system', their modification according to temperament and age, and their extinction at death (Barthez, 1806, v.1, p.33).

"The Roots of French Vitalism" *op. cit.*

This language of multiplicity, assemblages and connections will be very familiar to readers of Deleuze.

of assembling parts already given, they opposed that obscure power of creation and synthesis working spontaneously from inside outwards which is manifested by what we call life. These romantics recognized this power of life in societies no less than in biological organisms.[7]

Spring's characterization of vitalism is worthwhile:

Vitalism in this broader sense might be called a philosophy of affirmation since it is anti-ascetic, opposing all asceticism in religion and philosophy and destructive or negative intellectualism. … [Vitalists] are inclined to value intuition more than intellect and to glorify "life" as the ultimate reality. Pragmatism follows from this as a matter of course, for *vitalists naturally wish to heighten life and to further it in every way.* … [my emphasis]

Much importance is attached by vitalists to instinct or "unconscious spontaneity" which they view as superior to reason or cold intelligence. Instinct, moreover, has its social equivalent in tradition so that vitalists, as a rule, deprecate undue intellectual interference in social evolution, preferring to trust the irrational or non-rational continuity or spontaneity of life itself. Thus eighteenth Century rationalism and the *Contrat Social* of Jean Jacques Rousseau and their sequel, the French Revolution, are anathema to vitalists. …

Vitalists are advocates of intense living and emphasize the importance of strength of character—one thinks of the cult of energy of Stendhal, Merimée, Gobineau and Nietzsche. Vitalism is anti-intellectual and hostile to rationalism; reason proceeds by means of identity, while life makes for differentiation. Vitalists abhor the abstract notion of man brought into fashion by the *"philosophes"* of eighteenth Century France and the more logical and consistent among them combat the *"égalitaires"* and, in particular, the attempt of Rousseau the rationalist to create an artificial equality among men.

Vitalists tend to distrust the dispassionate use of the intellect and to deny the concept of absolute truth, because they favor

---

[7] Spring, *The Vitalism of Count de Gobineau*, p16-17

individual truths. They sympathize with illusion whenever it is seen to favor life.[8]

What Spring describes here is the vitalism of the Right. This line or branch of vitalist thought, from Gobineau, Stendhal and Nietzsche, to Ludwig Klages and Oswald Spengler, has been largely suppressed and ignored since the second World War, only coming to relative prominence once again in the 21st century thanks to the republication of works by Spengler and Klages,[9] and the popularization of Nietzschean vitalism by Bronze Age Pervert.

There are many similarities and overlaps between the vitalist thought of the Right and that of the Left; often the difference is in how certain ideas are applied rather than the ideas themselves. As Jonathan Bowden noted, the Left has always liked the part of Nietzsche's philosophy which is destructive and critical, particularly towards Christianity. Nietzsche's rejection of conventional morality informs both the leftist and rightist interpretation of him, though in very different ways. For the Right, Nietzsche's "immoralism" means that war, slavery, exploitation, and cruelty must be seen anew, not with the condemnatory eye of a moralist but with a biologist's and anthropologist's eye, in order to understand their functions in the life process. For the Left, immoralism means something else, perhaps best exemplified by André Gide's novel *The Immoralist*, written in 1901 when Nietzsche's corpse was barely in the grave, in which the main character uses Nietzsche's ideas as a justification for pederasty and homosexuality. One can see from this example that the split

---

[8] *ibid.* p11-14. Elsewhere Spring notes that "Vitalistic theorists are given to comparing societies to biological organisms." The clearest examples of this would be Oswald Spengler and Count de Gobineau. Leftist vitalism, in contrast, explicitly opposes the "society-as-organism" idea—see, e.g., Manuel DeLanda, *Assemblage Theory* and *A New Philosophy of Society*.

[9] For an overview of Klages' relation to *lebensphilosophie* see Nitzan Lebovic, *The Philosophy of Life and Death: Ludwig Klages and the Rise of a Nazi Biopolitics*, Palgrave Macmillan, 2013

between leftist and rightist interpretations of Nietzsche precedes World War 2.[10]

In my view, the key distinction between rightist and leftist vitalism lies in their different relationship to nature. Rightist vitalism extols and reveres nature, and looks to nature for its understanding of what life is and how it functions. Nature therefore means biology, animal life, and ecology, but with the key understanding that nature is unequal and predatory. This is especially true of Nietzsche and Klages. For leftist vitalism, nature seems to be the enemy, something to be overturned. They seem more interested in the grotesque than in the beautiful. In this way, "leftist vitalism" is something of a misnomer since it is often theory divorced from biological life; the conceptual and logocentric play of the intellect, divorced from the body.

*   *   *   *   *

The book which you hold in your hands by Gioacchino Leo Séra is a forgotten classic of Nietzschean vitalist thought. It was published in Italian in 1907 as *Sulle Tracce Della Vita (Saggi)* and translated into English two years later as *On the Tracks of Life: The Immorality of Morality*. The English translation was done by J.M. Kennedy, an interesting figure in his own right. He was a British writer and right-wing modernist who wrote for A.R. Orage's influential periodical *The New Age* and who translated Nietzsche's *The Dawn* for the very first English

---

[10] It is true that Nietzsche did quote approvingly the saying of Hassan i Sabbah that "Nothing is true, everything is permitted." However, it should also be noted that he did not necessarily reject the *conclusions* of traditional morality, but rather its method of arriving at them:

> I should not, of course, deny—unless I were a fool—that many actions which are called immoral should be avoided and resisted; and in the same way that many which are called moral should be performed and encouraged; but I hold that in both cases these actions should be performed from motives other than those which have prevailed up to the present time. We must learn anew in order that at last, perhaps very late in the day, we may be able to do something more: feel anew. [*The Dawn*, sec. 103]

edition of Nietzsche's collected works. He also wrote one of the first books in English on Nietzsche's philosophy, *The Quintessence of Nietzsche*, and translated Henri Lichtenberger's *The Gospel of Superman: The Philosophy of Friedrich Nietzsche* from the French.[11]

The translation and publication of Séra's book seems to have happened at the behest of Oscar Levy, the editor of the English translation of Nietzsche's collected works. Levy wrote a glowing review of the book in the December 7, 1907 issue of *The New Age*, and also wrote the introduction to the first English edition, which has been omitted here. A contemporary advertisement shows Séra's book listed alongside volumes by Nietzsche, Anthony Ludovici and Levy's own *The Revival of Aristocracy* as "Other Books Edited by Dr. Oscar Levy of Interest to Readers of Gobineau and Nietzsche."

Before the wars of 1914-18 and 1939-45, Nietzsche was largely seen as a philosopher of "aristocratic radicalism"—that is to say, a proponent of hierarchy, "order of rank," inequality, selective breeding, and the rejection of all comfortable illusions for the sake of raw, honest truth about life. In this atmosphere it was natural to read him in the same company as Gobineau —fellow theorist of "master races"—and to see both men as representing the same strain of vitalist thought, as Gerald Spring does in his book.[12] It was only after the wars that

---

[11] Lichtenberger would later write a lengthy analysis of German National Socialism in 1937, *The Third Reich*. For information on J.M. Kennedy and his associates such as Anthony Ludovici and A.R. Orage, who were also deeply influenced by Nietzsche, see *Conservative Modernists: Literature and Tory Politics in Britain, 1900–1920* by Christos Hadjiyiannis, Cambridge University Press, 2018.

[12] In the journal *The Nineteenth Century* from May, 1913 there is an article by Georges Chatterton-Hill entitled "Gobineau, Nietzsche, Wagner" which argues that Nietzsche knew Gobineau's work and was influenced by it. According to research conducted by Eugen Kretzer at the turn of the century, both Nietzsche's sister and his friend Overbeck confirmed that Nietzsche knew of Gobineau and held him in high esteem.

Nietzsche and *lebensphilosophie* first fell out of favor and then were rehabilitated in an altered, distorted form.

The work of the early modernist Nietzscheans such as J.M. Kennedy, Thomas Common,[13] Oscar Levy and others represent an initial engagement with Nietzsche's ideas devoid of political correctness and sheepishness brought about by the trauma of the wars. They were the British Nietzscheans, and they found in the Italian Leo Séra[14] a fellow traveler, but from a different direction. Whereas their thought and writings reflect an essentially Northern worldview, Séra is decidedly Southern and Mediterranean. This is significant not least of all because, as he notes of Nietzsche

> His doctrines are the aspiration of the north for the south, of the mind of countries deprived of sun and life for light, for heat, for the blue of the southern sky. ... Nietzsche's work is a *southernisation* of the northern mind, its refinement, its embellishment.

So who was Leo Séra? Various sources give his birth year as either 1870 or 1878 in Florence. He studied medicine and surgery in Rome, graduating in 1903. Most of his biographies online are brief and jump immediately to his career as a professor of Anthropology from the 1920s onward. He taught at Pavia, Milan, and then at the University of Naples beginning in 1926. Before this he was in Rome, Florence, and Bologna, conducting anthropological research in various museums. While at Pavia he founded the *Giornale per la Morfologia dell' Uomo e dei Primati* (Journal of Human and Primate Morphology) which was the first journal of its kind, and which ran from 1917 to 1923. Many of the articles published in the Journal were by Séra himself. The *Giornale*

---

[13] See *Nietzsche as Critic, Philosopher, Poet and Prophet,* the first English language anthology of Nietzsche's writings, which Common edited and translated.

[14] In his later work, he seems to have always used his full name, whereas *Sulle Tracce della Vita* was published in Italian and English under the name "Leo G. Sera." Thus we will use Leo Sera for brevity.

ceased publication because Séra was rendered blind by an illness, a condition which would continue for the rest of his life. He is remembered today mostly for his work in primatology, craniometry and human origins. He was one of the last proponents of the theory of polyphyletism, the idea that human beings have more than one evolutionary ancestor.[15] He was also the first to propose what is now called the Aquatic Ape Hypothesis, that there was an aquatic phase of human evolution, a theory which continues to be investigated and debated today.

Séra's academic work belongs to the later part of his life. His early years, during which he wrote *On The Tracks of Life*, are not discussed. In the memoirs of Eva Kühn Amendola, a Lithuanian woman associated with the Futurist movement,[16] she mentions that Séra was part of the Florentine cultural circle centered around the Theosophical Society, though it is unknown whether he was a member. If so, the Theosophical doctrine of "root races" may have provided inspiration for his later polyphyletist ideas. That Séra the Nietzschean was part of the milieu from which Futurism emerged makes perfect sense, since Futurism was more influenced by Nietzsche than Dada, Surrealism or any of the other avant garde art movements of the early 20th century.

Séra unquestionably knew Eva Kuhn's husband, Giovanni Amendola. The appendix to this book is largely concerned with responding to a review by Amendola, whom he calls his "good friend." Amendola is remembered today for being an opponent of Fascism who was attacked by Blackshirts in 1925 and later died from his injuries. Séra, despite holding

---

[15] For an overview of polyphyletism and Séra's particular theory of no less than six evolutionary stems for human beings, see "Welcome to the Twilight Zone: a forgotten early phase of human evolutionary studies" by Richard G. Delisle, *Endeavour* Vol. 36, No. 2, pp. 55-64

[16] She wrote under the pen name Magamal, a name which she took from Marinetti's novel *Mafarka the Futurist*.

Nietzschean views that would undoubtedly be considered far-right today, never joined the Fascists, perhaps because of what happened to his friend.

In 1935 Séra wrote the entry on "Race" for the *Encyclopedia Italiana,* which explicitly rejects the National Socialist doctrine of race and the existence of Jewish, Italian and Aryan races.[17] This was Mussolini's stated position at the time, and so it is unclear whether Séra himself believed this or whether he was pressured to conform to Mussolini's views.

His views in 1907 were certainly not such. In *On The Tracks of Life* he wrote:

> So we may see that, prepared by their vigorous social structure, and having arrived at the period of military civilisation, the late descendants of the former emigrants marched back again to the south, this time as invaders and conquerors. Athirst for heat, love, and power, they descended into the countries of brightness, the land of dark-eyed and dark-haired women, and by sheer strength and war founded their kingdom. Thus did the Goths and the Vandals in Spain, thus the Franks in France, thus the Goths, the Lombards, and the Huns in Italy. Similarly, it should seem that the Greeks were invaders who had come from the north, and imposed themselves as aristocratic and governing classes upon the native element, and that, having in time forgotten their own origin, they regarded as *barbarians* those who were not native Hellenics.
>
> But the finest and greatest example of this process is shown us by the Aryan race, which, having sprung up in the Pamir plateau, descended into India and founded the greatest and most superb of military aristocracies.

*   *   *   *   *

On the Tracks of Life is a remarkable exposition of vitalist thought which was in many ways a century ahead of its time. It is firmly rooted in biology because of Séra's medical and

---

17 "There is no Italian race, therefore, but only an Italian people and an Italian nation. There is neither a Jewish race nor nation, but only a Jewish people; and, the most serious error of them all, there is no Aryan race, but only an Aryan civilization and Aryan languages." ["Human Races," entry "Race," *Enciclopedia Italiana,* vol. 27 (Rome: 1935).]

anthropological training. Like Nietzsche, he is more on the side of scientific skepticism than of speculative and unfounded theories. He praises Hermann von Helmholtz, who was an opponent of vitalist theories of biology in favor of a more strict materialism. Considering that hormones were only discovered a few years before the book was written, it is remarkable that he was already speculating on their importance for individual character and development, as he does in chapter 4. Likewise his observations (echoing Nietzsche again) on the importance of nutrition and diet:

> A poor and deficient allowance of food, that is to say a dynamogenic supply, while it makes people all the more willing to submit to the yoke of servile labour and organic impoverishment, is likewise an instrument of political oppression, for weak and badly fed individuals are far from desiring liberty and independence, or, if they do sometimes feel such a desire, they do not possess the intellectual power of discovering what means they should employ to attain their object.

Séra also shows a keen grasp of human psychology. Indeed, two of his primary influences are Nietzsche and Stendhal, two of the greatest psychologists of the 19th century, each of whom has a chapter dedicated to his work here. The book opens with a chapter originally titled simply "Love," which we have changed here to "Love and Lust" since its true subject is sexuality and breeding as they relate to society. He is fully in accord with Nietzsche's statement that "The degree and kind of a man's sexuality reach up into the ultimate pinnacle of his spirit."[18] Sexuality is at the core of Sera's conception of vitalism; for him, vitality is virtually synonymous with virility. He develops the idea that "sexuality and sociality are connected by the closest ties; but this relationship is antagonistic: in complete opposition. *Sociality is in function the reverse of sexuality ... "*

---

[18] *Beyond Good and Evil*, sec. 75

Sexual, aristocratic, beautiful, are conceptions which are closely related to one another, if not, indeed, the same thing seen from different aspects. Thus I have already said that love, dominion, and genial creation have a common root and a common soul.

It is for this reason that the aristocratic individual is shown to be almost an enemy of sociality and of morality, because he is the representative, against these, of rights of race, strength, and virtue which tend, in their greatest and most glorious manifestations, to increase and perpetuate.

He also anticipates some of the insights of Rollo Tommassi, Heartiste and others, a hundred years earlier, as for example when he formulates the principle which Rollo would later call "Alpha Fucks, Beta Bucks":

From this point of view woman has the sharpest insight! With a single penetrating look and synthetic discernment she values and adjudges a man, weighs up in an instant all that she can draw from him and which she thinks may be useful to her; so that while she will submit her entire self with all the humiliation of a slave to one man in order to obtain even a kiss from him, she will make another pay a high price for her body, the price, that is, of . . . matrimony.

Séra's psychological insight is also on display in the chapter on "Modesty and Shyness" which prefigures Jung's later concepts of introversion and extroversion.

Chapters 2-4 concern the origin of society in the different castes of men. He defines what he calls *the aristocratic spirit* as:

A detached individualism, courage in every form, the spirit of initiative and enterprise, the love of adventure, of war, and of the chase, of the unknown and of the unexpected, are the distinguishing traits of those individuals who belong to the first type, traits which denote a healthy and vigorous nature. Leisure is their natural state, as it was also the state of primitive humanity, of which, indeed, they possess many of the characteristics. These are the men who are called "rulers," "masters," "governors."

The theme of leisure, which Séra treats and defends considerably, would later be developed by the Catholic philosopher Josef Pieper in his 1947 book *Leisure: The Basis of Culture*. In contrast to the prevailing and various worker ideologies of the time, Séra views work as such the same way that the Greeks did: as drudgery that drains the spirit of life. "[My] principal thesis—the identification of aristocracy, physical superiority, and repugnance to work."

The key question for Séra is this:

> Does the most desirable and highest advantage of society consist of well-being assured to all—the greatest happiness of the greatest number—in the tendency to mediocritise all abilities; or in opposing and confirming the differences, in widening the gap between rich and poor, between exploiters and exploited?
>
> Those who accept the first solution are democrats in all the different senses of the word; those who accept the second are aristocrats: and those who accept the first agree to accept for humanity a future resembling a deep, low-lying bog.

Like Nietzsche, he sees the Greeks as the high point of human achievement.

> *Hellenic civilisation signified perhaps the culminating point of the history of civilisation on earth, as it showed a perfect balance between interiority and exteriority, between form and substance.* This correspondence and harmony between real and ideal, between thought and execution, between the beautiful and the true, glittered perhaps like a transient meteor in the Greek sky. We at least with our Renaissance saw only a very much diminished light derived from it.

Central to Séra's worldview is "the psychological contrast between North and South" and their interplay in the development of civilizational and historical trends. He develops this idea throughout the book, especially in chapters 3 and 8. While his perspective is certainly centered in his Southern place of origin, and is perhaps somewhat influenced by the Mediterraneanist ideas of Giuseppe Sergi which were prevalent at the time, he is not at all chauvinistic or bigoted, and takes Nietzsche's ideal of the "Good European" as his own. In chapter 9, "Social Rhythms," he anticipates some of Spengler's ideas about culture and history, and makes some remarkable predictions about the rise of Germany in the 20th century. In the following chapter on the nature and creation of genius, he writes that "genius is liberation, an aristocratic mind's finding itself after having been held prisoner by inferior conditions."

As against the over-intellectualized, abstracted counterfeit of vitalism which would develop later, he writes:

> I will only say that in some men the strongest thought coincides with the most intense life, and that these men are, or should be, at the top of the tree. ... [I]n the highest stages life *coincides* with thought, and it is only when going down from the two parts of the hierarchical curve that we find either the predominance of life in its lower and more brutal functions, or thought more or less morbid with its abstractions and abstrusenesses. I maintain, however, that for the highest interest of life, its preservation, I incline to the first defect rather than to the second.

* * * * *

As for the change in the book's title, and relegating its initial title to subtitle, there are two main reasons. First, "The Immorality of Morality" seems to have been chosen for its shock value for a 1909 audience rather than for how aptly it describes the subject and contents of the book, which is not primarily or even secondarily a critique of morality. (Likewise, Séra's subtitle in Italian was simply "Essays," implying that the chapters are individual and standalone, but they are not—the book is a coherent whole and should be read as such.) The real subject of the book, as with any good book of *lebensphilosophie*, is Life. Although Séra does not use the term "vitalism," the word *vitality* shows up repeatedly in his evaluations as a principle criterion, as when he says that "the ideal of the higher man has its origin in the expansive instinct of a growing vitality, of a vitality which, having been compressed and diminished, returns to primitive grandeur and strength."

Of his philosophical position, Séra writes that: "I am certainly neither a materialist nor a positivist in the customary sense of the words, perhaps not even a realist; but neither do I feel myself to be an idealist." What he is, as I hope I have established here, is a vitalist, and that is the philosophy which his book expounds.

As for the original title, it has been retained as subtitle both because it was the author's choice and because it evokes the search and the quest that any good vitalist philosophy ought to inspire and guide: for *more truth, more power, more life.*

This book, then, is for "the higher man, the man who examines himself and finds in his own being the traces of a free and healthy life, of a profound force long handed down from generation to generation, who becomes aware of his own nobleness ..."

ROGUE SCHOLAR PRESS
February, 2025

Gioacchino Leo Séra

TRANSLATOR'S NOTE

In translating Dr. Séra's work, I have had the benefit of his and Dr. Levy's assistance in the elucidation of several references which were not quite clear to me; and my thanks are due to them both for their help in this respect.

Dr. Séra, in the course of our correspondence, has desired me to modify the text in places, and all such alterations are incorporated in this edition, which is not therefore a literal rendering of the first Italian edition. Most of the changes made are, however, not very important.

J. M. KENNEDY.

Author's Preface

To establish our conception of social life on its original basis; to reaffirm and, so to speak, renovate its *golden values,* the values which were created by the fresh and vigorous meditation of the earlier ages of mankind; to find, amidst the thick confusion of moral, religious, and political prejudices, false scientific conceptions, and out-of-date aesthetic formulae, the traces of a life higher than our actual existence; to discover a true life:—this is the task of him who loves mankind, or, rather, of him who loves to see men beautiful, strong, serene, and free.

The phenomenon of modernity—new by reason of its intensity; but by no means new by the predominance of certain forms of thought, instinctive and sentimentally inclined tendencies, in short, that peculiar state of mind which, in one word, however incomplete, we may call *democratic*—has perverted and corrupted thought in its investigations into human nature, the origin of many human facts; even into social development itself.

What is much worse is that these data, upon which we might endeavour to base a new construction, have been scattered broadcast, and even threaten to be lost altogether in the thick and ever-increasing cloud which hovers round these so-called modern ideas.

The keen searcher will but too well perceive that most of these ideas reveal themselves only by a subconscient dissimulation of many truths of which the so-called modern man has a hazy presentiment.

But, in so far as this dissimulation, or direct lying, is a vital necessity of our present condition, it is useful to the existence of modern man; for only with great difficulty will the fact be recognised, and with even greater difficulty will it be conceded, that the work most necessary to be done at the present time is that of investigating the *tracks of life.*

But, even if the programme I have just outlined be approved, I am sure to hear objections and ironical questions from all sides: "Do you, then, think that you are the first to arrive at a just conclusion as to the processes of life? Do you think you are the first to travel along these paths, and to reconstruct and connect those facts which have existed from the first ages of humanity; or do you think you have been able to penetrate further than others into the miracles which are every day repeating themselves before our eyes?"

To all such inquirers I would say that my object is simply to look at these things from a different and higher point of view: natural; amoral. As far as possible I wish to eliminate from my explanations anything that is merely the more or less disguised prompting of our own will or our habits of life, our modern mind and circumstances. To discover the eternal motive, the perennial rhythm of life, was my aim; but it is almost certain that I have not attained this ideal.

At all events, whether my aim has been attained wholly or partially, the merit will at least remain to me of having expressed the problem in its proper terms. And I think it opportune to discuss this aspect of the question.

The deleterious, anti-vital effects of the tendencies I have mentioned (it is evident that their aim is to level downwards and to render monotonous, in contrast to life itself, which is diversity and harmony) are manifested even more openly in practical spheres; but these effects can also be traced in the region of the intellect.

The overflowing mediocrity of present-day desires; the acquiescence in the lowest and most vulgar forms of living, due to the presence of conditions which, long unrevealed, have once more disclosed their origin in our own time, all tend to impose on mankind a physical, moral, and intellectual misery, under the appearance of a common and even universal benefit.

Many people would wish us to believe that not only is the period through which we are now passing merely a transitory phase, superior in general excellence to any chronicled by historians; but that it is, as it were, the prelude to a new and infinite melody: in other words, that we are now verging towards the calm, obscure, quiet region of general equality, solidarity, and perpetual peace. But it would be no great loss if such opinions were reserved for the politics of coffeehouses, clubs, or parliaments.

Such a supposition, like every other which concerns life in the full sense of the word, is always with us, even in places where we should never expect to find it; in the impartial and elevated regions of art, of science, and of philosophy. Whatever concerns the practical interests of men has an enormous influence, even in the most abstract spheres of thought; and it cannot be denied that this conception of life more or less defiles art, and philosophy, and science.

The entrance of common, plebeian ideas into the republic of knowledge has made knowledge itself more languid and weak; and knowledge, hiddenly or openly, is becoming more and more the approver and defender of conditions of life and modes of thinking which have a vulgar origin stamped upon them by the influx of people who hold merely vulgar intellectual views.

Let it not be supposed that only the so-called moral and historical sciences are suffering from the influence of this gradual change of view: it is reflected still further, for this particular species of automorphism which I am now considering is manifested also in many other directions. Democratic automorphism may be fairly accurately analysed in its relation to the biological and exact sciences: so many investigators are now desirous of contributing their mite of knowledge to the world, that even the most unimportant divisions of science are studied with the utmost minuteness; although the nature of this excessive specialisation is servile and mechanical. These remarks apply equally to the spirit in which scientific investigations are undertaken, as well as to the results of such investigations; whence we may see that, while in epochs of great worldly splendour science was free, personal, and aristocratic; now that everyone dabbles in science it has lost the initiating spirit, and become common, plebeian, imitative.

Philosophy itself, once the queen of wisdom and thought, has gradually become a useless, childish prattler—a logomachy of words ending in *ism, al,* and *ect.* Realism and idealism; substantial and formal; subject and object, fill page after page; but in the end nothing is determined. Nevertheless, according to the splendid sentence of Novalis, to philosophise is equivalent to *dephlegmatisieren, vivifizieren.*[19]

Art, and only art, waves from some high and lonely peak the banner of personality, and supports the aristocratic principle, the principle of the noblest minds.

And even art is menaced; and, what is worse, not menaced by iconoclastic ferocity, but by the corrupting flattery of Socialism, by educative ideals, by universal brotherhood, and so on.

The absurd and paradoxical consequence is that the intellect, the divine renovating force, threatens to be lost in the general shipwreck caused by the spread of education itself.

The masses are entering the realm of science; but their sloth of mind and body is brutalising it, perverting its discernible results, and retarding the progress of every new and truly creative energy.

Still, in this overwhelming mediocrity, there are some youthful minds to whom, amidst lazy indifference and hostile

---

[19] "dephlegmatize, vivify" - A reference to the ancient theory of the Four Humors. The Phlegmatic humor was associated with introversion and passivity.

murmurings, an internal voice whispers varied opinions. Uncertain opinions, however: since science now takes delight in vulgar instincts; science, whom tradition counsels these minds to take as adviser and guide; science, whom these minds are accustomed to consider as a profound and established force; science speaks through its more eminent representatives an unusual language, a language of indifference and timidity; and through the others, the greater number, pampers either stealthily or openly the most common and vulgar instincts.

On account of all this, then, there are many who believe there is some necessity for a vigorous renovation of modern and human standards of value, originated by a psychological criticism of our fundamental conceptions of what social life is. In this connection, far too many of our notions concerning some essential facts are uncertain and impure. Examples are the general conception of aristocracy, social development, the characteristics of genius; and, finally, our beliefs regarding civilisation itself are most chaotic and fragmentary.

The aim of this book, then, is an attempt to solve some of these problems.

*　　*　　*　　*　　*

Among these uncertain criticisms and signs of decadence, I believe a thought has been maturing in some minds:

That the renewing of our culture (not using the word in the sense that makes it almost a synonym for obsolete erudition), or, better, the revival of humanism, must await a return of general taste to philological study, or else, which is more likely in a generation saturated with the results of linguistic science, a return to that fruitful ground from which glottology[20] sprang forth at the beginning of the last century. I know of many confirmations of this supposition.

---

[20] An older term for linguistics.

Certainly the more deeply one penetrates into the study of human values, the more is one convinced that in the first stages of human history, when our consciences revealed themselves in their freshness and bloom, like a flower which until then had been sheltered in its bud, one could have a more just conception of human facts, a more accurate appreciation of human beings.

The intuitive knowledge of humanity considered aspects, affinities, and analogies, which the progressive analysis of later times has never been able to discern so easily, inasmuch as language, itself an analytic instrument, became more and more removed from those data to which it should have brought itself closer.

Primitive Indian poetry, for example, as was generally the case with the mental expression of early peoples, gave utterance to more vivid and comprehensive thoughts in its ingenuous synthesis than we can express in the more confused and irksome constructions of our modern languages.

In the luminous periods of human history, of which that of the Indian poetry mentioned is not the only one (although, perhaps, the most characteristic), these happy intuitions must have been relatively frequent, since the primitive mind united many thoughts that were then more or less artificially dissociated.

Modern glottology has given more attention to the formal factors of linguistic elements than to the signification of those elements with respect to their psychology, and their place in relation to the ultimate purpose of forming a true science of thought, which is really what most interests men. This is due to several causes. In the first place, these ingenuous conceptions, or, better, primitive intuitions, were confused by later developments, and especially by this very modernity I have spoken of; and, although they have left their traces on words and tongues, these traces are but few, and not easily recognised. In the second place *psychica*, to use the word coined by Techmer[21] in his celebrated scheme, has hitherto been prevented from developing into a really true doctrine exactly by the reasons I have indicated.

Certainly our hopes and efforts should in the very near future be turned to the formation of a science of thought which shall take its elements from many directions, although making use of glottology as its chief instrument. It will then be recognised that all other sciences are merely tributaries of this science of thought, which in truth is queen of them all. It is, however, very different from modern psychology, and this fact must be clearly understood.

Our new science will, of course, avail itself of the results of gnoseological criticism, as also of the results of particular scientific investigations; but it will at the same time have a well-defined basis, and will not consist of an unending series of purposeless syllogisms, which has too often been the case with philosophical systems.

Nothing, however, but liberation from certain presuppositions which, so to speak, we breathe in with the air of our modernity, can inspire our imaginations with these new visions, and then guide them in conformity with truths which already we faintly perceive. It is therefore necessary to put forth a preliminary work to vivify the stagnant air and remove obstacles from encumbered paths.

But, in order better to demonstrate the presence of certain requirements in contemporary thought, we must consider another coefficient.

German philosophical thought, from about the end of the eighteenth and the beginning of the nineteenth century, was undoubtedly very rich in ideas; but, even if some of the ideas matured, and helped to build up certain sciences—especially glottology, undoubtedly the greatest science of the last century —many of the germs of these ideas were sacrificed. Every new

---

21 Friedrich Techmer (1843-1891) was a German linguist.

progress of thought seems to me to have affirmed itself as a return to what I may call uncertainty of capacity; to pure speculation; the power of the mere idea by itself, which was the very starting-point of science in the preceding period. The science of a specified epoch appears after a certain time to have exhausted that susceptibility of development that was possessed by those ideas which fought with and emerged victorious from amongst others. What we gain in clearness and practical utility we lose in fineness, perspicacity, and richness of meaning; thus making inevitable a new period of chaotic fermentation, pure ideological treatment; a return to philosophy.

This is not the place to discuss this view, to which I give the value of a historical law of thought; but I have certainly many good reasons for thinking that a new philosophical period is preparing, and is just about to begin. But of that I will say more another time.

The inference to be drawn from the foregoing remarks is what I now assert: that if we are to arrive at any definite conclusion from future philosophical progress, our *concrete* knowledge of moral man must inevitably be revised; and it is my aim to give assistance in the revising.

This work, then, is merely preparatory; and, although it considers new aspects of distinct and particular problems, it remains in my mind quite subordinate to a higher and more distant ideal.

*   *   *   *   *

I may be permitted to add a few words to help to elucidate this work even more clearly.

Among my analyses, it will often happen that the reader will meet with a general and fundamental fact to which until now he may have attached little importance; yet which is, in my opinion, the centre and nucleus of very many human facts: sexuality.

What has been the origin of this silence on sexual matters, when these are in reality the most prominent in the life of every human being? Why do men, whether in works of the imagination or in the affairs of life, apparently wish to forget that they have a sex? They are never ashamed to confess their wishes for food or drink; yet they never care to admit sexual desires, although they may secretly acknowledge their influence. The common answer, "It is immodest to do so," is a tautology. The scientific answer referring to religious prejudices and the anti-sexual nature of all religions is very superficial, and determines nothing, since a further question at once occurs to us: "Why are almost all religions anti-sexual?"

These facts are too widespread and important to be explained by mere antipathy, aversion pure and simple, or even by the hatred of the "*senza donne,*" to use Morasso's acute argument.[22] All the so-called explanations already given really amount to a single affirmation: the affirmation of an anti-sexual principle in the present state of the human mind. And then we are confronted with the more general problem: "Whence arises this principle or tendency?" Simply admitting it for the present, all we can say is that man wishes, as it were, to keep his sex a secret, so that this intimate branch of sexual physiology remains little studied and comparatively unknown. He rarely admits things concerning which he has confused opinions; and sexual envy and sexual jealousy are the most common and deeply rooted of natural feelings, although the most misunderstood.

Nevertheless, from all the sexual facts I have been able to gather, I think much light will be thrown on intricate human phenomena. Among these facts is the relationship of sexuality to sociality.

---

[22] Mario Morasso (1871-1938) was an Italian writer who had a strong influence on Futurism. Among his works were *Uomini e idee del domani (l'egoarchia)* (1898), *L'imperialismo artistico* (1903), *La nuova arma (la macchina)* (1905), *Il nuovo aspetto meccanico del mondo* (1907), and *La nuova guerra* (1914).

The principle which imposes silence and forgetfulness on sexual laws acts with extraordinary vigour on men in general. If it is worth while to hide from them even the scientific knowledge of these facts, it is legitimate to think that this knowledge, if brought to light, would be of interest to society.

Of the first statement in the preceding paragraph it is sufficient proof to mention again the significant fact that the physiology of reproduction is still the least-studied branch of physiology; and certainly such a backward state of things must be partly attributed to the gradually acquired repugnance to investigate and consider this and similar subjects. In regard to the second statement, the thought occurs that this silence may have a protective value for society. And now I may hear the objection: "If these facts contain, as you say, the solution of so many problems; if the silence maintained concerning them protects the interests of society, would not great harm be done by bringing these facts to light?"

But I think the time has now arrived when more than one truth may be told that could not have been enunciated sooner. Centuries of abstention from speaking of these subjects, and the silence of great thinkers, have produced their effects on our race. By virtue of our morals we have become so correct in behaviour that opinions publicly expressed on these subjects are not likely to lead to the perturbations which might at one time have been expected. Our moral discipline has made us sober and tractable animals; our minds, when considering new problems, work in a cold and crystalline sphere, a region where hot blood and ardent passions never penetrate!

So also in a distant future, when social discipline shall have made man even better, more docile, and more *compos sui*,[23] the exterior bonds which at present bind him will be broken. For the rest, it is useless to oppose one's self to a current which is every day becoming stronger. Finally, if any one of these

---

[23] "master of one's self"

numerous problems can be solved, if some of these obscure thoughts which glide like phantoms across the minds of many thinkers can be gathered together and correlated, what then? Our nature has numerous, perhaps infinite, inner depths, of which whatever light we have been able to throw on the problem will illuminate only the first few. For the thinker whose chief delight lies in mystery and shadow there will always be a world of darkness; an infinite number of gloomy paths that may be seen spreading out from the initial grottos.

*   *   *   *   *

In this undertaking I could have composed a rigidly scientific work, or an elegant and aesthetic one; but the Italian public requires a work of life and movement, a fighting work.

I may, however, be accused of having written a *contaminatio* of psychology and physiology; and I answer that these two aspects of human reality are not so distinct as might be believed; and, moreover, I have not given any technical discussions; but have restricted myself, as regards physiology, to generalities.

As to psychology, on the contrary, my method is that of synthetic psychology in the sense that my work, whilst dealing with human truth, does not travel in the direction of knowledge by which one seeks to arrive at the hypothetical elements of conscious life; there may, however, be reflected in it some of that separatist movement in psychology which was originated by Dr. James.[24]

But, above all, I must make it clear that I am alienated from doctrinary psychology. In general, I have used those elements which I have deemed good and valid, without regard to their derivation; aesthetic, scientific, and philosophical arguments which often pass beyond traditional limits. In this way I hope I have avoided professional jargon, the

---

[24] William James

employment of which so often conceals limitation and narrowness of mind.

The remainder of the work has not been written in accordance with any particular method; indeed, it will be found that all special methods are the same in essence. One method, even when rigorously applied, leads only to subordinate truths; in my case the greatest generality possible has been sought. I should, however, like to add that, in addition to a systematic treatment of a complete social doctrine, I have endeavoured to establish conceptions susceptible of being developed; to bring forward ideas which are fruitful and easily applied; and I have not been at pains to seek out other facts which I could have illustrated by the light of these. In short, it is the ambition of this work to be a *fermentum cognitionis et cogitationis*, to quote an ancient philosophical motto.

But the ideas themselves do not take up much room, and, instead of a plain, expository style, I have often expressed myself in an aphoristic and polemical form. I have tried to make my work human; but not on that account trifling and inconsiderable. I am not the founder of a new school or system; but I have made an attempt up to a certain point; I have travelled by a new route. *À propos* of this, I will make one final remark. The different chapters may appear unconnected; some readers may think those on Stendhal and Nietzsche out of place. This is not really so; if I have been fortunate enough to express my convictions successfully, and if I have had the ability to guide the reader into the spirit of my ideas, those who read carefully will certainly perceive that, under the variety and inequality of the ideological treatment, the same deep current runs through all the book.

CHAPTER I

LOVE AND LUST

The manner in which one feels and conceives of love is the surest guide to one's personal character.

But, just for this reason, in the single word *love* are included many, even innumerable, states of mind, the extremes of which are, I am inclined to think, quite the contrary of one another.

These extremes are sensuality and affection. Lamartine has said, with much acuteness and penetration, "Il n'y a rien de si loin de la volupté que l'attendrissement."[25]

And Stendhal in *De l'amour*—a profound and subtle book, but more often obscure, through which, like stars on a cloudy night, sudden flashes of light appear here and there—continually repeats the words "tendre," "tendresse," "attendri" when he wishes to indicate the exact contrary of physical love.

From the confusion between these two species of love (which, even if one be derived from the other, are nevertheless very far apart) arose the innumerable controversies which occupied the poets and the philosophers who have discoursed, debated, or raved about this subject.

The two principal forms of love were raised up and made eternal by the literary school which created Don Juan and Werther.

It is not entirely without interest to consider that Don Juan was created in Spain, of which country it is no exaggeration to say he became the national hero, so great was his popularity at one time; and that Werther was created in Germany—in romantic, cloudy, spiritual Germany. But if Goethe himself, in

---

[25] "There is nothing so far from sensuality as tender emotion." (trans. Eugène Plunkett)

his Olympic and divine manliness, came to see in Werther a strange and monstrous being, this was not and is not the case with a large number of his countrymen.

L'Attendrissement, or sentimental love, is the extreme conception; the most profound modification of primitive love; or, to be still more exact, it is the final stage to which the primitive rough sexual impulse has been brought by all the many causes which have operated on it in society: and the truth of this statement is seen in the fact that where these social causes have operated most strongly, owing to particular reasons which we shall have occasion to note (as, for example, among the northern peoples), love in such places is, generally speaking, nearer to the Platonic than to the sensual conception.

It must then be observed that the action of these social causes often results in an effect which we call morbid, even when speaking of persons belonging to the southern nations; but only when we find such an effect together with other abnormalities in their moral life; but the doubt always suggests itself that such a mode of loving must surely always be a sign of vital decadence, even in cases where we attribute it to some peculiarity of race, such as a diffuse and collective manner of feeling.

I mean that an idealised and complicated love, a love enriched with a thousand blendings of sweet and tender colours, the embellishment of poetry of spring mornings and of the gloom of autumn, a love made human, indulgent, compassionate: physical love, transformed into ideal love with its sublime devotions, the complete alienation of one's own person: this love resembles those delicate and fragile plants which are all changed into flowers under the influence of a forced culture in a warm and moist atmosphere; all this frail and weak life seems to be devoted to a work of beauty which clothes their slender limbs with the brightest and most gaudy colours.

Who knows whether this *humanised,* spiritualised love, enlarged in spirit and intimacy, the love issuing from magnanimous affections and sublime sacrifices; who knows whether this, like that monstrous growth, is not the sign of the early extinction of the species, or at least of a vital diminution? The flowers of that plant which are the joy and satisfaction of our eyes have lost their true natural function by the artistic but deforming force of artificial cultivation; their stamens, their pistils have become infecund, and are no longer serviceable for reproduction.

And, then, what is this pure, human, and ideal love, this dreadful and terrible longing for another individual, this absolute necessity for one single person, but often, too often, the undefined consciousness of one's own incapacity to carry out a clever, subtle, brilliant amorous conquest? What is this desire to possess another being to communicate with, to find comfort in, but always, infallibly always, the sense of one's own weakness, and the dim realisation of the truth that two weaknesses may together amount to an appearance of strength? What is all this talk of eternal, unique, absolute love, but the exaltation, the raving, the delirium of the agony of the love of a former time; a strong, undefined, promiscuous, free, and serene love?

An inward contradiction and a subtle error are innate in the greatest and most delicate love, so that this contradiction and this error are the greater the more such love is "noble" and "worthy."

He who nourishes such a love comes, in fact, to conceal the sad thoughts that oppress him so as not to vex the beloved object; to be silent about the faults and blemishes which, in spite of the veil of illusion before his eyes, he discovers in the loved one, in order that he may not afterwards have to reproach himself with the infliction of humiliation and suffering. Worse still, since whoever feels love in this way is sensitive and imaginative by having no reason to grieve over any possible injury to the other, he tries to extend his own range of vision, to deepen his compassion, going even so far as to accuse himself of hardness of heart, of narrowness of mind, and of lack of indulgence.

And what does all this amount to in the end?

To put the superior and refined being at the mercy of the coarser and less noble one—the one who has less sensitiveness and intelligence; in other words, it leads to a highly immoral consequence if we would consider it from the point of view of social utility.

But it may be objected that the satisfaction of the lover is entirely personal and contained in himself, that *his* love *only* constitutes the true joy and superiority which he feels; but the answer may be made at once that such an egotistic and egoistic position would hardly be admitted even by the man who loves in this way; who feels, and feels reasonably, that his behaviour is inspired by disinterestedness or altruism.

On the other hand, however, he himself should recognise that all his abnegation does not in any way benefit the loved object, because it leaves it in ignorance and does not improve it morally—and of this abnegation, moreover, the one who loves most always possesses the largest supply; and in love there is invariably one who loves more and one who loves less.

It is better in every case to amend any little discourtesy, any frequent small infringement of the absolute rule, than to apply it rigorously, without reckoning the miserably utilitarian consideration that the one who is the object of these attentions, but is unaware of them, is not and cannot be grateful for them.

The practice of the good for itself, of absolute altruism, associates of the purest, greatest, and most disinterested love, is barren of results, and indicates a nature wrapped up in itself, and afflicted with a hidden impotence to act on men and things, and with a certain incommunicability.

The good for the good itself is an ideal aim; but it is outside the scope of life, for it does not appeal to men. Instead of moderating them, it encircles them, so to speak, pities them, and embraces their defects and merits in a single look.

But universal comprehension and compassion are usually accompanied by philosophic inertia and indifference rather than with active virtues, and are very nearly related to impotence and weakness. Moreover love, that function which looks towards a specific end, is subjected to well-determined physical conditions; it is a work of our spinal centres, to use a physiological expression; but woe to those who would elevate it, who would make it cerebral or even worse! we may refine it, so to speak, but we shall debase it at the same time.

And yet we as *men*, and as social beings, are unable to free ourselves from this deviation.

When the strong and egoistic tendencies of physical love are overcome and conquered by the rising intellectuality and morality of love, that is a sign that the energies of the race are becoming exhausted, that the race is getting poorer; and, although we may perhaps admire its final red and golden twilight, we must, as dispassionate observers and philosophers, witness the signs of its early death.

That love which delights in sacrificing itself before the loved object, which is not daunted even with a refusal, which does not feel itself offended, and does not hate: that love is indeed marvellous and almost angelic, it is true; but it often indicates a weak and crushed individual, a being on the path of dissolution.

We may in general admire it (and, in this regard, may not this general admiration be a perversion of taste, the symptom of a vast decadence?); but we cannot but recognise that its essence is revealed to the judicious eye as an expression of a life that renounces itself, an individuality that is no longer capable of living.

Many different kinds of love have been established; but these have no right to be taken as distinct and special forms, as they are only particular varieties between these two extremes, and take a blending of diverse colouring according to the nature or the dominating passion of the individual. This may be said of the love arising from one's fancy or vanity, or of the other kinds.

As the supreme interest of the race is contained in love, to the manner of feeling it are very closely joined the most essential qualities of any individual: those which concern his social person, and determine his actions and reactions on society.

So that, as much as the instinct of possession and of direct and material mastery is manifested in love, so much the more will it be purely physical, and the indication of a psychologically strong and primitive character, of a nature rich in strength, of a temperament strong in vital forces.

A very close relationship connects physical love with the instinct of mastery and possession: these, indeed, are two things which are rarely separated; but on the other hand it is a characteristic of ideal love to find in it the greatest disinterestedness and altruism.

In so far as ardour and the power of the amorous desire are the expression of organic vigour and of robust temperament, and not of morbid impulses—derivatives from changes of the nervous and psychical process of the sexual act (since pathological elements enter into it), this ardour and this power are, within these limits, the manifestation of a strong and profound vitality, of a really living and active organisation, the sign, in a word, of perfect and entire *vitality*.

To such organisms is naturally entrusted the task of transmitting to the future the strong animal type of the species *man*, since active sexuality and perfect vitality are companion and parallel phenomena.

And it is easy to understand why this should be so, for it was by means of this sexuality that natural selection was able in the past to assure the prevalence of the strongest and healthiest individuals, i.e. through reproduction on the greatest and most extended scale by those who were physiologically most robust was the species propagated and assured. The association of the two temperaments mentioned above—amorous warmth and vigorous vitality—is one of the laws of the animal kingdom.

It may be objected that, in properly *human* development, elements other than organic strength and vigour might be introduced to confuse such simple premises (I do not speak, be it noted, and the reason will be seen by and by, of *muscular* strength and vigour), and that intelligence, laboriousness, or some other qualities, would assure individuals of possessing the security of existence, and hence the propagation of their own progeny. This is undeniable. But I reply to these critics that the influence of the human period is still fortunately very small, and that in our physical and moral organisation we still feel strongly the confused remembrance of millions of generations of animal-like individuals who have preceded us, and for whom life had no end other than the act of sexual intercourse.

I repeat that love is still fortunately the principal act of life; and in this we are closely related to all other animals, without reckoning that it is not the most laborious or the most active, in a word, the most moral men, who assure the propagation of the human species, since these latter are not they who are organically the strongest.

In fact, it is well known that the most warlike peoples are the most devoted to polygamy, and Plutarch and Plato have already remarked that those nations most sensitive to the pleasures of love were also the most warlike and courageous.

About this statement of facts there are many prejudices and wrong opinions, due to the ideas of Schopenhauer as expressed by him in his celebrated *Metaphysics of Love.*

Let us direct special attention to the following considerations.

The morals of fidelity, of chastity, and of temperance are the sexual morals of the altruists, of the partisans of the good, and the so-called virtues. Now it must be observed that in essence such a sexual morality in its greatest extension and most rigorous application is contrary to the interests of the species in at least one fundamental: that of its continuity. In general, it may be said that the altruism of the individual, if it were generalised as desired by moralists and preceptors, would have a harmful effect on the species as a direct consequence; whence, translating this application into physiological terminology, we may say that the sexual morality of the altruists, as it leads to infecundity, is a sign of degeneration, as it represents the greatest effort to free one's self from animalness.

On the other hand, the sexual morality of free love, inconstancy, erotic wandering, is the morality of the egoists, the encouragers of the full development and complete satisfaction of one's own needs, and cannot be carried on without encroaching upon the rights of others.

Such a morality, acting for the whole advantage of individuals, or at least of some individuals who would be aggrandised, strengthened, and exalted by it, is on the other hand favourable to the fundamental interest of the species, as it represents its continuity by means of its strongest champions. It is only after centuries of Christian sentimentalism and of Jewish sadness and weakness (the Hebrews were the most anti-amorous people of antiquity) that we can have given up our convictions to the contrary, and made altruism the moral formula most favourable to the development of the human race. Egoism and its sexual morality are the vital conditions of him who lives well and is in sound health, and it is to the interest of the race to be propagated by means of the most active and healthy individuals.

There exists, therefore, a kind of double antagonism, whereby that which appears blamable from the point of view of our *social morals* is justified by the exigencies of the race; and that which seems only a boast in the eyes of us sociable and domesticated men is blamable from the naturalist standpoint.

In short, this antithesis is due to the opposition in the interests of the animal species to those of the homonymous social species.

It follows from what I have said that I cannot agree with Morasso, who holds that the sexual instinct "leads the individual to a series of acts and desires, of gains and losses, which are almost always harmful to him, and certainly tend to diminish his forces and to prevent his energy and individuality from being employed for themselves alone." He, in my opinion, mistakes the pleasure which the individual looks for in the satisfying of his sexual impulse with the result which is obtained from it; in other words, his point of view is not very different from that of the "snare" which, according to Schopenhauer, is held out to us by Nature. He therefore confuses the hedonic aspect (which we should only consider as psychologists) with the teleological aspect of the fact—with Nature's object, that is to say.

Now what the individual is conscious of is only the pleasure which he pursues, and it is still an essential *datum* of positive psychology (not doctrinary or, worse still, Christianising psychology) that the quest of sexual enjoyment is one of the principal characteristics of a strong and animal vitality, of a soundly egoistic constitution.

That afterwards, with the act of copulation, the individual undergoes a considerable loss of substance, and hence of life, cannot be affirmed with equal certainty; at least, in the absolute sense in which this is generally understood. We shall return to the consideration of this question; but nothing whatever of a psychological nature can be affirmed with certainty until it is known what pleasure is or signifies. And in truth we are very far from possessing this knowledge.

If pleasure were the cognisance of an increase of energy, as several thinkers have held, it might be admitted that the difference between gain and loss—between the increase of strength experienced subsequently to the pleasure received, and the diminution of strength through seminal loss—was to the advantage of the individual.

But we need not venture to state useless hypotheses.

For the rest, if individuals with more marked sexual characteristics are to make the greatest sacrifices, which would be the outcome of Morasso's idea, they could not go beyond the limits of a few generations, which is unteleological and contradictory to experience.

With restraint, aggravation, the multiplying of social ties, surrounding ourselves with a rigid morality and, above all, the institution of marriage, which takes away the woman from the absolute rule of the man, the conception of love, as we have already emphasised, is gradually being deprived of its traits of animalness, of egoism, and of purely physical desire—in other words, it is changing into poetic love, Platonic love, sentimental love.

It is said that troubadours and poets have contributed to the production of this new form of love. This may be; but it may then be asked why troubadours and poets have felt love in this way, and it is at once apparent that we have not advanced one step towards the solution of the question.

Putting this problem on one side for the moment, and dealing with the matter from observation alone, we may say that such a form is more common among the northern peoples than the southern, and if we take this fact in conjunction with the other two of their relative sexual coldness and their later development, we may affirm that: *sentimental and poetic love is the love of the chaste and cold; or, better, sentimentalism is the amorous effervescence of cold people.*

This statement is not in discord with the fact that the first loves of young men, the first early erotic trials, are sentimental, since an embryo erotism is not more active than an insufficient erotism, and must act on the sensibility and on the imagination to the same extent and in the same manner.

An interesting question, when different sexuality among different peoples and individuals is spoken of, is this:—

Is the different degree of intensity of the sexual impulse, the greater or lesser portion of the life of a race which is given up to love, an immediate or direct function—the expression of an organic attribute with which men and nations are endowed in a greater or less degree: or may it be that in these ethnic groups and individuals, whom we call less sensual, is to be found some purely psychological mechanism which subdues the love instinct, so that these men and races are only *apparently* less sensual?

It is of some consequence which answer is given, because behind this question there is another and more important one concerning the relations of the sexual function with, and its influence upon, intelligence and conscious life. In other words, this question may be formulated thus: Does the lesser sexuality correspond to a lesser intensity of the organic function, or is it an effect of education—a purely psychical fact?

I think that an affirmative reply should be given to both the alternative questions. The two processes should often appear together, and the psychological process must give way to the other after the lapse of time, as the possibility of the development of the subduing mechanism must be based upon a diminished general vitality, that is, upon an organic fact.

   *   *   *   *   *

In those countries most given to love, woman forms a plastic atmosphere of ideas and sentiments, and creates a public opinion which is the dominating factor upon the actions of man.

In whatever disguise it may appear, this is the law that is in force in such countries: The only thing worthy of a man who is truly manly is an amorous conquest.

For this reason it is evident why other high aspirations, quests of knowledge, and desires to accomplish heroic actions, are neglected—even sometimes openly opposed, or treated by public feeling with some ridicule and contempt.

A warm atmosphere, tinctured with a rosy erotic blending, the very air wafting little shivers of voluptuousness, seems continually to titillate these races, and to keep them in a continual state of Dionysiac exaltation.

In general, however, even in those countries less devoted to love, woman is less influenced in her judgments upon man by preconceptions and by moral sentiments, which proves on one hand her greater proximity to the state of nature—the primitiveness and *innocence* of the feminine soul; and, on the other hand, how the attraction, the unconscious choice of woman is something profound and natural, and that, contrary to moral stratifications and beliefs, she is guided by the inherent and eternal necessity of the species.

Therefore the purest woman, the sweetest, gentlest, most chaste, and most decent woman, if she will inquire into her hidden feelings, and if she will give their real name to certain other feelings which take illusive appearances called social contempt and moral abomination, but which are in reality masculine moral valuations (or, rather, valuations of one section of males, the less fortunate as against the more fortunate), valuations which the woman possesses and suffers without *feeling* them as *hers:* this woman, I repeat, if she examines herself thoroughly, will often find in herself an inward and hidden wish for the victor, for the *homme à femmes,* for the Don Juan, for the man who employs his time in preparations for and in the work of seduction.

For, alas! how often is the supposed antipathy of a virtuous woman for a man who is the idol of another woman only the instinctive and desperate defence of a heart that is conscious of its own weakness? is it not a dissimulation against one's self? And when one of these women perceives the true nature of her feeling, there begins for her a fierce inward battle, if her modesty is strong and her nature ardent and passionate; and little trifling occurrences will torture her anew every moment. Laclos's picture of Madame de Tourvel[26] is a good example of the melancholy spectacle of such minds.

But there are even more dreadful situations when two different loves fight with one another for the possession of a woman's heart.

This possibility proves the enormous distance which separates one species of love from the other. Thus a woman, with all her tenderness and goodness of mind and heart, can love a man whose moral loftiness, prayers of devotion, and nobleness of feeling she values and esteems, and yet feel her inmost and secret viscera vibrate with a very different quivering at the mere sight of another, a man *par excellence*, a man who has all the traits of masculineness: the Ruler, the Master.

This is the tragic case of the heroine of *L'Amour est mon péché.*[27] But if her greatness of mind, her sensitiveness, all her moral being become repugnant and rebel at the treachery, if by the perfection of her feeling she even allow it to die away rather than acknowledge her fault to the man whom she feels she loves, she has none the less fallen; and the exigencies of Nature have once more declared against the laws, the impositions, and the violence of morality: "Let the most agreeable, attractive, and amiable woman belong to the strongest, most ardent, and most loving male."

---

[26] In *Les Liaisons dangereuses*

[27] "Love Is My Sin," a novel by Helene du Nouy.

For the rest, such contests of the feminine mind do not always turn to tragedy; but often to comedy.

From this point of view woman has the sharpest insight! With a single penetrating look and synthetic discernment she values and adjudges a man, weighs up in an instant all that she can draw from him and which she thinks may be useful to her; so that while she will submit her entire self with all the humiliation of a slave to one man in order to obtain even a kiss from him, she will make another pay a high price for her body, the price, that is, of . . . matrimony.

Woman is in general less moral than man, for she is more natural; but I should call her amoral rather than immoral: moreover, in her tastes and preferences she is usually the exponent—the index—of what is most advantageous for the race, even in opposition to the rights of society.

Young herself, she will not hide her admiration for the man who is handsome, brilliant, strong, rich, and unreasonable, and her secret sympathies are for those men who are even rather violent and overbearing, to the disadvantage of those who are gentle, quiet, and laborious; "good," in a word: as mother, she will often have a greater regard for her more uncontrollable children, and, in opposition to the husband (who, thinking of the social future of the children, redoubles his severity, and tries to institute a proper system of discipline), she will often take the side of indulgence and liberty, and will have her children healthy and strong rather than clever and wise.

It is undeniable, on the other hand, that woman is charitable, and able to console and to comfort much better than man.

This statement may appear to contradict what has already been said. But it does not. Woman owes her charity to her physical weakness and to her state of bodily inferiority, and, besides that, her charity has an eminently natural character. She is tinctured with, not to say formed by, maternity, which is the altruism of woman; a substantial altruism, since it implies

ON THE TRACKS OF LIFE

with pregnancy and parturition a huge sacrifice of life and matter. It will thus be seen that the altruism of woman is almost a natural phenomenon, and that of man a social phenomenon; the first is, I should be inclined to say, physiological, the second psychological.

In accordance with this estimation of the altruism and of the love of woman, we may observe that maternity among us Latins alienates the wife from the husband more than is the case with the peoples of the north. Among these latter the bonds which depend upon higher and truly human acts of affinity, choice, and mutual consent prevail in marriage over those which originate from the needs of the race; and the affection existing between the married pair is not overcome by the love for the offspring which is born and grows up.

On the other hand, how many unions among us southerners continue to have a semblance of reality only on account of the existence of the children!

It is often said that the psychology of woman is made up of contrasts and contradictions. In one sense that is true; but we must before all make clear some fundamental points in her nature.

Woman, whatever may be said by the poets and by a certain madrigalesque psychology, is a more monotonous and more uniform being than man: the chromatic scale of her characteristics is not far extended, for she is a being nearer to nature than we men are. The forgetfulness or ignorance of this fact has caused, and is still causing, much bitterness to the idealist, the man who thinks, and explains also the rancour with which he has judged and continues to judge woman.

Woman is less moral than man because she has almost always been idle.

And the fault of that is certainly not hers. The nations have been very few in number who employed woman in ordinary work, since the deforming and brutalising effect of this did not escape their observation, and the natural indolence which may have induced men to utilise the services of women as beasts of burden was checked and overcome by their desire to preserve and perfect her as an instrument of pleasure. The moralising action of work had little or no effect on the physio-psychic organism of the women, directly, at least; and they to a great extent passively imbued the aspects, ideas, and moral sentiments which were acquired from and found almost solely in the men.

The domestic labours to which she has since been destined are not nearly so toilsome and deforming as those of man; and we need pay no attention to this legend about the domestic activity of woman: an activity which really consists in giving a great deal of attention to unimportant matters. It may, however, be recalled that all this was *desired* by man, and was submitted to by woman.

Woman had to become aware of this state of affairs, which she did with a certain wonder and surprise, as her relative coldness did not enable her to perceive the actual value which man was setting on her body. And, as is the case when we have an incorrect or too low opinion of ourselves, and we try rightly or wrongly to adopt a higher point of view, our aspirations and desires, having acquired an unlooked-for daring, rise suddenly above the equitable: so woman made man pay heavily for the irresistible need which he felt for her, and she has given to the . . . thing a greater value than it really possessed. And this was another injustice of man, who thus compelled woman to develop herself in one sole direction !

This more *natural* aspect of the psychology of woman being granted, it at once explains her preferences, her so-called weaknesses, and her affinity for those men who, as we have said, represent the primitive animal type; and yet men, or, rather, idealists, complain of her nature, and say that woman is the despair of all reasonable men, and that she does not understand deep and sincere thoughts and feelings. Poets, too, have showered imprecations upon her; many voices have been lifted up to bewail the unhappiness of genius in love; and, in addition to all this, we have the brutal harshness and abuse of the pessimists, in whom there was rightly seen to be a great sexual deficiency—a more or less concealed impotence.

But it must not be imagined that the opinions which have predominated in literature in regard to certain subjects (especially woman and love) are by any means the expression of general human knowledge. This would be a great illusion. Prose writers—sometimes also poets and artists—form a section by themselves within a larger section of *workmen,* and, consciously or unconsciously, they are subjected to the influence of the special morality of work.

But, besides the world of thinkers, writers, and moralisers, there live and vibrate sundry forms of sentiment, action, and individuality who, even if they despise literature and art, are not on that account less sincere or potent: but rather the reverse!

And this shows the infinitely greater compass of the chromatic scale of masculine personality, which, however, if it is more extended from the standpoint of sociality than that of woman is perhaps outdone by it from the opposite standpoint of naturalness.

Only too often do writers make erroneous generalisations about love and woman, from which arise common opinions that have no right to stand for what is really the truth, and have no more authority than that of the writer himself.

I wish to make it clear how this error arises.

Those who *write* about love and about woman have for the most part a certain type of mind peculiar to themselves, a fixed range of ideas and sentiments; but, on the other hand, those who really *know* woman and can tell us the most interesting things about her do not write at all; but live and let live.

The variety of blendings of character in men is very large, much larger than in women. But, on the other hand, there are probably reciprocal laws of attraction and relationship having a certain regard to whatever concerns the means and circumstances of the seduction practised by one sex on the other.

So, therefore, the man who is thoughtful, calm, hardworking, and reserved will easily fall a victim to the charms of one of those women who are usually called "dangerous"; a shy man will be caught by a coquette, and, vice versa, the ardent man of amorous initiative will choose his companion among women who are modest, retiring, tender, and affectionate.

It may be that every individual looks in love for his psychological integrant; he instinctively looks for those qualities and traits which he himself does not possess, or, what is more probable (since even love is only a struggle for the mastery), the stronger being—the one who is provided with the more subtle and seductive ways—succeeds in conquering the weaker.

Now, to a certain extent, and within certain limits, some activities, which I will call social, and which are becoming more developed in society, are contrary to the virtue of seduction, at least in so far as it partakes of animalness and nature. I do not wish to consider that in its present state the battle of love is fought with the very means and weapons which society itself gives to those engaged in it. But in the acquisition of such social means as riches, knowledge, and the authority which comes from one's position, the faculty of natural seduction is lost or considerably diminished.

And from the knowledge of this fact springs the misogyny of a few writers, and their hatred for woman—the enemy who is often victorious.

Behold, then, an original and ingenuous idealism converting itself into an erroneous pessimism which is often blind to the most evident truth!

Man is in general a moralising animal, and that is his weakness in his relations with woman. It would be better if he were to make up his mind, and find out which is the more agreeable to him: the woman who is voluptuous, beautiful, and fascinating, the instrument of pleasure, the Phryne or Fiammetta;[28] or the woman in the higher and more noble sense of the word, the Andromache or the Miranda.[29] Instead of either of these, however, he often chooses the proud woman, charming and playful, and would like to teach her morality, instead of providing himself with a whip, as the wise old woman advised Zarathustra; he longs for the voluptuous woman, haughty and playful, and forgets that she has teeth and finger-nails.

And yet, O pessimists and abortive Panglosses, would you think of waging war with the lion that would tear you in pieces, the poison-darting serpent, the eagle that would bear you away in his talons ?

Nevertheless, you fancy you can bargain with certain women in this way, and you are disquieted and enraged when they sometimes remember that they are beasts of prey!

But, it will be asked, what then are the probabilities of love for man—the higher man, the man of the future?

It is possible that a third phase in the history of the relationship of the two sexes is about to open—or in the history of the battle of sex, as Viazzi[30] calls it. If in the first phase man overcame woman by his bodily strength, if in the second woman had the advantage over man (if not in name at

---

28 Phryne was an ancient Greek courtesan (*hetaira*) who became one of the wealthiest women in Athens. She was charged with impiety but was acquitted, allegedly because she showed her breasts to the jury. Fiammetta—Italian for "little flame"—was Maria d'Aquino, the muse of Giovanni Bocaccio.

29 Andromache is the wife of Hector in *The Iliad,* and Miranda is the daughter of Prospero in Shakespeare's *The Tempest.* Both are traditional models of feminine virtues.

30 See note 20

least in fact) by the development of her qualities of cunning and subtlety, who can say that a new era may not now be beginning in which man will turn woman's own arms against her and conquer her once more? Some people expect and predict the approach of a phase of conciliation and peace; for my part I am not convinced that progress is made by acquiescence and repose; but I believe with Schiller that out of war comes everything that is most beautiful.

Let us outline the probabilities of love for the higher man, the man of future humanity.

The scruples, the delicacy, the chivalry of man towards woman, his compassion for and generosity shown to her weakness, are often an extreme proof of masculine stupidity, the clearest expression of the absurdity of his being; just as his horror of feminine lying, and his noble design to redeem woman, to exalt her, are nothing but illusions, new and more subtle appearances of man's rooted credulity and of his suicidal wish to deceive himself.

Woman is another species within the species *man;* a more aristocratic species, that is, more handsome, more false, more immoral, or, to express it even better, amoral; she is nearer to nature than man is, and, like nature, heedless of and indifferent to that order of motives which we call ethic.

The higher man, the man who examines himself and finds in his own being the traces of a free and healthy life, of a profound force long handed down from generation to generation, who becomes aware of his own nobleness: such a man must learn to love feminine lying, and the handsome and untruthful woman. In proportion as she is clever, rapid and ready, so ought the true male to be shrewd, enticing, and insinuating; he should overpower her with her own weapons, subdue her, crush her without her feeling the yoke, make her the slave and the agent of his wishes and the instrument of his pleasures.

Warned by experience of the diminution, the dispersion, and the ruin of many of his companions by female blandishments, he should devote all his energies to redoubling his acuteness so as to avoid falling into her meshes himself.

I do not preach a crusade against women, like the Schopenhauerian misogyny or the dull and unjustified invectives of the Fathers of the Church: the dismal result of the union of impotence with envious rancour. The lying of woman, the lying against which, O men, you are revolting, is desired by life itself, it is a natural thing.

The lying of woman is lost in the shadows of her conscience, even more often than not it is quite obscure, and the amiable being is seriously convinced of the truth of that which is after all only the product of her imagination.

Even her deliberate lying is only the continuation of what has already been imposed on her by nature; and how, O men, can you condemn a being who, at that supreme instant of love —at that moment when voluptuousness becomes grave and serious—is, as if by the unexpected presence of a God, forced by an unwritten law to simulate repulse and flight?

The acknowledgment that women lie should not be held by an intelligent man as belief in an absolute and proved truth, but only as a pretext of his to rid himself of a woman when he is tired of her; a justification which gives to his moral nature the force of a pretence and the support of a conviction; even if he does not want to play with the woman like a cat with a mouse, or to let himself be deceived and run risks through using up his own entire strength.

Why, again, should we worry about this so-called womanly deceit, and perceive treachery and duplicity in every act of woman? Let us accept without too much sadness the pleasure which she offers us so graciously and pleasantly; moreover, our jealous susceptibility originates from our exclusivist and limited masculine self-love, from unwillingness to grant our lady friends the same right to love as we concede to ourselves.

And, if it be objected that this latter is logical and consonant with the exigencies of society and of nature, I answer that men should subtilise and refine such relations by raising themselves above both nature and society, and so cease to be their slaves and victims.

Let us rather be thankful, and accept with candour, frankness, and coolness the gifts that woman offers us with so much simplicity and grace; let us especially prevent our imaginations from setting such a value on woman as shall make us appear unworthy of her; and let us not defile the beauty of her acts with our fantastic notions of sin, deceit, and crime. For the rest, there is every reason to believe that those who declaim against sensual love have not been born for it; so that they think woman, whom they find themselves unable to conquer, is therefore only a sink of perfidy. The man who is born for love is less subtle, and delights in woman with simplicity and innocence.

We ourselves, more refined and complex, shall take delight in her not only as an instrument of pleasure, but also as a good game, a magnificent game, relishing with wise voluptuousness the joy of her ten thousand dangerous and terrible seductions. Strengthened with our science, we shall teach her to serve our interests, our desires, and our aims; we shall accord her even the supreme luxury of making her believe in the immortality of love—*her* love—and we shall hide from her eyes her own real nature, her frailty, and her tendency to fall; in short, we shall make her more beautiful and more glorious, we shall make her our own creature, the work of our own full maturity.

But one day we shall be tired of this also, for a higher truth will appear to us, and we shall feel that we are on the threshold of true greatness. Then our own art itself will seem to us something immature, something precocious and forced; a beauty of forced growth; a remedy for and an attempt made by our hearts, always afflicted with the disease of sentimentalism, an artificial flower of our inner consciousness;

and perhaps the moment when we perceive all this will mark our real freedom. And we shall then love woman with the gentle and faint recollection of a past time, with the remembrance of strong and deep sentimental love, purified and exalted by recent experience; we shall love her with a love resembling the tender colours of twilight that form the highest wisdom of the day, and our passion will awaken the distant echoes of our hearts, as a gentle sea breeze raises little specks of foam that crown the little waves—the echoes of bygone tempests.

Nothing further will then disturb the limpid sphere where our intelligence dwells, and where our ardent will to power is concentrated.

The pure poetic love of our youth will not have been felt in vain, but it will have discarded all its dross, all its ineffable imperfection, coarseness, and simplicity. No longer will it be bitter jealousy, the irritation of one's self-love, the false protestations of an eternal affection, or a thing of artifice and dissimulation, but it will be the indulgence that springs from the clear knowledge and the security of the man who is above any form of acting, every kind of attitudinising. And, when man has arrived at this stage, he may be sure he will receive a magnificent reward for his wisdom; that any superior female mind—any woman in whom the highest intellectual vigour is coupled with the ardent virtues of the female sex—will readily yield up her entire self in the surprise of hearing the unexpected revelation: "Nothing belonging to thee is hidden from my knowledge; all thy good, all thy evil, thy blemishes and thy virtues: all are clear to me, and I love thee all in all. I now perceive thy real and deep sincerity, the sincerity which is hidden in the depths of thy heart, as the generative power is hidden in a flower under the deceptive appearance of a bright and seductive corolla. Thou art before me as nude as Phryne, and all my desire is kindled at the sight."

At such a time falsehood, truth, and cheat are only vain words without meaning, since we must hide nothing from each other; our love is so great that nothing must be concealed, for we can let nothing impede us that contributes to thy pleasure or to mine. We are both free, and every time either mankind or the world dispels the illusion of our eternal desire, our eternal longing for pleasure and for knowledge of each other, every time that a new face out of a thousand attracts us and then disgusts us, we shall come back to each other until—who knows?—until a decaying, crepuscular wisdom reunites us for ever.

CHAPTER II

WHAT IS ARISTOCRATIC?

In every age and in every place there have been, and are, fundamental and contrary forms of human character, synthetic unities of sentiments, ideas, and actions, all of which, acting reciprocally in an identical manner across the course of history, must have given rise to social phenomena which, in their essence, have been continually reproduced, although to a superficial observer they may seem dissimilar.

The two extreme forms which I shall outline in the following pages may to some readers appear schematic and arbitrary; but I myself look upon them as psychological types rather than as figures, as characters rather than as living persons.

These two types, however, coincide with the characters of the men whom we see around us every day, who form part of life, and, what is more, create it. This remark applies more especially to the first type, as it is more in evidence than the other.

Moreover, the existence of these two contrary forms explains every human fact to us from a natural standpoint; and such differences of character may be found, in the main, at least, by the patient investigator, in facts and aspects of life which are very different in appearance.

In examining any aggregate, or any social group, even the collection of the few persons who constitute a family, we may note, socially speaking, some differences with respect to the manner in which these persons participate in the labours and the advantages of the aggregate.

There are individuals who, giving to the group but a small portion of their energies and activities, succeed in obtaining the greatest remuneration, even more remuneration than is usually given for the particular kind of work which they perform.

There are others, on the other hand, whose condition is just the contrary of that described in the preceding paragraph, who, giving all their energy to the work to be done, receive in return a wage much lower than what their efforts entitle them to.

The proportion between giving and—a purely economic relationship —is the expression of character in a social sense, i.e. of the *personal value* of the individual, and is of the highest importance in social dynamics.

Social character—that is, the method and the extent of asserting one's value, and of acting upon one's fellow-men—is not by any means the gauge of the value of any individual; but we need not consider this argument just now.

A detached individualism, courage in every form, the spirit of initiative and enterprise, the love of adventure, of war, and of the chase, of the unknown and of the unexpected, are the distinguishing traits of those individuals who belong to the first type, traits which denote a healthy and vigorous nature. Leisure is their natural state, as it was also the state of primitive humanity, of which, indeed, they possess many of the characteristics. These are the men who are called "rulers," "masters," "governors."

These are the representatives of what I call *the aristocratic spirit.* And I must here call attention to the fact that the aristocratic spirit only partly coincides (and even then more in appearance than in fact) with the spirit which is the mental and psychological inheritance of our present aristocracies. The aristocratic spirit stands in the same relation to the mental and sentimental possessions of our aristocratic classes as a living body does to an embalmed corpse, or as the personal creation of a man's genius to the mere tradition of a school in art, in literature, or in science.

Daring and bold—often just because they are upheld by their great confidence in and their high opinion of themselves —they do not shrink from enterprises which would make others of even greater skill and experience hesitate; and yet they succeed better and more quickly than others, for life needs men of prompt and decisive action rather than unreliable and doubtful ideologists.

Their strong personality, powerful and indomitable activity, thirst for sensations, and restless curiosity, are ill adapted, or not adapted at all, to the discipline of regular work, and they are incapable of giving attention to or occupying themselves with any labour which requires steadiness and calmness, their tendencies being all towards physical life and the pleasures of love.

The most salient traits of such men are a certain violence, more or less dissimulated by their habits and the conventions of society; a frank and sincere egoism (I mean an egoism not timid or despicable, which does not dissemble and seek to hide itself, but seizes liberally upon everything it thinks suitable); and a wish, everywhere and always, to force their own personalities upon other men.

I must here remark that when I speak of egoism, violence, and a tendency towards leisure, I do not attach to these words any condemnatory significance, or any moral sanction. My task is, so to speak, that of a naturalist, and I use certain words because they stand for certain things; but I pay no attention to the moral colouring ascribed to them. It is very true that our mentality, hedged about and consubstantiated with moral valuations—since morality is of all the circumstances of our existence the most diffuse, and also in a great measure the state of those who think and write—cannot free itself quickly and entirely from that particular moral colouring which is an adherent feature of the objective meaning of those words which are the instruments of our inner life. I hope nevertheless that this book of mine will help someone to learn to repudiate certain out-of-date forms which should long ago have been relegated to their proper places in the realms of prehistoric thought, in view of the continual interchange of ideas between the higher and lower classes of men, and these out-of-date forms I speak of should form part of the patrimony of the latter.

These moral qualities which I have mentioned are exact parallels of those external physiological qualities which are seen in the appearance and bodily activity of the physical type of man. The spirit of action in such men is rapid, almost instinctive, always sure; suited to and followed by happy results. It may be supposed that such virtues are the expression of physical vigour, a certain equipoise of humours, and a primitiveness and freshness of temperament.

This capacity for violent deeds, this instinct of destruction, this audacity, which, as we have seen, are characteristics of the aristocratic spirit, are found in men who devote themselves to love and amorous conquests—compelled to do so, indeed, by their own impulses and constitutional needs—and these qualities give their behaviour, appearance, and ideas a distinct and special impress; although their habits, and the necessity for charming others with graceful and delicate manners, might deceive many people on this point.

Thus in the elegant Don Juan, under the appearance of politeness and courtesy, we find these same fundamental traits; so that, just because their manners are insinuating and enticing, and correctness and gentility are habitual to them, they are armed all the more dangerously because these weapons are hidden and pointed.

Such an affinity between the two types is significant, and reveals an element common to both, namely, a vigorous vital activity which is concentrated in and hinges upon sexuality. Moreover, sexual love and the domineering spirit are, as we have already said, companions and even brothers.

Love, and the control of others, are the strongest and most primitive outlets of action, and the indisputable fascination which men of these two categories exercise is the fascination that attends men of vigorous action, since action is the most fervid life, the most robust life; and all that is strongly vital is furnished with the attribute of beauty. It is interesting to see how some of the psychological signs referred to before are still part of the female ψυχή,[31] except that in women who are physically weaker than and in conflict with men, they are more prominently tinged with cunning and deceit, in the eyes of men, at least.

The infallible and sure choice of a woman when she is in the presence of one of these men is a certain sign that such men are dear to nature, since woman is unconsciously the herald and the judge of nature's petitions and sentences.

Now, even a beautiful and delicate woman, when she sees that she is the object of the attentions of a Lovelace or a Valmont,[32] or if she finds herself courted more or less openly, will perhaps be shocked by some trifle which will reveal the brutal character of the man to her keen intuition; but yet behind this jar to her feelings there will always remain the fascinating influence which comes from these strong creatures.

Woman admires more readily whatever is natural, formed, precise; she admires character as an insuperable and infallible form of action; and nothing disgusts her more in a man than indecision, fear, doubt, hesitation, and reserve, which, however, are often the qualities of the man who thinks and feels deeply. Women in general think that man should take, or know how to take: whether it be pleasure, riches, or . . . herself. Even in the poorest and most wretched woman there is always something

---

[31] psyche

[32] Robert Lovelace, from Samuel Richardson's novel *Clarissa*, and the Vicomte de Valmont, from *Les Liaisons dangereuses*. Both characters are archetypal libertines and playboys.

of the feeling which prompted the women of the middle ages to give themselves up as a reward to the bravest and most distinguished knights of the joust and the tournament.

The Greeks, whose mythology is a magnificent work of human knowledge, had already idealised this fact when they made Mars the conqueror of women and goddesses, and the beloved of Venus herself, in preference to good, honest Vulcan, the laborious and jealous net-maker.

In the type which is the exact contrary of that to which I have hitherto been referring there predominates a certain state of depression, or at least an attitude partly of calmness and partly of inertness.

These forms are more favourable for the production of a methodical and moderate activity. Such a type of man clings more or less strongly to the idea of duty, that is to say, to a moral idea; he is weak in his outward expression, rather slow, of small imitative capacity, taciturn, and provided with a powerful sense of inhibition which almost overpowers him, and makes him hesitative, unsteady, and uncertain. All these characteristics indicate a poor vitality. But the most important fact from a biological standpoint, and the key to the type of man we are speaking of, is his amorous coldness, which is accompanied by an inefficacious and extremely poor power of seduction.

Since the intensity of sexual life beautifies and animates the whole personality, and moreover is manifested in that group of attitudes of aggression and initiative which are directed towards the overcoming of woman, this intensity is once more revealed when one sets out on the conquest of social benefits.

The man who is not, so to speak, a good love hunter, will most probably make but a poor figure in life when competing with other men in the struggle for success and ease; and it would be safe to wager that, even with greater merits and personal worth than others, he will not be successful in securing these advantages in life to which his merits entitle him. And this is due to the fact that the means by which a man may come successfully out of the struggle for ease and wealth are the same as those which he makes use of in his amorous conquests. Therefore where one man is lost because he will not dare, another wins because he is rapacious.

In this regard it may be said that, from an internal and subjective point of view, the way in which men distinguish themselves is the spirit, the state of conscience by which they *take* their share of the benefits of life.

It should seem that there are some who take the greatest advantages that life offers and yet always keep themselves on the credit side; and others who take scarcely anything, and even then with timidity and suspicious looks, as if fearing to be unworthy of it, or dreading that they may have to give it back. These have the so-called "bad conscience," a perennial dissatisfaction which is common to all men who are weak, sickly, crushed.

Affections, sentiments, and moral judgments will naturally differ, and even up to a certain point conflict, in the two classes of men, and, whilst one will set the highest value on virtue, work, goodness, and altruism (or, if not altruism, at least on not injuring one's neighbour), another will maintain his views from what we may call a rather amoral sphere, or, at the worst, from the standpoint of egoistic morality.

It would be a mistake to suppose that individuals who act in this manner profess immorality. Immorality is a form, a category, a classification of those who manufacture morals, and the aristocratic spirit lives above everything that is devised by man and imposed artificially.

Moralists and moral men are wrong in believing that what they call "evil" is always wished for, sought by, and accompanied with this "bad conscience." That may be the case with moralised individuals who for some cause or other station themselves beyond the pale of the law; but it does not happen to those who live and move in complete disregard of and above the law. For the rest, these two moral forms (we may so call them for convenience, although one only has a right to the name) exist apart from each other, not only in different individuals, but in one and the same man. It may therefore be said that some of our own actions are inspired by one form and some by the other; and even that in certain periods of our lives one form prevails and in other periods the other.

From the most superficial and common observation it will appear that ardent individuals who are intensely devoted to love accustom themselves to work with some difficulty, and this proves the opposition between the sexual instinct and the social instinct: if, indeed, we may speak of the modern man as possessing a real social or gregarious instinct, and if it would not be more to the point to speak of gregarious tendencies. Whatever this sexual instinct may be, it asserts itself in opposition to the social instinct; and it is by the prevalence of one or other that individuals, societies, and nations are distinguished. Therefore the peoples of the East and South, who have their sexual tendencies strongly developed, have not the same spirit of sociality or solidarity which is so remarkable a feature of the sexually cold northern nations.

The aristocratic spirit in the classical times of Greece and Rome is revealed to us in the literature, art, and thought of these peoples. All this paganism, of which classicism is the intellectual formula, may be said to be the psychological representation of the word ἄριστος in its ancient and original acceptation, that is, in its physical and bodily meaning of strongest, most vigorous: Christianity, of which romanticism was the later intellectual formula, was developed in a different manner that might be compared to the transformation of the conception of excellence indicated by ἄριστος, which after Plato's time came to stand for spiritual and moral excellence, goodness, virtue. It may be said that a great part of the history of morals is contained in the evolution of the meaning of this word.

It may not be out of place to observe here that, although similar changes of meaning are to be found in many languages, philology cannot give us much assistance in compiling a history of morals, for their origin has to be sought in an extremely remote period.

The contrast in these two established types of character is very great. But, to find out whether a person belongs to the one or the other, we must not, in reckoning his mental value and his more or less noteworthy intellectual contribution, trust in appearances only, or even in what he himself thinks, his personal convictions, and his professed doctrines. For a man may be endowed with the aristocratic spirit, and yet be an ardent apostle of liberal and democratic ideas.

Did not this often happen in the case of Lassalle, the finest and most dazzling figure in the history of socialism? His influence on the politics of his time, and the fascination which he exercised on the society of the period—a fascination, indeed, which enabled one of our modern Italian poets to make him a figure in a drama—are due to the fact that, in spite of his socialistic ideas, he was one of the aristocratic spirits, if only because of his giving up his entire person to the inflamed and genial propaganda which he carried on.

Need I say that the two types which I have endeavoured to characterise are seldom found in a pure state? But we find in all individuals a combination of the types outlined. These two extreme forms, I expressly repeat, are valuable inasmuch as they are useful in determining certain dynamic points in the development of the individual and of society; they are opportune points of view which we may use as new and secure foundations on which to base the genesis of complex social products, and to establish a true conception of progress.

*   *   *   *   *

In everyday speech there are other distinctions made which have an approximate moral or historical value, the actual substance of which, however, has not hitherto been precisely ascertained. I shall try to bring these into the light of a psychological examination.

The first step will be to discriminate between the two meanings of *aristocratic* and *distinguished,* which are generally confused in common language. There is a great difference between what I call the *aristocratic spirit* and that special quality which is somewhat inexactly called *distinction.*

The essence of the first-named is an expansive, eccentric, exuberant, rich, and violent activity; its psychological nucleus is the will to power, its physiological base is an intact and vigorous vitality. The aristocratic spirit is that fullness and integrity of personality which will have nothing to do with the shackles of routine restrictions, the limitations of a particular state, the bonds of any one class or profession, and, above all, the moral and physical diminution due to the degrading influence of work: it is the greatest knowledge of individuality.

Every special trade, occupation, or profession, in so far as it comprehends a certain number of actions and duties which are constantly repeated, creates a special mode of feeling and thinking, a restriction of the mental field, a *bosse*, a special mediocre figure— in short, a deformation of moral and physical personality.

Moreover, everyone knows how it is possible to recognise a man's ordinary occupation by certain traits, certain peculiarities of an individual's appearance.

Of course, the wealth and consequent leisure which a man obtains by working, and which gradually efface the deforming effects of work, may in more or less time result in a complete moral and bodily transformation.

In truth, it would be more exact to say that some particular characteristics distinguish a person whilst betraying him at the same time; but as most men are beings with particular characteristics and personalities, who, in choosing practical occupations, have followed one bent or inclination more than another, it will be more convenient to apply the word *distinguished* to those individuals who do not show these deformities or particular traits at all.

Distinction therefore is only an *effacement* of every marked particular, a deficiency of characteristic traits, which can go so far as to obliterate anything personal and original—and therefore worthy and strong—which the individual may possess.

Distinction is just something undefined and vague. Most certainly it is not beauty—more often the contrary—and it is exactly this absence of characteristic traits which is the result of ease. An individual's own characteristics may be and often are unheeded and of small importance just by reason of their peculiarity; but they are sometimes expressive of originality. Now, distinction levels and suppresses every salient quality, and is therefore often insipid, flaccid, and flabby; something that shows impoverishment of blood, anaemia, functional degeneracy.

Distinction is a privilege of the upper classes; but it is an imitation, a poor copy, of the real aristocratic type. In most cases distinction is a social mask; a kind of deceit which those who possess it turn to the disadvantage of society; setting a higher value on what is really moral and physical poverty.

As *bon-ton* is, according to Madame de Staël, the means by which most people hide their narrowness of mind, so distinction allows the tired and the exhausted to give a very different value to their persons, and to deceive others into adopting this estimation.

For the most part, distinction springs from decadence of the aristocratic type, and is in such a case regressive.

The so-called aristocratic classes of today—I specially insist on this—are for the most part of the *distinguished* type, not the aristocratic type, of which distinction is but the counterfeit and the false image.

Distinction is the heritage of the descendants of the true aristocrats, who are the founders of aristocracy in the usual meaning of the word, to whatever class they belong. The true greatness of a race is that of a single individual, the man who initiates it: those who follow him live at the expense of the ideal or real patrimony handed down for many generations until it is extinguished in impotence and sterility. The aristocratic spirit is the true golden value; distinction is merely the paper money which represents it.

But in the varied forms of character and being there is continual progress or regression, so that distinction is therefore in other cases (much less numerous, however) a kind of "recovery," an expectation, a promise.

In the same way in which Nietzsche speaks of Epicurism, distinction may be a stage of progress, a preparation for the aristocratic mind, and it is just this that happens in the progressive refinement of the so-called middle-class type. This is in its turn a transformation of the plebeian type, or, to use a word now consecrated in psychology, it represents the "recovery" of the plebeian type.

Behind these vague and uncertain words plebeian, middle-class, distinguished, aristocratic, the careful searcher will find real differences of physical constitution, and especially of nutriment.

The individual who is called plebeian is of the extreme human type, in which, either by the hereditary action of evil influence (which is manifested in an organic congenital deficiency) or by a defect of nutrition, or, as is more often the case, by both, life is maintained in a very low form, reduced to the minimum, in fact, with an almost miraculous balancing of incomings and outgoings, represented respectively by little and bad nourishment, and by the force and energy he devotes to his work; or, worse still, whose individual patrimony will be consumed with the vital decadence of his organism.

The consequence of this is, from an anthropological standpoint, a continual and progressive deterioration, and the degradation of the corporeal type, and this too accounts for the oppression and impoverishment of this class in the social and political sphere. For, in proportion as the members of this class are weak and debilitated, so much the less resistance do they make to the encroachments of others, even when such pretensions are to their disadvantage.

The common meaning of imbecile—a man who is foolish enough to act contrarily to his own interests, who submits to encroachments upon his rights, and suffers others to live at his expense—is entirely psychological; but, like the Romans, who took *imbecillitas* in the sense of physical weakness, we must not forget men's bad dispositions, and physiological poverty and misery, precisely to which, in my opinion, is due debility of activity and of one's own person.

As already stated, the plebeian type gives way to the middle-class type, and such a transformation is due to the improvement in conditions of existence. Granted that the plebeian type seems to us like an actual want of organic balance—almost a diseased state—the middle-class type acts as a kind of recovery. Let not my statement be thought strange, for certainly a great part of the middle-class state of mind is in accordance with what I say under this particular head. That indescribable mixture of meanness, wretchedness, restraint, and ridiculous prudishness, which has been the subject of so much scoffing by poets and artists (Heine's Philistine, for example, is the incarnation of all these traits) corresponds to the form of life and thought of imperfect and unhealthy beings.

If new conditions of existence assure the weakened old workman of a better state of life, a certain feeling of ease, the primitive defect is always apparent, for the traces of the ancient origin of the plebeian classes are revealed in their habits, customs, ideas, and sentiments. From a physiological standpoint, proofs of my statement are found in the frequent change in their vital processes, which takes place as a result of their growing stout (the humorous epitaph of "fat bourgeois" is not merely a literary expression), and, from a moral standpoint, that they are continually occupying themselves with trifles; paying great attention to their habits and health, thinking that dangers lurk everywhere, vanity, and, often, an entire contentedness with their station in life.

On account of all this weakness, incompleteness, limitation, and still more by their manner of acting towards others, there is something rather unsympathetic about the middle classes.

There is a magnanimity about the plebeians in making a continual sacrifice of their persons and often of their own lives with a stoicism which, if it be sometimes unknown to themselves, is at other times really superior disdain. With few or no attachments to life, they often show themselves indifferent to it; and, both in their disputes and in the risks they run, they exhibit a courage and indifference to death which are found only in brave men.

By the complete yielding up of themselves which they are always doing, and by the dissipation of their own lives, the plebeians bear some resemblance to the aristocratic type, and this latter type has much more in common with the former than with the middle-class type. Individuals of this latter class appear in all their acts as diffident and timid beings, having learnt from life to recognise that their own weakness renders them liable to be crushed at any moment; they seem to move about protected by a cotton cuirass, and will not expose their bodies to the fray. They are unable to forget the minor virtues of economy and prudence, which enabled them to rise and obtain wealth; and they seem even morally to be miserly of themselves and of their sentiments. They do not live sincerely in the presence of their ideas; but like to keep them in their *arrière-pensées,* in the back room of their brain, and to hide themselves behind a system of prejudices. It may be said that all their moral life is only an apparatus of preservation and conservation, and that they bide their time and go on accumulating, in the same way that their social function is the accumulation of wealth.

This aspect of incompleteness, transition, and preparation of the middle-class type—and consequently this admixture of ugliness and weakness (beauty is found only in the person who has attained his object)—was deeply felt and expressed in contemporary literature by Flaubert.

In him there was always a struggle going on between his past and his future; between his own actual feelings and the ideal of expansion and aristocratic liberty of superior art: an ideal which he always seems to be on the point of attaining, yet never attains.

The aristocratic type springs from all classes; it expresses, so to speak, the strength of the species, and may arise sporadically everywhere. When it issues from the lower grades of society, its strength is shown in its ability to overcome the difficulties by which society opposes the rise of an individual.

It is only with difficulty that we can realise the weight of these obstacles.

To form an idea of it, let it be remembered that in most cases the rise of an individual is not the work of one person only; but the consequence of the activity, the intelligence, and the ambition of several generations of the same family, and that such a success requires a combination of circumstances difficult even to imagine.

The aristocratic type possesses an eminently ascendant force, and accomplishes in its own life what would normally not result for many generations.

Napoleon is an example of a man who verified the most daring, not to say outrageous, stretch of the imagination.

When we take his origin and the conditions of modern times into consideration, he appears to be perhaps the champion of this admirable species of men. The great warriors and conquerors of the middle ages are the only prominent examples of this type. But in Napoleon we are confronted with something abnormal: for we are in the presence of Genius.

The aristocratic type bears a certain resemblance to the criminal type, a resemblance which is derived from the primitiveness and the nature of the strength which they possess in common; but, while the criminal is beyond the limits of the maximum ancestral variableness permitted by society, the aristocratic type is within these limits, and is an element of health and strength for society.

The aristocratic type differs from the average type only psychologically, while the criminal differs from it in physical appearance.

For the rest, in the almost infinite number of types into which one may endeavour to divide the mass of human personality, the aristocratic and the democratic types do not occupy places so far from one another as that occupied by the so-called average man.

In the extended sense of aristocratic type, but outside of it, we have the criminal and the immoral man as excessively atavic elements (having, however, a general signification of force and conservation of the animal type). In the extended sense of democratic type, but outside of it, as excessively progressive elements, with the signification of the decadence and the degradation of the physical type of the race, we have the apostle, the hero, the ascetic; arriving finally at the man who accomplishes the most extreme renunciation of the individual in the sacrifice of his sexual duties, whether by abstaining from their performance, or by real and effective emasculation.

CHAPTER III

THE ORIGIN OF SOCIETY

There has hitherto been deplorable confusion between the problem of the origin of society and that of the origin of the so-called human races. This latter has been the subject preferred, and in dealing with it sociologists and anthropologists have unbridled their imaginations, which, unfortunately, were not always of a high order, but sometimes even rather lame.

It is true that the two problems are closely connected with each other, but this does not mean that at the same time they are not quite distinct.

I think that any conception formed of the origin of society should go back for its deductions to the question of the origin of races, and that it should thence in the first place turn to that our critical investigations.

But whilst the first problem has a wide general range, it is a problem of philosophic importance; the second is a scientific problem, and its solution is in a continual state of change. While to solve the first we must use general—i.e. critical and psychological—methods, we use, or should use, other particular means for solving the second: the instrumentality of glottology, history, physiology, and anthropology.

To tell the truth, I think that while to the former question we may give an answer which is likely to hold good for some time, to the latter we can give only provisory replies, as to all scientific problems which are susceptible of being further amended and even radically negatived.

In any case, it is certain that on the genesis of the phenomenon, which we must admit whenever we accept the evolutionary theory of the origin of man, viz. the natural formation of society, we can only express suppositions and draw deductions, since we do not possess, and cannot even hope one day to possess explicit and directly demonstrative documents.

But modern psychology, more enlightened and conscious of itself, can legitimately try to do once more what has already been done, diffidently and unconsciously making use of our present sparse knowledge, fragmentary facts, and, above all, of analogies, the true scope of which is as yet not ascertained. I mean that, to carry out our design, we should employ the results of closer and more exact modern psychological investigations.

To arrive at an approximate and sufficiently satisfying hypothesis upon this question, we should take as our starting-point those data with which anthropology furnishes us in regard to human origin.

It appears to be at present certain, both from inductions of a general kind—on the habitat of the higher animal species as well as on the climate of the tropical zone—and from particular inductions founded on paleontological discoveries, that the terrestrial zone, inhabited by the human progenitors and the so-called ancestral forms of our species, was the tropical zone of the great Australasian continent.

It is not necessary to restrict the limits of this zone to any island or group of islands, or to any limited division of land, especially as it is very probable that the islands of Borneo, Sumatra, and Java, which some modern anthropologists would wish to be regarded as the cradle of the human race, belonged to an extended continent, portions of which comparatively recent geological displacements have submerged.

For the rest, the polygenical origin of the human race, held at the present time by almost all anthropologists, is hardly compatible with the restricted localisation of the place of origin of the human race, and, for our hypothesis, it is necessary only to admit it as very probable that primitive humanity lived in a warm zone of the earth's surface.

The analysis which follows will be the application to this question of abstractions and principles drawn from what we have observed, from what surrounds us, from the life in which we have our being. This may be—indeed, is almost sure to be —criticised; but I should like to ask these presupposed opponents: What up to the present time has been done by all the thinkers who have considered this question that is essentially different from this, except to reason on explanations of phenomena of origin, and analogies drawn from restricted and particular observations of other kinds of human facts? And they do this without thinking of it into the bargain, and with the most immodest presumptions, often believing they have built up the strongest possible arguments, yet never perceiving that the weakness of their theories was due simply to the peculiarity of the analogies by which they were tempted and led astray.

An example of what I say is seen in the influence which the historical view of the barbarian invasions has certainly exercised upon the formation of the theory of the immigrating and civilising Aryan race.

Our own theory will be completely and conscientiously analogical; but it will be based upon the larger and more extended human fact which is always present behind the most diverse conjectures: the psychological contrast between North and South.

The collective state in which the forerunners of our species lived cannot have been very different from that in which many of the higher animals live at present, that is, in groups of a variable number of sexual couples: the first rudiment of the human family.

It must, however, be remembered that with the sexual troop, the band, or with the biological family, as Morasso calls these aggregates, we are still in the sphere of animalness and not of sociality. It will not be denied that the real existence of these bands or families may have contributed to the constitution of society; but they were *only the materials*, the simplest *elements*, out of which society arose.

The necessity for this latter sprang up and was developed by virtue of another principle, very different from that of reproduction and sexuality; a principle which we can discover and affirm by analysis, but of which we naturally cannot follow the distinct and particular specifications without running the risk of feeling, and with some reason, that we are only writing bad poetry. In other words, we may affirm the range and value of society; but it would be an exaggeration to pretend to be able to follow its individual application. This principle is of another order, viz. *economical.*

The conditions of existence of our prehistoric ancestors were relatively good. In a climate at once very warm and humid, nature easily brings forth foods in the form of fruit, herbs, and roots, as well as what may be obtained by hunting; and, indeed, by reason of the climate itself, there is little need for a large amount of nutriment to renew the bodily losses, especially those of animal heat in the cold of winter, or to resist any other unfavourable occurrences.

The greatest difficulties in their lives must have been due to the other animals, which of course abounded in the tropical zones, and this fact necessarily favoured the development of those qualities that assured continued existence, such as courage, ferocity, and strength.

As, however, the number of groups increased by the augmentation of individuals, this nutriment offered by nature without work, *without any activity whatever,* that is, *with the view of fulfilling an aim,* began to get less plentiful, and struggles between the groups began to take place.

At the beginning such quarrels may not have been very frequent, or at least not very serious, since the area of ground permitted, in case of dispute, the choice of new settling-places equally favoured by nature.

The warlike state gradually became more intense, until at last those bands who were less numerous, or composed of the weaker individuals, were defeated and compelled to abandon their territories to the conquerors, emigrating afterwards to more unfavourable districts, generally to the northern countries. This process had to be repeated again and again in course of time, both among the groups who had emigrated and those who remained, provoking continued emigrations, and ending at last in the gradual occupancy of the temperate regions, until finally the polar regions themselves were reached.

I strongly emphasise this *dynamic* and *internal* process, in the first place because the spread of the human species over the most diverse regions was often regarded as something capricious and casual, and in the second place because it indicates a primordial difference of origin between the populations of the south and those of the north.

In these circumstances certain characteristics of man came to be developed which were not at first appreciated or heeded; perhaps not even perceived. Chief among them were industriousness, economy, foresight, etc. It is natural to suppose that where one's nutriment could not be obtained by more direct means perspicacity would be sharpened, and that new, slower, and more indirect means would be found.

So, then, in the weak and conquered races this quality continued to be developed. It afterwards became inherent, and from it must have come all the *humanity* of man—voluntary attention. This latter, indeed, requires a certain diminution of primal instincts and animal passions; it was born under the influence of grief and privation in the mind of weak people, from a kind of lowered vitality or organic impoverishment. Of course, voluntary attention was at first interested; it was incited by actual need, and thence, having become a real and proper autonomous faculty, was susceptible of being freely applied for distant and indirect interests.

It is, of course, understood that each of the emigrating groups mentioned above preserved those hierarchies, those divisions between rulers and subjects, with the functions allocated to each, which it had possessed previously.

All we have explained is, of course, schematic and approximative, but such explanations must be taken on general lines, since it may easily be supposed that the simplicity of the premises given above will be changed by particular or contingent elements. So, to state an instance, as a result of one or more successive immigrations into a territory where a preceding group had already arrived, new and more complex relations would arise between the former immigrants and the new-comers.

Those who in this way had come to settle in districts where the fertility was poor or the climate rigorous, finding the conditions harder, had to do their best to survive; had to submit themselves to a continual discipline; and had to exercise their minds constantly in considering schemes for supplying the deficiencies of nature. In this manner, and with this mechanism, arts came into existence, the first of them being agriculture and pastoralism.

Pastoralism represents, perhaps, the turning-point between the purely parasitical existence of primitive man, who took his food wherever he happened to meet with it, and the active existence of social man, directed to a predetermined end.

Agriculture is, on the other hand, genetically the first true, real *work*, and represented also what was to be the prototype of *work*, with all its physiological and psychological consequences to man.

As regards the distribution of duties among those composing the emigrating bands, the weaker members were those who had to work, doubtless the women and the slaves especially. Work came into existence at the same time as slavery, and was the first duty of the lower and inferior men.

Human intelligence was formed at the same time, having its first dawn in the realm of necessity; a long time before it inaugurated the beginning of liberty.

Conditions of existence gradually became harder and harder, work became more methodical and widespread, and in time greatly extended its ramifications.

These two phenomena were the most characteristic of social progress; but another was developing on the same lines: the transformation of moral judgment, the ideal sanction of work. Indeed, this latter, by its increasing diffusion, was gradually losing that character of inferiority and lowness which it owed to its origin amongst the weaker men and the slaves. This stamp was imposed on work by the estimation of masters and rulers, who created the appreciations, or, to use Nietzsche's word, the values.

Moreover, we may remind the reader that similar judgments prevailed in their entirety until a very short time ago, even for the highest form of work, viz. intellectual work. It will be recollected that in the middle ages noblemen boasted of their inability to read, or even to write their own names.

The progressive change of scene and climate in emigrating groups wrought, as a consequence, notable alterations in their temperament and character.

The natural psychological character and the vital inferiority originating from downtrodden and conquered individuals were increased still more by the influence of the social necessity for work, which acted by way of further developing certain aptitudes and suppressing others.

This is equivalent to saying that the complication of these conditions acted in the sense of creating racial characteristics.

So, therefore, agility, vivacity, promptitude, all the characteristics of those organisms of the sunny southern lands gradually diminished and in time gave place to their opposites.

The theory (or hypothesis, if this word be preferred) of the origin of the species *man* in the tropical regions being granted, it is very probable that the primitive corporeal type was brown-eyed and blackhaired, similar, or nearly so, in temperament to the present-day southern peoples.

The type with white skin, blue eyes, and fair hair is, to judge from all appearances, a transformation of the primitive type consequent upon climatic and telluric influences and changes in food, which for a long time operated on those groups that had emigrated in a northerly direction.

It is difficult to say by what means such modifications were effected. Moreover, the corporeal characteristics referred to above are only the more manifest expression, the anthropological index, of differences in their states of blood, and in the composition of their organic elements.

The causes which give rise to these changes, by repeating themselves again and again, gradually established such changes as definite characteristics of race; so that, when people with blue eyes and fair hair form part of a southern nation, anthropologists rightly see in them traces of northern blood. This must have been especially evident about the time of the barbarian expeditions into the southern countries.

These organic modifications were nevertheless favourable to the development of sociality, as this is strengthened by a diminution of animalness.

An objection, apparently reasonable and convincing, will be made to the idea set forth above. The northern peoples—at least, those who are northern in comparison with us Italians, and of whom we moderns have the best knowledge—far from being weaker than we are, are, at least at present, stronger and more vigorous; and of this we have undeniable historical proofs in the splendid prosperity of English power and in the promising Germanic youth, in conquests extending all over the world, and in recent wars. The war of 1870 showed the superiority of Germany over the Latin nations, and the marvellous colonial development of England is an amply convincing testimony of the vigour of her sons.

But there is an answer to these observations.

Those ethnic groups who were compelled to lead their life in unpleasant regions and in cold climates were forced by their necessity to strengthen their organism and train it up to war. By the tonic action of the climate, and the need for an active life, they developed their bodies in the direction of *a greater muscularity*, just as their thought was developed in the direction of an increase of *will-power.* Certainly many of them must have perished, but little by little the others acquired qualities of resistance which finally gave them the upper hand.

A physiological parenthesis may be allowed here.

An increase of muscular strength does not signify, *by itself alone*, an increase of organic vigour; this is something more intimate and profound, it is an antecedent and an attribute of animalness, and is founded on the nature of the organic elements, the chemical qualities, of humours, blood, and lymph, in their natural balance: in other words, it is independent of the predominance due to the exercise of some system. And that is what I call the organic temperament, which receives its strength and its complexion from sexuality.

Muscular strength depends upon the unilateral development of a fixed and almost solid tissue, susceptible of being influenced by exercise, which is of relatively small importance in determining physiological qualities (e.g. resistance to disease, immunity, quickness of material exchanges). A proof of this is that an athletic constitution, which is acquired exactly by the predominance of such tissues, is not the best constitution that could be desired.

Muscularity is a reacting state, something secondary (produced by the influence of sociality), and is a substitute for a preceding weakness; it is an adaptation which one's state of weakness allowed in order that the end of society—work—might be attained. And that must doubtless have happened when people first began to live together, when the work of human hands had to be directed against the opposing forces of nature.

Greek mythology incarnated this value of muscularity in the person of Hercules, who well represents this reactive, not active, force, this adaptation and transformation of an element of a certainly lower value.

We cannot here disclose all the reasonings and arguments upon which our thesis is based; these will be specially dealt with in the next chapter.

The mass of circumstances outlined above developed a greater muscularity in the race, which, however, probably deteriorated in organic vigour. As a proof of this I may instance the coarseness of features, the heaviness and ruggedness of facial lines, and the predominance of fatness and of lymphatism in the northern races.

On parallel lines to this development was that of the increase of will. The rise of this aspect of psychicity, and the hypertrophy which it shows in the races of the north in comparison with its small development among the present races of the south, are consequences of what I have referred to.

The will, in this way, is shown to be a *human* faculty, social *par excellence*, we may say.

Of its origin—its northern origin, so to speak—one proof is the contempt in which it is held by the southern nations, who make constancy and tenacity synonyms for a certain obtuseness, and who on the other hand have a higher opinion of intelligence and rapid intuition.

It must of course be understood that the action of the causes upon which we have laid stress in the development of the process of sociality does not go beyond certain limits.

It is true that by the repetition of the same process of the elimination of the weak, and by the progressive emigration towards the north of those who were ostracised, the most distant regions of the earth, even to the Poles, were populated; but it cannot be said that these emigrations favoured indefinitely the development of sociality. This seems to have continually taken its centre of greatest intensity towards the north, since the theory that the advance of civilisation was always towards northern lands is now firmly established and is certainly in agreement with phenomena and causes which do not differ from those outlined by myself. But it is logical to think that where life is confronted with obstacles of great physical difficulty (perpetual ice, fields of snow, etc.), it is almost impossible for this influence to be reflected by the circumstances of the surroundings on the character of the people, and that in the only too unequal battle, human strength, so much inferior to that of nature, must succumb.

The ethnic groups remaining behind in the more temperate or absolutely warm regions, not having the stimulation of voluntary labour directed to a determined end in the necessity for maintaining life against the difficulties of nature—not having, in a word, the stimulation to work— remained in a lower state of civilisation, and especially in a state of political separation. They passively received the conquests of civilisation which came down to them from the north, sometimes in a quiet and pacific form, more often in a violent and warlike spirit.

Thus by the disciplinary action of natural circumstances, and of an inner organisation which took from it its necessity and strength, these ethnic groups acquired cohesion and vigour, and increased in strength to such a point that they became not only warlike groups, but also groups organised and prepared for war.

The nature of this acquired strength, muscularity, let me repeat, sprang up like a reaction, a kind of retrogression, as if one had been inoculated with a new virtue which a state of weakness allowed to get into human organism. Further, in one of the following chapters, we shall be able to see, in a few sentences which I shall devote to the origin of militarism, the confirmation of this theory. In the meantime, I may say that the warlike organisation of barbaric states or nations, like present-day militarism, which is a repetition of it, is not a primitive, atavic fact, as some believe, but is a comparatively late form of evolution. Warlike organisation was shown to be a particularity of the development of those ethnic groups who had emigrated towards the north. That is to say, only when an iron discipline imposed by nature had increased its power in a social aggregate during evolution, did warlike organisation come into being.

So we may see that, prepared by their vigorous social structure, and having arrived at the period of military civilisation, the late descendants of the former emigrants marched back again to the south, this time as invaders and conquerors. Athirst for heat, love, and power, they descended into the countries of brightness, the land of dark-eyed and dark-haired women, and by sheer strength and war founded their kingdom. Thus did the Goths and the Vandals in Spain, thus the Franks in France, thus the Goths, the Lombards, and the Huns in Italy. Similarly, it should seem that the Greeks were invaders who had come from the north, and imposed themselves as aristocratic and governing classes upon the native element, and that, having in time forgotten their own origin, they regarded as *barbarians* those who were not native Hellenics.

But the finest and greatest example of this process is shown us by the Aryan race, which, having sprung up in the Pamir plateau, descended into India and founded the greatest and most superb of military aristocracies.

India, that wonderful laboratory where all kinds of human experience are commingled, in whose religions, political institutions, philosophies, and books—thousands of them as yet almost unknown and unread—are to be found so many treasures of human wisdom: India is the country where the process I have described is found, as it were, crystallised in all its purity.

Rarely, however, did these northern races long retain their power. They declined more or less rapidly, mingled with the inferior and subjected elements, were finally absorbed, and disappeared.

It is permissible to suppose that the chief cause of this was their inadaptability to the climate; this is almost certainly the cause in a few special cases, as, for example, the rapid extinction of the Vandals in northern Africa. Perhaps, again, this shows that the supposed vigour of the northern races is more apparent than real; or, rather, it confirms the more muscular nature of their energy.

We may, however, add that, if they disappeared as lords and masters, their influence made itself felt from time to time in the rise to new power of those nations with which they had become commingled, even after their disappearance. Who can say that the Italian Renaissance may not have been due to the many admixtures of northern blood in the middle ages, or that the same reason may not have accounted for the greatness of Spain under Charles V?

It may, in my opinion, be affirmed that all the greatest civilisations arose from the fusion of these two elements, the northern and the southern; the one active, the master and the organiser; the other passive, which provided the plastic material. For these reasons we ought perhaps to conceive of the development of civilisation as an exchange between North and South, a real and material ebb and flow of energies. Even the hypothetical fact (which, however, judged by itself, contains much that is probable) of emigrations towards the north, and that other fact recorded in history of the return of large human groups towards the south, constitute, so to speak, the two phases—objectised, as it were—of a general rhythm which will be better understood further on.

As we have found, in physical causes, a limit of the development of sociality towards the north, so we must see in the torrid climate the reason of the decadence of some civilisations. It is very probable that India owes her conditions of general slackness and lethargic slumber to her extraordinary climate. This, however, weakened and restrained the conquering Aryans who had come down from the north.

We may summarise by saying that society came into being through the insufficiency of the nutriment offered by nature to our pre-human ancestors, *and became established in the fundamental fact of work.*

We cannot speak of society without noting this phenomenon; and a final analysis will derive its origin from an economic principle: *the disproportion between the number of the inhabitants in a state of nature of a green zone, and the quantity of food which the area of this zone itself can offer them naturally.*

At this stage it is interesting to note how the tradition of many peoples has spread with the creation of myths and diverse fables; the obscure remembrance of certain facts analogous, in essence, to those we had already known and expected.

It seems to me that, for example, on the basis of these facts we may give a tentative interpretation of the myth of original sin and of an earthly paradise, myths which are found not only in the sacred writings of the Hebrews, but also in the folklore of uncivilised peoples.

The myth of Eden, as being a place of painless and pleasurable life, would thus be a transformation and a fantastic idealisation of recollections of places and of countries where life might have been more easily led owing to a richer and more exuberant soil, especially recollections of epochs previously to the introduction of work. The doctrine of original sin, however, would be merely the moral translation of the economical contrast between the number of living persons and the quantity of food, a contrast the origin and responsibilities of which primitive mentality evidently attributed, with justice, to the sexual instinct; but which later, with the gradual obscuring of the discerning faculty, and the prevalence of the sentimental point of view over primordial intuition, was afterwards changed into a most gloomy and unnatural religious doctrine.

At any rate, the real and objective elements can easily be recognised in the myth. Adam's ejection from the earthly paradise and the Maker's sentence: "In the sweat of thy face shalt thou eat bread!" is only the dramatic elaboration and the mythical metamorphosis of the data of the fact, i.e. the necessity for work, due to an excessive increase of participants in life.

This idea could certainly be further developed; but this is hardly the place to do so, as I wished to introduce it merely as an argument in defence of my views on the general process upon which civilisation is based.

Coming back to the subject, we may say with respect to the inner organisation of these groups which were, as we have seen, driven out of the richer territories, that this was to a certain extent already regulated, and continued to be formed according to the principle which governs the relationship between rulers and ruled, between the strong and the weak, the principle which I laid stress upon in the preceding chapter.

This principle is that the strong men, the masters, should live in ease and idleness; and that the weak men should supply them with the means of life. This is a fixed, stable, primordial element of an origin older than society itself; based perhaps on the most remote animalness, for it is a relationship having its origin in brute force.

Sociality found this relationship already existing, and fresh social formations were adapted to it. Work, however, went on increasing the distance and the difference between the weak and the strong, for its whole weight was felt by the former, whilst the latter lived in idleness.

The different theories of the present time as to the development of civilisation (the oldest and best known being that of the so-called Aryan or Indo-European race, whether Scandinavian or African, of Sergi[33]) do not by any means solve the problem of the origin of society.

At the most, they may aspire to be called ethnographical or anthropological conceptions; but nothing more.

The problem of the origin of society is, I say emphatically, of an almost exclusively psychological nature, and our only hope of bringing light to bear upon it lies in the employment of psychology. For the rest, the discoveries—for we may certainly call them so—of Nietzsche in the genealogy of morals, which are so many experiments in primitive psychology, have perhaps contributed more than anything else to bring us nearer to this end.

The different theories of a single race to which our European civilisation is said to have been due are only generalisations founded on the analogies of great historical phenomena which took place at much later times—I refer to the emigration of large bodies of people from one part of the world to another. But, in our case, these emigrations explain nothing, for, when we speak of emigrating peoples and civilisations, we do not attempt to explain the origin of the people itself, or of its own civilisation.

In other words, the conception of society is contained in the conception of race, and the anthropological problem is a corollary of the larger and more important problem of the origin of civilisation.

Morasso, in a book containing many genial and fecund ideas, passes an acute and legitimate criticism on these theories, as having been put forward merely to explain the origin of society, a general proposition which in substance is

---

[33] Giuseppe Sergi (1841-1936) was an Italian anthropologist who argued for the supremacy of the Mediterranean race against the Nordicists of his day.

reduced to the affirmation of that primitive element, the relationship between rulers and ruled, between the strong and the weak.

He has to that extent succeeded in making some progress towards a full explanation; but his theory still lacks the affirmation of that element, the *economical* element, which, in my opinion, is essential.

Owing to the absence of this datum, many of his particular ideas do not appear to be convincing and complete, although some of his intuitions are most happy, and he has clearly expressed one of the principal explanations. To give an example of the defect of his method, I shall quote just one passage: "It is not a class difference which separates two members of a community, the well-to-do from the worker; but a difference of race." With that he evidently puts back the solution of the problem of the origin of a *community* to that of a race; but a race, in general, is such because it is the result of a long social discipline; and in this way not a single step in advance is made.

It is not a difference of race, as he believes, for that would mean postponing indefinitely an explanation of the facts; but it is physical differences, or differences of temperament, and psychological differences of character, which are at the bottom of social hierarchies.

Diversity of race may have still further influence, it may make the differences I have mentioned even more evident and palpable; but its presence is not *necessary;* it is often even particularity of temperament and of character enlarged, multiplied, and established in a common type. Such it may, however, be sometimes; but it does not always happen, as Morasso holds, that the different classes in the body of a community result from victory over a community which a stronger one has conquered. This process is purely accidental, and at all events it does not give us an explanation of the hierarchic differences in the heart of the two communities themselves, which existed previously to the defeat of one by the other.

In so far as the community already rich and free, and afterwards conquered, with its members made slaves, was a community, i.e. an aggregate, there pre-existed in it on one hand a warlike and parasitical aristocracy, and on the other hand a collection of downtrodden people—the workers. Conquests on the part of other bands probably made slaves of the former masters, setting up new rulers in their stead; but the hierarchy still existed, for the distinction which it presupposes precedes the social fact, and is even contained in its very nature.

Thus Morasso says in another place:

"The thriving community, rich in possessions, and superior in culture, in which many individuals did not work, was envied by the miserable surrounding communities, condemned to the severe labour of work; these latter finally rose, ceased their labours, and fell upon their rich neighbours, whose rulers they became, making the former masters their slaves."

From a psychological standpoint, it is difficult to conceive how these "miserable" people, who were "condemned to the hard labour of work," could conquer those who were rich and strong.

To grasp at wealth and wrest it from the hands of those who held it, one must be in possession of a certain amount of health and riches, since it is well known that want and poverty always render man less capable of fighting and winning.

All these contradictions are due to the fact that Morasso has not observed what the essential element was that characterised society; and while he clearly distinguishes one inherent, eternal, animal element, he overlooks the other new, progressive, and more properly *human* element: work.

CHAPTER IV

WORK AND MORALS

The necessity for production: here we have the extreme formula which synthesizes the causes of those particular developments which we call social; the key that unlocks the mysterious characters in which is concealed the secret of the origin of society and of the phenomena which are dependent upon it, or closely connected with it. Ethic and aesthetic emotions, sentiments, and judgments have their remote starting-point in these necessities; from thence they arise and are concreted into functions of society.

This chapter will be a general development of what I have already affirmed in a few words, in the same manner that the following will be a corollary of this: an exemplification of two of the principal emotions of social character.

I do not here pause to consider the numerous definitions which have been given of work. Rather do I regard such definitions as being too often a pastime of philosophers who have nothing else to do. It has always been possible to make one's self understood by the world without making too much use of definitions, even without reckoning that at all times when ideologists have been pleased to attempt to give definitions they have always had to end by confessing their inability to do so.

I take the word work in its economic sense as a purely social and human phenomenon, and not in a mechanical and physical sense. The free, spontaneous, and immediate activities which are shown by animals with the view of satisfying certain momentary needs are not work, or at least not social work. It is true that leisure cannot be spoken of in an absolute sense; inertness in animal life does not exist at all; but, as we distinguish certain determined acts by the name of work, so we distinguish others by the name of leisure.

The nature of these latter acts has to be characterised by freedom, pleasure, and, above all, by being accompanied with spontaneous attention. Those acts which we call "work" are distinguished from the former, at least in origin, by being compulsory, difficult, and accompanied by voluntary attention. As such, their fulfilment, at least in the beginning, is not easy; and is imposed on individuals only by means of limitations, diminutions, pains and penalties.

Those writers, therefore, seem to me to be very summary and superficial who, dealing with the origin of society, have passed lightly over this fact, as if the imposition, however gradual, of a law and rule like that of work had been such an easy matter for primitive humanity.

In this way we are entertained with the story of the primitive Aryans, who are made to appear a pacific people, governed by patriarchal customs, devoted to pastoralism and agriculture, an ideal example of wisdom, so to speak: as if such a state could not but be the indication of a great deal of progress in civilisation, and hence bringing no new light to bear upon the subject which interests us.

The process of civilising was a dynamic and internal process, as we have said; one, that is, which had its *raison d'être* in itself: which is but saying that it availed itself of the qualities, virtues, and different human forces which it found at hand, to make them act on and among themselves, and beyond themselves on nature.

It is difficult for us, and the result might be doubtful, to reconstruct with our imagination, however guided and restrained by vigorous self-criticism, what we take to be the mind of this originative humanity; nor is it worth while, as nevertheless Renan, speaking of the origin of language, thought it was, to examine and bear in mind the moral and mental life of savages and children, who are, to some extent, reproductions of the spirit of primitive humanity; for modern savages, by reason of their having remained in an uncivilised state, show that they are different from those who finally produced civilisation; and children are beings upon whom centuries of civilisation have exercised a strong influence, and who are brought up by personal education and training.

We must not, however, assume an entirely sceptical point of view, and, without giving an unqualified assent to these hypotheses, we may keep before us the value of some observations which are certainly just.

One of these is that the adaptation of mankind to work, although slow and gradual, must have been painful and difficult for primitive humanity.

Common observation has shown that lively, active, and exuberant individuals can but with difficulty be induced to work; as it is also not easy for them to sustain a continued effort at a given task. Some individuals, then, rather than others belonging to a group, were compelled to work; and we have already seen that these were those whom we have generically called weak.

When, however, we speak of weak and strong people in primitive humanity, it must not be thereby understood that in the first period there were any of these feelings of quietness and benevolence or mildness of spirit which we observe to be the inheritance of a great many men of modern times; and, in the second period, all kinds of ferocity and violence. Weakness or strength must be interpreted in a physical sense, and as an entirely relative datum. As a whole, the psychology of the two qualities differed in kind rather than in degree, and coarseness and barbarity were the heritage of both.

The diffusion of work must therefore have taken place with fierce battles and painful crises. The subjecting of those barbarous natures, those bodies habituated to the greatest and most entire liberty; the restraining of those powerful and bestial appetites, those savage and impulsive carnal tendencies which had hitherto satisfied their unbridled lust; the setting of this animal laziness and indolence to work, attention, and effort: all this was not done in a day, or without the spilling of much blood.

This coercion was forced on man, philosophically speaking, by external circumstances and by his joining with others in aggregations; but it found its real and concrete agents in the heart of every community among the stronger men, who used every means in their power to compel the weaker to work.

Some thinkers have held that in love the individual makes a sacrifice of himself to the race, and have endeavoured to derive the sacrifice of the individual in society from this love sacrifice.

There are several errors contained in this opinion. In the concession which the individual makes of his sexual energies, there is not, hedonistically, any sacrifice at all . . . quite the contrary! But even physiologically we cannot affirm that the embrace entails a definite loss to the organism.

The physiology of reproduction is still in such a rudimentary state that nothing precise can be definitely affirmed on this point; but I believe I am right in saying that an exact knowledge of this complicated question will have many surprises in store for us.

Sacrifice is, on the other hand, evident in work, in which we can see there is a giving out of energy, and also a certain psychological effort to overcome the instinctive repugnance which one feels towards it. Since the free individual in an animal state consecrated his entire activity to himself, and as he lived, so to speak, in a smaller world, he had far fewer possibilities, being, however at all events, in a complete and integral state. In society, on the other hand, he sacrificed his whole person to production, his development being thereby greatly modified and even altered and deformed.

The ends and advantages of the race are not, as some hold, contrary, in general, to those of the individual. One confusion in particular has led us into this error, the change in our conceptions of "race" and of "society," a change which it is but too easy to make, but one which can lead to the most absurd consequences. The social fact is, in a certain sense and in a certain measure, a formation superimposed upon nature, and is in relative opposition to her.

It must be added that as time passes repugnance to work is gradually disappearing by force of habit, and is even being formed in the north into an ethics, and even a hedonism, which magnify and idealise it: it is, however, worthwhile observing that such abstract sanctions have a protective and preserving value *in the sphere of work itself.*

To bring forward a final objection in this adverse thesis, looking at the matter from the point of view of those who admit the sacrifice in the love embrace, it is difficult to understand how sex, in the historical epochs of dissolution—in which the individual began to acquire greater liberty, and gave himself up in a greater measure to his instincts—in the most egoistical epochs, we might say, could find its greatest satisfaction in the so-called "corruption of manners."

The assertion which we have many times repeated, that work arose with the weaker men, as at the present day it is the function of the lower classes and individuals, may seem an absurdity on account of current prejudices in contemporary opinion; but these prejudices are for the most part of democratic origin, and have moreover penetrated into science and falsified some of its conceptions.

Is not the vulgar error of judging human facts on the basis of implicit or explicit principles, more or less defiled, of *personality*, the same error as that of all scientists, who, unconsciously or deliberately, judge of the same proposition as being within the sphere of morality?

So, then, on this special subject of work I have never known any one to think naturally and not morally, who considered it from an external point of view. In this chapter I shall bring to light fundamental analogies and concordances which will explain the genesis of this fact, and I shall also try to dispel some of those prejudices which I have mentioned.

We shall find in one special kind of work—intellectual work—certain data which will serve, generally speaking, for all forms of work: for in this kind we have the clearest knowledge of the conditions which favour and determine it.

It is a well-known and ascertained fact that many great men showed considerable delicacy in infancy, being weak and sickly in health. By examining our knowledge of many such men, scientists have been able to establish the hydrocephalic constitution of the brain, especially that most acute observer, Dr. Peris. It may even be affirmed with some probability that the notable size and heavy weight of the brains of great men are signs of the residue of an old hydrocephalus.

Without wishing to give my assertions a general and axiomatic character, it may be deduced from these observations that a certain physical and moral weakness and susceptibility restrain these children from violent exercises and the noisy, active play of childhood which would naturally be manifested at their age, and direct their attention to precocious thought and day-dreaming, this being the physiological base of the meditative and poetic habit of puerile imagination. In other words, such characteristics would favour an inclination to matters of the intelligence.

We may easily find similar facts in the biographies of many great men; but especially evident is the case of Newton, whose life, feelings, and ideas are, for the most part, very interesting for the curious psychologist who is examining the conditions which favour the development of the intelligence.

Without wishing to go into further details, it is sufficient for the question under discussion to recollect that, as a child, Newton was so delicate that it was feared he would not live very long; and the first four years of his life were passed in the country, where his parents, hoping that this would make him stronger, had taken him. The same may be said of many others, including Goethe and Napoleon, to mention only the very greatest.

It was of course to be expected that this weak youthful constitution would be strengthened as time went on, and this was exactly what happened in Newton's case. He became very strong indeed, otherwise his intellectual labour would have been impossible. Therefore the conditions most favourable to such work are found when the organism has been strengthened and invigorated, without the loss of the habit of activity of thought.

Social work, as an extended and diffused phenomenon, originated in similar physical dispositions. The weaker people, if they desired to live, had to submit to work and to develop that faculty which may be said to have been born with work, *attention,*.

The quality which more than any other has enabled man to achieve all his progress, all his glory, and to acquire the magnificent greatness of his genius, had a humble origin. The *will to live*, restrained and oppressed by brute force, was set free by the spirit of weak and conquered individuals in the form of voluntary attention.

This it was that made the world smaller, reducing it to monoideism, deepened it, enriched it by numberless underground ties, and finally gave to man the superb edifice of science and omnipotence, by means of which the lower and weaker man became in his turn a lord and master. Further, grafting itself upon the ancient brute force, it adorned man with a new light, and gave him an incorporeal brightness: spirituality.

It must be understood that when I speak of strong, healthy, and lively men, I do not refer to muscular energy, or to ability to work in general.

There exists in public opinion a generally entertained belief that a healthy and vigorous individual has need for the activity of work, and feels the want of it like a painful sensation. I will not insist too strongly on the very obvious reply, which, indeed, contains some truth, that such a need is only an illusion due to habit; but I shall reply by referring to what I have previously said, namely, that muscular temperament, the development of which is determined by work, is not by any means a strong and originative temperament. It is rather a transformation of the primitive temperament determined by the exigencies of sociality.

A proof of this is the fact that the psychology of a man of muscular temperament is the psychology of the quiet, active, and hard-working man, often as yet limited in intelligence, and of somewhat restricted morality.

We see this still better in the extreme type of muscular athlete. The athlete is a disproportioned individual, who often shows himself deficient in other respects, liable to diseases of the heart, of low sexual power, very often dull. The muscular strength which is often exchanged for real strength is a particular human product; i.e. social, not animal: it is a result of sociality, the consequence of a particular exercise, of a unilateral development which issues from the plebeian practice of work. This peculiar origin of muscular strength is more evident in the northern peoples, whose predominance in the contemporary world is due to a strength the value of which is, in truth, inferior, just because it is of a muscular character.

The healthy, good-natured, and vigorous individual, in sound health and strength, is really thin and emaciated, as the aristocratic races are thin and emaciated.

A digression will be pardoned here, one which, moreover, will bring forward new arguments to support what I have said.

The habit of work, imposed by centuries of sociality, has rooted itself in such a manner in men's minds as to make itself felt as a need of methodical activity, even in classes and individuals who do not need to work at all. This need is revealed in sport. But the fatherland of this phenomenon, where, among all the northern nations, it is now seen to be most widely diffused, is England; and this is another proof of what I have said. Sport is a residue, a remembrance, of old habits of work; it is like a plebeian and democratic survival in individuals or classes who have become independent by the plebeian exigencies of work; that is, in the aristocracy or higher middle classes.

Now, it is a very curious admission that, although the real essence and remote origin of sport are found in something very different from leisure, the socialists of Germany and England, notwithstanding this, voluntarily take up that which, according to themselves, has an apparent stamp of aristocratic idleness!

For other reasons it is worthy of note that this custom has not made much progress among the leisured and rich people of the southern countries, where it is at least much less widely spread. Among the aristocracy and rich middle classes of the Latin countries sport has had but a small vogue, because leisure is more innocent and natural for us southrons, and does not take such peculiar disguises.

I should like now to bring forward an element which I believe has not hitherto been observed by anyone, and which I think is of great importance as regards the diffusion and the historical affirmation of the social phenomenon "work."

I refer to the effect—I might almost say the *historic* effect—produced on the race during many ages by widespread diseases, epidemics in the broader and more modern sense of the word, as civilisation became more and more extended.

This may seem strange, but I do not think I exaggerate in any way. Epidemics which, in the conditions of growing communities caused by the advancement of civilisation, must have found richer and more fecund soil for their own dissemination, certainly contributed very greatly, in lowering vitality, to spread and to strengthen the necessity for work.

It is well known that those recovering from severe and exhausting illnesses are generally in a better state, morally, than they were previously, and that an illness often completely changes a hard and stubborn disposition into a submissive and yielding one.

A certain pride and even cruelty of character are indications of an animal and even, perhaps, brutal nature; one, however, healthy, strong in will, and full of life. These epidemics, acting on a large scale, struck a blow at the vitality of the race, and occasioned like changes in the human type, which had the effect of taming its primitive ferocity and of refining the habits of men.

But there are numerous other proofs of my assertion that *a diminution of vitality is at the base of sociality*, and such proofs may be found in many different places.

It is known, for example, by educationists that the liveliest, strongest, and healthiest boys cannot easily be made to accustom themselves to the discipline of work; and not only this, but also that, if the infantile organism is allowed to become strengthened and hardened by freedom of action, or in the confused and joyful pranks of childhood, it is almost impossible, after a certain age, to adapt the child to work at all.

Education evidently reproduces in a certain guise the mechanism which acts on man in the early formation of society; is it not, indeed, limitation, inhibition, impoverishment of all a child's expressive manifestations? We may easily see this in children who are learning to read and write. Everyone knows that there are some boys who have to be severely punished, even with bodily pain, before they can be induced to pay the requisite amount of attention to their studies.

Again, what is pain but a lowering of vitality, the aim of which is to render possible the acquisition of a special habit, which, given a healthy and perfect state of body, is difficult? And this remark applies not only to the punishments of children, but also to those inflicted on adults.

It is odd that no one has hitherto grasped the real meaning of punishment, that it is a diminution of life which makes possible, at least theoretically, the application of a social rule which is, in substance, a yoke: and that delinquency, far from being a destructive element, is an element of strength and eminently conservative, at least from the point of view of race, inasmuch as it indicates a certain strength of natural resistance.

We have still another proof, unassailable, because almost proved by experience, that a vigorous vitality, and especially a strong sexuality, which is its greatest manifestation, are fundamentally contrary to work and to methodical activity.

This experimental proof is given by our domestic animals, which we render incapable of producing young when we wish to make them serve for our own uses, just because only then is it possible to adapt them to our needs.

I shall give the reason of this in the following chapter. Let us now consider other analogies which, as they are more important, may be brought in here.

The possibility of the perfect carrying out of several given acts of any kind of work, which means the more or less complete realisation of a given end, is based on a psychical activity slow rather than hurried. On the other hand, Conolly Norman has observed that the highest faculties of mental life, judgment in the intellectual sphere, criticism, comparison, the examination of the logical connections of a subject, and the ability to regulate one's own feelings in the sphere of morality, are often those most affected with mental diseases, which are the mental forms of exaltation of physical life.

Again, melancholic forms are characterised by a stoppage or by a slackening of mental activity, but they themselves are not diminished or even disordered. And, whilst keeping within normal range, a certain melancholic turn of mind favours, at least within certain limits, this faculty I have referred to; this is therefore the state in which an individual who has such a disposition is said to be more teachable, more docile.

This, too, is the reason of the difference that exists between the people of the north and those of the south in their susceptibility to the influence of education. Education means inhibition, and this is easier for the cold and melancholic temperaments of the northerns than for the ardent and, so to speak, maniacal minds of the southrons. Again, this is why the former excel in all work, including mental work, which requires much application and tenacity, and, in a general way, in all kinds of work, especially at the present time, when the value of intelligence is more and more giving place to that of will.

We have hitherto been speaking of conditions which favour the habit of work; let us now say something about those which determine the incapacity to adapt one's self to the fundamental necessity of social life.

Repugnance towards or incapacity for work may have several origins. It may be the reaction of a healthy disposition, a too healthy and exuberant physical energy, which does not adapt itself, or adapts itself unwillingly, to discipline or to the rules of a methodical and moderate activity.

Perhaps this kind of repugnance gives rise to the inadaptability of some savage nations—the Redskins, for example—to civil life. This repugnance is not recognised by modern science, which, in spite of its impartiality and objectivity, *often in its theses does nothing but reflect and establish as axioms the conservative truths of its state, that is, those propositions which serve to maintain it, and the implicit postulates on which the possibility of scientific activity is based,* not to mention that this logical process is spoiled by the *ad personam* error.

In other words, the scientist is a workman, and, in affirming what is sound and normal, he often does nothing, however good his intentions, but hypothesise his own disposition and theorise on his own mode of life: the ideal mode of life, the physiological type.

Seen from this point of view, a certain doctrinary psychology, and often even psychiatry, fall into the same error as the older morality, which was only the pretension of one race of men to make laws for all the others; even psychiatry in some special doctrines, as in that of moral insanity, accepts only too easily all the suggestions and prejudices of morality.

In the meantime, in spite of all this, the fact still remains unshaken that the variety of human characters, a variety which moral doctrines would wish to reduce to uniformity, is one of the chief conditions of life and of the continuation of the existence of society.

The types of activity which our morality more or less explicitly condemns (aristocratic tendencies, sexual and economic dissipation) have, in my opinion, a very high function for the race, and render possible the propagation and continuation of human society, which would otherwise, from many deteriorating causes, die out.

But, coming back to our subject, there is still another kind of repugnance to work; that of weak, unhealthy, neurotic, and exhausted people. An essential difference, however, separates these individuals from the first-mentioned, since, with the first, repugnance to work is accompanied with an easy conscience; with the second, in most cases, we may observe remorse and dissatisfaction with their state of life.

For the majority of men, such as they are in the present organisation of civilised societies, work is a necessity which has gradually become fixed in a need for generic activity; for very few, relatively speaking, is it a real joy, particularly if the work is routine and not creative.

In this sense creative work is quite different from the other ordinary work, which I call servile: creative activity has many of the psychological characteristics of spontaneous activity, which is always present, even when the individual can enjoy aristocratic *otium* in the broadest sense of the word; so that one might say that *otium* and spontaneous activity were one and the same thing.

Let not the reader be wrongly impressed with what I say.

There are some truths which science seems, as it were, unwilling to assert in a loud voice, fearing the danger to society which might be aroused by the promulgation of such truths, supported, as they would be, by so much authority and influence; fearing also that the knowledge of these truths would occasion a change in the standard of one's conscience, and hence in the balance of those human activities which we call "society."

But it must be confessed that true science is not made in this way. I go so far as to declare that science must affirm even those truths which implicitly deny it. And, not to give my thought the appearance of a paradox, I will add that a truth which denies the *very basis* of a science, or, rather, of a certain stage of thought, must belong to some higher form of knowledge to which we are becoming worthy of attempting to ascend.

Now that we have observed the inner conditions which favour the habit of work, let us see what are the consequences of it.

Work is not, as very many people ignorantly proclaim, and a few hypocrites who live in idleness preach, work is not the best and most desirable state of existence for mankind. Why, indeed, should there be such a fretting and scrambling for wealth if work itself is said to be the chief aim of life? My statement is proved by facts which anyone may observe, by things among which we live.

The apology made for work resembles just a little too much the methods of those who, living in a poor, mean room, cover its bare whitewashed walls with pictures cut from illustrated papers; or it even more resembles the procedure of a prisoner who, to delude himself into forgetting his imprisonment, painted on the walls of his cell a representation of a free and open horizon of sea and sky, and ended by believing in its reality!

Look at the mind and body of a peasant—a man who is tied down to the hardest, most absorbing, and most lowering typical kind of work: look how all his being bears the stamp of his life, the deformation of his yoke! Work on the land is work *par excellence;* but it, even more than any other, imprints the stamp of organic degradation.

One should note the close relationship between the words *labor, lassus, labefactus, labes,*[34] which express the complete psychological inferiority of the workers.

How, then, has our esteem for work arisen, all the ideality which surrounds it?

Whatsoever state or condition tends by a natural law to make itself the centre of universal life, to make people believe that it is the only desirable condition for all men: such a state or condition tends also to attract others to itself. But, in the present case, this aspiration is much more illegitimate, for work is only a means (even perhaps a transitory means) by which in present-day society (this itself a state of aggregation and not a necessary form) it is possible for a large number of individuals to live, who, however, on account of this necessity, are mutilated, reduced in vitality, made into slaves.

And since the facts are as I have stated, and not otherwise, we can argue therefrom that wherever the human and social factor, work, was produced, there were two groups in society: the one organising and directing, and, so to speak, parasitical; the other one ruled over, labouring and exploited.

I do not wish a feeling of contempt for the one class, and of pity and revolutionary propaganda for the other, to be attributed to these ends. To my mind, such a division (which, moreover, is clearly defined only between the two extremes of the social scale, every intermediate degree being a blending of

---

[34] *lassus*: faint, weary; *labefactus*: to cause to totter; *labes*: a cause of ruin

the two elements, by which the individual is at the same time and in a varied degree ruling and ruled), to my mind, I repeat, such a division seems to be more real and natural than a social distinction, and thence above any criticism based upon moral estimations. This is due to natural, physical, and psychical differences in the species *man*, and every free spirit must recognise that all higher rights, that is, the rights of the species, are for the masters rather than for the subjects, since the preservative function of the race is confided to the former, as being the stronger and more sexual.

Work, then, is a transitory social, and not a permanent factor, with determined and special conditions of development. It is natural that it should have some morals, aesthetics, and hedonism; but such morals, aesthetics, and hedonism have no right to be imposed on all men, since they are only contingent and transitory.

The true student of morals, to carry out his design, should be neither moral nor immoral; but amoral.

For this reason, Morasso's conception of work, although it comprehends the principal character of work which determines its moral and physical consequences to man, is not entire, complete, or scientifically impartial. His greatest merit is that of having shown the diminishing, anti-aesthetic, and restrictive influence of work on personality: this result, I may add, is in accordance, on one hand, with the psychology of voluntary attention—which is monoideism, that is, the restriction of the mind to a single object—and, on the other hand, with the physiology which teaches that work gives rise to toxins and vitiations which poison and corrupt the organism.

It is apparent that the influence of such agents, prolonged through centuries on races subjected to the servitude of work, or on classes domineered by other classes, has left an ineradicable mark on such races or classes, and that we now bear on our own constitutions the more or less noticeable traces of the slavery of our ancestors.

But Morasso was obliged by the very originality of his point of view to exaggerate its colouring, and to neglect the contrary views of work which are, moreover, widely diffused in public opinion, and generally accepted.

There is in addition a contradiction in his argument, which is however more apparent, perhaps, than real. Did not Morasso perceive that in making the extension he did to "the act of accusation of work" he thus condemned intellectual work itself, and hence his own writings? Unless perhaps he wished to include cerebral activities in an entirely separate category: but this would not be right; and I do not think he intended to do so. Such a contradiction is insuperable unless a distinction is clearly made between creative work and productive work, or, to be more explicit, creation by work, which I have done.

But there is more to follow. Everyone will perceive that when all the social classes make up their minds to work no more, society will soon be menaced by hunger. There is thus in Morasso's ideas a sprinkling of truth which was too much exaggerated, and which, as regards some aspects of the phenomenon *work*, was not fully matured.

Again, he entirely forgot to examine the psychological value of wealth, to which work must necessarily bring us. Now, wealth has precisely this reintegrative function, helping to beautify a personality which has been lowered, mutilated, and brutalised by work. Wealth is the means by which many individuals in present-day society, differently from those in society of the past, can bring their own persons to completion and perfection. I think that, previously to my having done so, no one has specifically pointed out this reintegrative value of wealth, with which value is closely connected the spread of wealth among a whole class which was at one time heavily oppressed—the middle class—which takes from wealth its rising character, and its particular state of being. Now, it must not be forgotten that in the present state of society work is the *only* means by which the majority of men can hope to attain ease; and this necessity, while, as we have said, it has its origin in their particular disposition, exercises in addition an extraordinary influence on their whole material and moral life.

But, just for this reason, ease remains the natural and superior state of both primitive and modern man. All beautiful things grow out of leisure.

On the other hand, however, I cannot agree with those who hold that society is not an imprescindible entity, at least in the sense of an economic necessity.

Granted the increase of living persons on a given territory, and the present conditions of alimentation, society is an unavoidable necessity—at least, if we do not want to arrive at anthropophagy. It may be that the future is reserving for us the liberation from such ties. This has already been predicted, in view of the great progress made in chemical synthesis; and a chemical genius, Berthelot, has predicted the important consequences which society of the future will derive from this. But even in this case, in spite of the deep and radical changes in all social relationships, society will still be necessary.

The psychologist can scarcely imagine all the radical transformations in our moral life, in our sentiments, in our ideas, even in our conception of life itself, that will result from a discovery which will render alimentation exempt from all pain and fatigue: for the economic necessity for production has moulded, animated, and coloured every ideal development of our psychical life.

We have seen how, of the two fundamental instincts of life —nutrition and reproduction—the first, being related to the possibilities of production offered by our planet (in respect to its extent: the extent of fertile and cultivable, of tropical and polar zones)—determined the development of work and of society.

Liberation from society, however partial, would signalise the beginning of a radical transformation in psychic as well as in social relationships. The solution of the problem of nutrition will then, indirectly, exercise an enormous influence on that of reproduction, or, rather, of love.

The chief obstacle which, in the relationship between man and woman, prevents the sure and infallible sexual instinct from appearing—material instincts, with their first and most specific determination, viz. nutrition—will thus be avoided. The removing of this obstacle will have a great and ameliorating influence on sexual relationships and in the amorous choice which, especially on the part of the woman concerned, is false, and overwhelmed by calculations of worldly interests. In this connection we may recollect the enormous amount of untruth which the woman contributes to present-day unions: dissimulation due merely to her own position, and not to any special fault of hers. We may also recollect how much kind-hearted, honest, loving mothers advise and torture their daughters to take advantage of the first opportunity, binding their bodies with a legal matrimonial chain to some man whom they regard almost with aversion. We may also call to mind how often, and with how many tears, a woman pays the price of her fidelity, and how much remorse she feels for a fault which is not hers.

There will always remain, even in the most favourable cases, numerous causes of complication in relationships which at first sight seem so simple; but there is no doubt that a greater amount of truth, sincerity, and justice will be brought into our sexual life.

But all such progress, it may be recalled, is within society, and I do not see how it can be withdrawn from society, as some hold. However much we may desire the individual to be developed and uplifted—and this is possible only after a long social development—we cannot even think of such a possibility absolutely outside of the limits of society.

And here we meet with a problem as old as the world itself; but one which continually crops up in the modern guise of specious antisocial theories: Can men ever live outside of the limits of society?

The answer can only be in the negative; even if it were granted that men would renounce all the refinement brought into life by society, and all its advantages and comforts; even granted that they would agree to return to a savage state, they could not live on a virgin soil away from other human beings. With the present forms of production and nutrition, human work consists principally in field labour, and is unavoidably necessary. And even if science found simple and economic methods by means of chemical synthesis, the very existence of science and of laboratories would imply a society.

Summing up what has been said above, we may affirm that sexuality and sociality are connected by the closest ties; but this relationship is antagonistic: in complete opposition. *Sociality is in function the reverse of sexuality:* such is our final formula. This, it should be clearly understood, is not to be taken in an absolute sense, for it is evident that sexual attraction, which springs from an impulse, is a fact which helps—in the family circle, for example—to draw social bonds more tightly together.

In this case, however, we may easily observe that a sexual impulse of a similar kind has already been modified by sociality, and has no longer its primitive force and violence.

The opposition I have referred to has not been brought to light until now, and yet it may be said to be the secret origin of many ideal developments which have taken place in society. All our morals, and a great number of our emotions and sentiments, have their *raison d'etre* in the existence of this antagonism.

The knowledge of particular and concrete conditions, both psychological and physiological, which favour work to the greatest extent, the knowledge, to use a biological expression, of the *optimum* of society, is most interesting, since all morals are only a theoretical transposition of the complexity of these particular conditions into an ideal, transcendental, and general form: a form that is imposed on all members of society by means of practical rules or formulae.

We have seen some of these conditions in what precedes, and we shall shortly see others.

It is of importance to observe how the spread of such formulae was achieved under cover of a kind of cajolery with promises of material and spiritual advantages; but especially spiritual promises made through religion, which, imposing on mankind a belief in another world, constituted a very strong support for morals.

Limitation of activity and mutilation of too pronounced and exuberant personalities—which were characteristics, through real, actual work, of the stronger men, of oligarchies or aristocracies, in the early ages of society—came in due time to be carried out by still more abstract and spiritual means; but this was made possible only by the progressive intellectual development of humanity. Violence, cruelty, and ferocity were the first instruments of coercion in so far as they were employed against members of the community itself, and not against foreigners or other communities. The desire to impoverish the weak and to subdue their struggles, to dominate the stronger individualities which might possibly arise from amongst them, was the first form of legality, that is, as a direct entity for the maintenance of the State.

The State itself—using the word in the widest and most abstract sense—owes its origin to two extreme forms of activity: the one organising, directing, dissipating of the strong men; the other, the working, economical activity of the conquered.

Any different conception of the State is Utopian, for, as an aggregate, it must be based on dynamism of this nature. If such facts are not so apparent today, it is because the warfare has assumed a more mental aspect; that is to say, it is fought with intellectual weapons in the intellectual sphere; but it is always being waged.

However much good men, philanthropists, and humanitarians may wish and endeavour to render such struggles less intense and to lessen the differences, it will never be possible to eliminate them, since the essence of the State is founded upon these dissonances. Moreover, we endeavour in all our institutions to increase the distance between us and nature, to arrive at an ideal of goodness, at the realisation of a dream of ease and peace, forgetting that the strength of our institutions lies exactly in the amount of *naturalness* which they possess and maintain, and in the more or less clever utilisation of the particular virtues of each one.

With civil progress, however, material and exterior influences and interventions gradually became substituted for interior differences and interventions proper to the individual himself. This must at first have been due to the stronger men threatening the weaker, and afterwards to the menace of a power higher than all other powers, a power which was inimical to every action which appeared to be unjust.

It is only here that we can properly speak of morals, and we must therefore affirm that morality came into existence with religion. If it later became independent of religion, that does not necessarily imply a denial of its origin; nor will it be further denied that, for the greater number of coarse and uncouth men, morality without religion is something almost inconceivable: because in these men we may still perceive the causes which, in primitive humanity, occasioned the menace of ills to come, either in this world or the next.

The first origin of morals is confused with the origin of conscience, and it is unreasonable to hope to bring any light to bear on this argument. We may, with our analysis, discover something that has not been mentioned before; but we shall not arrive at the true beginning. Nietzsche had this impossibility in mind when he gave us his *Genealogy of Morals* (note that he does not say *origin* of morals); but he made a great mistake in this direction: that of misunderstanding the importance of the sexual fact in his explanation of the genesis of the phenomenon of *morality*.

Such a truly fundamental importance is confirmed by the fact that all primitive morality is prevailingly sexual, and is directed to the end of obstructing the amorous instinct and impulse. Of exactly such a character is the morality of religion.

"In all pessimistic religions the act of generation is regarded as bad in itself," says Nietzsche. And pessimistic religions are those founded by weak, poor, and low men: democratic religions, ethical and sentimental in character rather than cosmogonic and aesthetic. This is due to the fact that religion, which is the highest creation of the spirit of sociality, takes from the nature of the latter its antinomy to sexuality.

Some sociologists and biologists, who are rather superficial, and therefore ready to condemn or to deny importance to the highest facts of the mind—facts which nevertheless should make everyone think—never forget, when speaking of religion, to attribute to it the cause of the social danger which arises from the presence of so many numerous and different sexual anomalies, affirming that the religious anti-sexual prejudice, which hinders a natural impulse, causes its abnormal deviations. I do not hesitate to declare that such accusations are foolish.

We especially see reproduced in the inhibitory and restraining function of religion, often with greater intensity, the character of every social phenomenon: in other words, in religion is concentrated, sublimated, and, so to speak, crystallised, this tendency towards sociality determined by work.

And, in so far as religion is a complexity of positive formulae, it is only in its far-off finality a transposition of what is useful and helpful for production or work. I will not deny all the other intellectual aspects from which religion might be considered; but I say emphatically that we cannot attribute to the *origin* of a human fact that which is the very complex final product, or result, of civilisation.

The efficacy of morals on our life, the inducement by which certain determined precepts succeed in exercising a directing influence on our conduct and on our acts, seems now almost mysterious, for we no longer see the menace of real and positive bodily harm on the part of others, or the menace of future spiritual ill in another world by the intervention of a supernatural power.

And this is because, having attained its end of creating an inner mechanism to guide the actions of individuals, the importance of the means by which this end was attained gradually declined, until the means themselves were no longer perceived.

Why, it may now be asked, did religion look upon sexuality as almost an enemy; why also did religious men of all shades of opinion do so; until at last those of a strong sense of duty came to have such a profound antipathy for everything relating to sex?

In replying to this question, we may be helped by some religious precepts and teachings, the nature of which is quite clear.

The practice of fasting, of abstaining from meat on certain determined days, of penitence, of a discipline carried as far as the wearing of a hair shirt on the skin, and even whipping—a form of penitence employed by the more fervent members of certain religious bodies—are all, in their essence, means of vital depression.

This has been the object of religion in the past: to depress vitality and animal exuberance, and in this regard we see the essential character of all society exaggerated and raised to its apogee, including that mass of facts and phenomena the aim of which is to favour the development of work.

Religion, which is, so to speak, the accentuation of the social phenomenon, was of such great importance because it was chiefly a protective aid to work, and, if it did lose its value little by little, it was because its function was at an end, or had even been assumed by other forms of conscious life.

But, as happened also in the case of many other phenomena, religion, or, rather, some particular positive forms which had been invested with the religious spirit, developing on their own account, lost the ties which connected them with reality, and even became obstacles in the way of social development, for they depressed human energies more than was necessary. We may recall the sublime, but useless and dangerous deviations of asceticism, and of religious emasculation.

For the reasons indicated religion combated sexual intercourse and love, since this latter is psychologically, and perhaps physiologically also, an active and aggrandising factor of individual personality.

Numerous statements have been made respecting the relationship of sex to the remaining physical organism and to conscious life, which, at least in their absolute form, reciprocally contradict one another, but which are nevertheless true in certain particular applications.

In this way, some have boasted of chastity as the higher state which allows of the extrinsication of human energy in more noble, refined, and intellectual forms: such, it is known, was Renan's[35] opinion, who made his own the saying of that ancient thinker who held that, in a philosopher, sex should mount into the brain.

In this way also some have declared that physical floridness, that state of sound health which is shown in the

---

[35] Ernest Renan, author of *The Life of Jesus* (1863) which Nietzsche criticized in his writings.

fresh reddish complexion of temperate youths, is due to chastity.

Others, on the other hand, say that a moderate but active exercise of pleasure is a necessary condition of health for all physical and psychical functions: and others again hold that sexual dissipation is the supreme law of every strong individuality, and the characteristic of a fine and magnificent virility.

How can these diverse opinions be reconciled?

We must before all observe that sexual physiology has been completely neglected, and that, with the exception of the researches of Brown-Séquard,[36] the subject is quite new. I think that the reasons why our knowledge of the reproductive functions has remained in such a backward state are almost all moral. At any rate, the fact remains that very little in regard to this matter has been proved.

I shall put forward some critical opinions of my own on this question, opinions which may perhaps be the starting-point of researches and experiments.

It is known that the sexual glands have a twofold function: one of external secretion—this is well known, for reproduction depends on it—another of internal secretion, discovered by Brown-Séquard. That portion of glandular secretion which is reabsorbed by the organism has a tonic and stimulating action on it; to this action is attributed the production of the so-called secondary sexual characteristics, that is, the increased growth of hair and beard, the development of the voice, etc.; but its influence would be specially noticeable on psychical life, determining the psychological characteristics of virility.

It must certainly be admitted that this twofold secretive function is of unequal intensity in different individuals, thus perhaps constituting a property which characterises one's individual organic strength, considered as vital capacity and

---

[36] Charles-Édouard Brown-Séquard, 19th century physiologist and neurologist.

vigour of the germinative plasm, of which an individual is only the trustee.

The sexual act implies an immediate loss to the organism, perhaps because a part of the internal secretion is suddenly scattered externally; but at the same time this sexual embrace acts as a stimulant and intensifier to secretion itself, at least within the limits of an ample and rich nutrition and the age of youth. It can thus be understood how it helps indirectly to augment the intensity of seminal absorption, and to raise the organic tone.

The lassitude and exhaustion which follow prolonged venereal pleasure are necessary, as for every organic activity the acquisition of a greater excitability, and therefore of a more intense function, is always obtained by means of an excessive stimulation which is evidenced by pain and vital diminution. Hence the exercise of venereal pleasure is perhaps a means by which the organism is capable of acting on itself, of refining itself, and of making itself more valid and resistant: in a word, of making itself virile.

The indefinite development and increase which, by such mechanism, should be theoretically admitted, is limited, on the one hand, by the fact that the genital glands (forming part of an entire organism, and depending on it) cannot acquire an excessive prevalence without changing the balance of the systems necessary to life; and, on the other hand, by the fact that indulgence in sexual pleasure, if it grows into a habit, does not fail to direct externally, in the way of sexual dissipation, those energies which should be reserved for the organism itself. That is seen, for example, in many libertines and Don Juans, or in mere masturbators, who at times present the appearance of eunuchs, that is, of individuals whose vital functions are affected by a certain characteristic torpor due to the absence of internal secretion.

It is perhaps to be supposed that the relationship between the internal and the external secretion of the seminal glands is changed by excessive and protracted indulgence in venereal pleasures, in the sense that the internal secretion diminishes to the advantage of the external, chastity having the contrary effect; but whilst a prolonged period of chastity certainly diminishes the intensity of the complexive secretion, and hence of the internal secretion also, frequent and intense indulgence tends to augment it.

I am convinced that the phenomena of creative intelligence are closely connected with sexuality, and I will explain in the following sentences the different points of view which I have put forward. Chastity is of much help when it is accompanied with a natural vigour, that is, when the glands themselves perform their functions intensely; and especially when sexual inhibition, through lack of the artificial and exciting stimulants so frequent in our life, is not so difficult and painful as it usually is. But, as this state of things is not often found, better conditions for the intelligence are perhaps those of periods of sexual abstention after periods of love and pleasure, as in these periods the internal secretion will be considerably increased by the preceding stimulation.

In general, however, it may be said that creativeness is a companion of sexuality.

In this sense we may mention the well-known fact that the greatest expansion of a civilisation, whether in political greatness or in the flourishing state of arts and sciences which naturally follows thereon, is usually accompanied with an extended quest after sexual pleasure.

After what we have said, we may here state the reason for the opposition between religion and morals on the one hand, and sexuality on the other. Many writers have pretended to explain this by saying that we have got into the habit of considering the sexual act as a collection of shameful things. But this is just the question: Why and how do we habitually sanction such an opinion of an act which is in itself the most natural that can be imagined ?

This point of view was not adopted purely by caprice: and they still more foolishly deceive themselves who condemn religion especially on account of its opposition to love: religion, one of the very highest and most marvellous human facts, in that it had a high and important mission to carry out, a mission which only a mean and narrow-minded science, constructed for the use of vulgar publicists or self-styled freethinkers, could misunderstand. With its antipathy to sex, religion not merely gave form to the exigencies of sociality and production, but also pleaded the cause of spirituality and intelligence in man.

Amorous pleasure, affirming itself in two ways contrarily to these exigencies, both as a tendency of every strong and brutal nature to leisure, and as a means of exalting and aggrandising vitality, comes to be opposed to that which favours work.

But those who accuse religion and morals of being the principal obstacles to love, especially physiologists who hold that religion and morals produce, or at least favour, a large number of amorous diseases and perversions, forget that the rise of a religious and moral problem in modern minds, that is, the suggestion of the possibility of relinquishing religion and morals, is really due to the fact that we have become intimately (which is equivalent to saying really) religious and moral.

Religion and morals had a task to carry out, a finality, and only now that they have accomplished their task, and because we have been transformed by them, do we feel the need of coming away from them as the butterfly breaks and issues from the cocoon, which nevertheless protected its formation.

Our limbs, having become too weak, feel, so to speak, the weight of the chains which at first they bore with ease and almost without noticing them. It is because we have become too moral that we feel the need of coming away from morality, which, indeed, tends to suffocate us, although it exercised a beneficent function in the past.

Thus is explained the great modern success of immoralistic doctrines, without necessarily concluding from this that we have become more wicked and corrupt. The immoralist system of Nietzsche is only a great attempt to free ourselves from morals intellectually; and the attempt is that of a people who are too profoundly moral, and who at the same time take pleasure in great theoretical constructions.

In the opposition of religion to sexuality we may therefore see another proof of the anti-sociality of love, and we can only conclude that religions have watched carefully over the interests of sociality.

We often hear of a greater morality, a sexual kind, in the northern countries. This is rather inexact. If by morality we understand a collection of positive and imperative precepts and formulae, which would tend to establish a certain mode of conduct—which, in my opinion, is the correct interpretation of the word—it is logical that these formulae should be less frequent and less conscious where inhibition of instincts, sexual instincts in particular, is a feature of organic qualities, such as coldness, and of a certain natural calmness. So that the pretended greater liberty of morals is only apparent, because, in these northern countries where the limits and restrictions of love are settled by nature herself, all other restrictions imposed by custom are hence rendered useless.

Sexual inhibition, which in cold countries is a physical fact, and as such more certain, must have been imposed by means of formulae and commands, that is, by psychological means, in the more southern countries, at a time when, for many different reasons, the necessity for production was felt to a greater degree than formerly.

And hence arises the finer, more delicate, and more conscious nature of southern morality, which took its special colouring from the Roman Catholic religion. The morality of this religion, especially in respect to love, is a masterpiece of perfect knowledge of men and their needs—at least, in past times. If we moderns now find ourselves ill at ease in our religion—as the northern nations did before the Reformation —it is because we have made some progress on the path of sociality, and have now become, in a certain sense, more northern.

Roman Catholic sexual morality was that which suited nations inclined to pleasure, to the pagan conception of life, to amorous ease; and its anti-sexual character is perfectly commensurate with the necessity for repressing a strong tendency. It may be remembered that one of the first acts of the Reformers was to proclaim freedom of love and marriage for clergymen, and that the ex-catholic monk, Martin Luther, got married to the ex-nun, Bona, an act which is apparently hardly capable of setting an example of good manners and customs, but which was an effectual return to chastity.

For the rest, as flesh is weak, temptation near at hand, and circumstances often favourable, the Roman Catholic religion found in its indulgent casuistry a moderating of its moral rigidity, and, making use of its enormous power of renovation of conscience in the practice of confession, it knew how to be the religion which was best adapted to the times, to places, and to men: which is, after all, the aim of every human institution.

In my arguments I have purposely always spoken of Roman Catholic morals and religion, for I think it is the most expressive of the religious spirit, and of all other forms closely connected with it in the real and positive aspects which it incarnates: but what I have said will, generally speaking, apply to other religions as well.

CHAPTER V

MODESTY AND SHYNESS

The continual increase of those tendencies and dispositions which I call by the one word sociality—using this word to indicate progress in that direction which is contrary to naturalness—proceeds with the progressive spread and generalisation of a collective psychological state, in which depressive emotions, or at least conditions of calmness, quietude, and methodical activity predominate.

Obedience, dread of authority, and modesty, to mention only a few of the feelings which were developed in society, are more or less related to fear.

Contrarily to what some superficial sociologists and psychologists have said, the feeling of fear is not at all a characteristic of the primitive mind of a savage. The savage may be seized with a feeling of alarm before something which appears to him mysterious or supernatural, but he will never be afraid when anything happens that requires an immediate employment of strength, boldness, rapid defence, a quick attack, the sure glance.

The aims, conditions, and necessities of social development will, on the other hand, only too often bring about a general diminution of those primitive qualities and instincts, as also of every form of personal potency. The development of these so-called social emotions was, as will be seen, contrary to sexuality; but in so far as this asserts itself as a salient and most prominent fact of animal life, to that extent is it the principle most liable to attack in its manifestations and its acts.

As we have already stated, it seems that our greater humanity has been acquired to a certain extent by the loss of those physical and moral qualities which are closely related to

sex, and, among them, courage and enterprise. All higher
ethical formations, as we have already seen, and a large
number of laws, rites, and customs, take sexuality into
consideration: I shall try to show how such an aim still remains
the obscure finality of two emotive states which possess a
psychological value of the first importance: modesty and
shyness. I should even be inclined to think that such emotive
forms are the more advanced aspects of a constraint which
was in former times more brutal and apparent. Thus, these
forms, although now *inner and   spiritual*, are not less efficacious
means against sexuality, which latter therefore finds its
limitation, not in exterior force or in the coercion of the
strongest males, but in psychicity itself; in the inner minds of
individuals.

Modesty and shyness, it is said, are as much male as female
characteristics; but we must observe that the sphere of true
modesty in woman seems to include that of shyness, as this
latter, which is by itself a hesitation, an incapacity for action in
general, accompanied with a particular sentimental state, takes
a special colouring and becomes more evident to man in the
field of amorous action.

And by such a distribution between the two sexes, modesty
has a general character of passiveness, whilst shyness has an
aspect of hesitation and oscillation.

It cannot be absolutely and laconically said, as most people
do say, that modesty and shyness are depressive emotions.
Such a denomination is rather inexact, and the physical signs
with which both are accompanied will perhaps bear out our
opinion. The blushing arising from modesty and shyness may
perhaps indicate that, apart from processes of paralysis and of
a diminution of the energy of active and spinal centres, there
is a stimulation of inhibitory and cerebral centres, due to an
afflux of blood to them; that is to say, there is depression and
exaltation at the same time. Both the conditions mentioned,
especially shyness, are not pure and simple emotions; but

contrasts, clashings of opposite forces, with the final victory of the inhibitory force, a victory, however, which is assured only after many oscillations.

Curious indeed is the argument of the Lombrosian[37] psychologists in regard to the modesty of man, which is simply an embryo or a larva of emotion that is confused with shyness. These thinkers say: modesty in man is *in reality* greater than in woman, and moreover it would be so *in appearance*, if important elements—the chief one being the initiative part which man takes in love—did not change the primitive resemblance.

I should like to ask these men by what extraordinary logical process they discover the presence of a phenomenon which *would be*, if there were not already other causes which are established as contrary to these, and which exist in every case. The argument given above, it seems to me, might indeed be considered as a marvellous trick of legerdemain ... only that there is another more convenient and justifiable name for it which ... I shall refrain from giving. And here a statement on my part appears to be called for.

I have a kind of discreet esteem for the work of the Lombrosian school in connection with the psychology of woman, of love, and of sex (although, in essence, it is only a derivation from and a development of the Schopenhauerian doctrines of love), and it especially seems to me that an independent follower of this school, Viazzi, has said many things which are, in a great measure, true.[38]

But the final impression which we receive after reading what has been written in modern times is this: The hatred of woman and sex, which dictated their bitter invectives to the

---

[37] Cesare Lombroso (1835-1909) was an Italian physician, criminologist and eugenicist.

[38] Pio Viazzi (1868-1914) was an Italian politician, jurist and philosopher, author of *La lotta di sesso* (The War of the Sexes) and *Sui reati sessuali* (On Sex Crimes) among other works.

fathers of the church, is in the main more or less subtilised and armed with scientific reasons in the ideas of all modern thinkers who have dealt with the psychology of woman. In other words, love is still considered *from the sphere of morality:* even with all the pretensions to an impartial and natural conception of the facts. But what is most evident is that such *impartial* psychologists have not yet been able to overcome the traditional obstacle of masculine egoism. Thus Viazzi, on the other hand, condemns feminism, of which he has not grasped the *moralising* value: he nevertheless speaks with a certain veiled bitterness of the astuteness, the deceit, the fine and subtle policy of woman—all these tortuous characteristics, in short, by which, in what he calls the second phase of the battle of sex, she has acquired hegemony, in fact, if not in name.

It is truly a case of pleading guilty to one of the accusations of the weaker sex against the stronger, namely, that of our insatiable masculine egoism!

Feminism is a movement which a final analysis shows to be due to the greater participation of women in social work, in production. This fact has moralised woman, giving her a desire for example to be sufficient unto herself, and to be independent—but it has brutalised her!

Now, Viazzi complains of this brutalising and this diminution of femininity, not perceiving that a great part of the fascination of the eternal feminine lies exactly in this psychology of deceit and artifice which he condemned a few pages before. I may add, moreover, that the words artifice and deceit are too moral, too human, to be correct; to approach more closely to truth and justice it would be necessary to add *unconscious;* and the coupling of these words, if logically absurd, would not be so psychologically, since it would be the reproduction of feminine reality across the visual system of masculine sentimentality.

Sed de hoc satis: for one thing results from all this, and it is that man is a glutton without equal, who wants what is sweet without giving up what is strong, and even requires both qualities in his female friends!

Modesty is a social emotion in the twofold signification of a phenomenon caused by society, and a protective phenomenon of sociality; it is not spontaneous, whatever may be said to the contrary; but is imposed by education. This latter is only a recapitulation in brief of the influences which operated historically on society; and is proved also by the fact that it is more rigid and severe in those races for whom external circumstances were most difficult.

Modesty in children is only a *notion*, not a *feeling*, such it becomes only at puberty. It is strange how the knowledge of this simple fact has not been sufficient to correct the opinions of certain authors, who believe it to be stronger among certain races than in others. Thus Krafft-Ebing holds that it is stronger and felt to a greater extent in the northern races, whilst Venturi,[39] with perhaps more truth, assures us that it is more conspicuous in southern peoples. This is doubtless true if we consider Venturi as referring to Italy in particular.

The emotion of modesty is in fact a state which originates in the struggle between two forces, that of sexual instinct and that of cerebral inhibition, acting by means of mechanism still unknown to us, but certainly real, and formed in the higher centres by the action of centuries. Now, the whole intensity of emotion comes from the relative strength of these two forces among themselves, and this strength varies to such a degree that the greatest emotion is found when these two forces have developed to such an extent as to be about equal to each other.

The northern races are sexually cold; that is to say, their sexual instinct is not very active, or *vice versa* their forces of inhibition are more vigilant (at least these latter are connected

---

[39] Silvio Venturi (1850-1900) was an Italian psychiatrist, director of an asylum in Catanzaro and author of *Le degenerazioni psico-sessuali nella vita degli individui e nella storia delle societa* (Psycho-sexual Degeneration in the Life of the Individual and in the History of Society).

with the former, perhaps owing to the weaker strength of the sexual instinct) to an extent that this series of interior oscillations, actions, and reactions, which constitute modesty, cannot be established. The contrary, however, must be said in regard to the peoples of the south, whose sexuality is limited more by the exhaustion caused by the climate to all general vital functions than by inhibitory inner causes.

For the rest, the future may perhaps have in reserve for us a scale of passions corresponding to our different temperaments, a correspondence, indeed, which in general and on the average undeniably exists: we may, however, now take it as certain that modesty in its greatest efflorescence is peculiar to temperate forms of morality.

Evident proofs exist of which I affirm: one of these is the almost unexpected appearance of modesty in a girl when she first begins to menstruate. The contrast with her preceding behaviour is sometimes truly extraordinary, and exactly corresponds to the conception of the rapid rise of a new force, which encounters the resistances already established by education.

There are, as is known, little children who, although bright, sharp, and unconstrained before puberty, become all at once reserved and timid, until finally they arrive at a stage of the most awkward embarrassment.

Modesty is therefore a proof not only of integrity and of purity, but also of a discreetly strong instinct, and in this we see also one of the seductions and functions of modesty, which until now has not been clearly elucidated, although it has been somewhat loosely and confusedly put forward.

For the rest, it is very difficult in such arguments to say anything entirely new; but it may also be stated that a truly exact examination of social sentiments and emotions has not hitherto been made. We find ourselves now in the presence of these phenomena as before material bodies which are being formed by successive crystallisations, so that we may perceive and describe sufficiently well what is on the surface, the most recent stratifications; but no further. In the matter of the history of sentiments, we can only approximately deduce and imagine their past.

In the meantime, however, we may affirm that modesty cannot be explained by a change of meaning, as is the case with other feelings, and if we cannot see in it either the identical reproduction or the simple enlargement of what it was in a remote period, we must yet affirm that our modern conception of it tends to multiply its conscious elements and to intertwine its relationships, whilst keeping within the limits of the original theme.

Thus, modesty, having had at first a particular and concrete meaning, which constituted as it were the almost imperceptible nucleus of crystallisation, continued to add to it secondary significations and functions which gradually complicated its nature. *A particular attitude of woman determined the instinct of mastery and sexual desire of man, who imposed certain precise and material limitations by means of violence,* was the first element around which other concordances were deposited, although they were developed separately up to a certain point. Such deposits were repeated several times, so that the older strata were finally lost to view under the more recent, and so on to our own times, in which modesty has taken such a delicate and human aspect, just because only the newer acquisitions are present to the mind.

The generic feeling in woman of her own inferiority in respect to man—a feeling which attains its maximum during the act of sexual intercourse—is the primitive psychological element of the emotion of modesty. Such a fact is truly originary, for we find it in animalness itself. The females of animals seem to bear the violence of the male with some pain; in some species of animals the male has even to hold the female firmly during the sexual act so that she may not run away. This is, however, less noticeable in the superior animals, in the highest mammifers, especially in the primate types, where, while the female has still a generic fear of the male, she takes a greater share in the sexual act. Finally, in the species man we find a still greater share taken by the female in love; and this fact, be it noted, is being accentuated with the increase of sociality.

But how is this vague feeling of inferiority utilised? It is here that the general principle which I have established becomes apparent.

When society began to be settled, the unlimited promiscuousness of woman's loves and conquests came to be circumscribed by the fact that males, being obliged to devote a great part of their activity to a search for food, could not afford to waste this activity in amorous conquests and love struggles. Besides, the expenditure of energy which love called for must have been still further increased by the fact that woman was afflicted with the same necessities (since she had not yet come to live in that state of comparative leisure which society afterwards generally almost assured her), and must therefore have shown herself more unwilling to comply with masculine desires. It must be added that the weaker people, forced to the drudgery of searching for food, must also have suffered a direct and real limitation on the part of the stronger, who took a greater number of women to satisfy their desires.

In such conditions as these the exigency certainly arose of preserving for one's own use the only woman whom one could have: the first dawn of the monogamic system. This, in the beginning, was neither a free choice nor a moral act; it was a form of life assumed by the weak under the direct oppression of the strong, as almost all human progress was at first; and it was only afterwards that psychical contagion made this spread amongst all classes.

Perhaps jealousy also arose in such a state of things. We have proofs of it in facts shown by common observation, the value of which, however, has not up to the present been correctly interpreted. Jealousy is, so to speak, a half-way condition—a mixed state—for it implies the vision or the vague feeling of a higher state of liberal and unlimited sexual activity from which one is at present excluded; but it is also an act of mastery; it indicates besides that a new element, however poor and scanty it may be, has entered into sexual relationships: spiritual love.

Jealousy is more common among the more amorous peoples; it is well known that the nations of the south and east are extremely jealous; but it would perhaps be too much to say that this is the sign of very great sexuality: it may certainly be affirmed that it more than anything else proves the existence of a strong spirit of mastery and a robust instinct of property. On the other hand, a very great genesial power is undoubtedly accompanied with a certain *insouciance* and erotic vagabondage.

A man with a strong sexual instinct can with difficulty submit to having only one woman, or a few; and such a man does not know what jealousy is, at least, in a lasting characteristic form. He may perhaps be jealous for the time being, but no longer. Jealousy is the special trait of the man who endeavours to keep one woman for himself, as he may think he could not easily win another, either on account of his own defects or exterior difficulties. But it must be added that a love entirely without jealousy, which is often found among the northern peoples, a profound and spiritual love, is the associate of a nature which does not feel any incitements towards sensual love.

Jealousy is the psychological form which prevails in the amorous life of males in a society where masculine desires have suffered limitation, and where the adjustment of sexual relationships is on the point of passing to the monogamic form, or has already reached it: not, however, without many obstinate struggles, and more, perhaps, in name than in fact.

For the rest, all this game of sentiments and emotions repeats, in a mild and attentuated form (because it is psychological), those former conditions on which we have laid stress, and into which only physical relationships of strength enter.

Rich, healthy, and vigorous individualities make victims of the less healthy and vigorous, or of the poor and the weak, not merely materially, but with economic and organic impoverishment. Certain feelings of weak people, such as jealousy, resentment, and impotent envy, have long had a deleterious effect on their physical and moral personality; and these feelings therefore appear to be more recent and refined means for affirming the superiority of the strong even in the mind of those who are subjected. They are in such a way real instruments of torture, mortification, and oppression.

Thus forms of depressive emotions symbolically reproduce the former conditions, and renew with interior mechanism that which was at first really an exterior action of outward forces.

In this way woman is flattered by and satisfied with the jealousy of man, since it puts him in a state of inferiority, and gives her a proof of her dominion. These artless, gracious ladies say they like to see a little jealousy in a man, for this, they say, is an associate of love; but in reality they like a jealous man because the fact that he is jealous is a proof of their power and puts the man into their hands. Indeed, even when an excess of jealousy leads a man to beat his mistress, she only holds him a closer prisoner by means of the most essential interests of life; and it is on this account that a woman would rather be beaten by her husband or lover than slighted.

The man who is free and master of himself is indifferent to this feeling, which, indeed, puts whoever experiences it in a state of dependency and servitude. The jealous being, far from disgracing his companion—for jealousy, as many have pointed out, indicates a want of confidence—is a disgrace himself, for he shows himself to be unworthy of a special and continued preference; and the man who feels strong and vigorous thinks rightly or wrongly that he is one of those who are most worthy of preference, if not the only one.

Coming back to the subject of modesty, this sprang from the necessity of preserving one woman from the interference of outsiders and keeping her for one's self alone, and, to help in attaining this end, this pre-existent emotive and generic element given by a sense of inferiority was made use of, and reinforced by effective masculine violence in cases where a woman failed to do what was right.

To this element others with different functions were added much later: they even belong, properly speaking, to the epoch when woman took a greater part in the work of love than previously, to make up for a diminution in the male activity of conquest. These elements have already been examined so often that it is hardly worth while repeating the deductions. Let us rather give a few words to those cases which show a lack of modesty.

Lack of modesty may be of at least three kinds.

(1) When the accomplishment of the sexual act is irresistible and violent, being based on a very strong instinct to which no difficulties can be opposed—difficulties which, indeed, never come to the knowledge of the individual. This form, if morbid cases be excepted, is very rare, and I should be inclined to call it amoral.

(2) When, on account of extraordinary coldness, the sexual act has become so rare that inhibitions of it are no longer conscious, but organic. The performance of the act does not then seem unlawful to the conscience, as it does when it is frequent and intense; but in such a case it appears, on the contrary, to be merely the satisfying of a natural and lawful desire. This form I should be inclined to call hypermoral.

(3) When the want is caused by a rough experience of life, and a voluntary quest of pleasure for itself. This variety may truly be called immoral, and it is, in my opinion, the sign of a perversion and likewise of a deficiency of sexuality.

Thus it is that in the want of modesty, the sexual profligacy of some women—particularly among the higher and more cultured classes—we cannot see a more ardent desire and a stronger sexuality; but a real amorous deficiency and inaptitude. Want of modesty is a grave failing in any woman, which must be taken into consideration when judging her value, together with any other masculine characteristics shown by so-called superior and cultured women. A woman who is not capable of an infinite complication of *ruses,* blushes, hesitations—real or formal modesty—reveals a grave defect in her femininity; I would not say with others: "She is only a woman"; but rather: "She is a woman no longer."

For the most part the desire for sexual intercourse in such women is not dictated by an actual need, but is an entirely cerebral exigency, a suggestion which is breathed in with our southern air. In other words, such women are by nature cold, and practise love only as a graceful sport.

Modesty did not arise, as Venturi thinks it did, in order to act as a defence of feminine personality; it is one of the numerous means for attaining a much wider end, an end which is above the rights of an individual, if indeed it does not overlook them altogether. Its specific location was in woman because a passive function in the sexual act was destined for her; but the principal function of modesty was not individual protection. I do not therefore think with Venturi that without education woman would learn modesty at a more advanced age by way of bitter experience, for the good reason that experience . . . only destroys modesty, does not increase it. There are very many different exigencies to account for the origin of modesty!

The chief cause, the most remote reason, must be looked for in the fundamental antinomy between sexuality and all those psychological conditions which we have examined that favoured the manifestation of the phenomenon of *work.*

This truth is in the main common to all more or less specious and deceitful appearances, and, although it is a product of analysis and abstraction, we must nevertheless see in the fact it expresses the origin of all the specifications of our moral life, which as a whole had the aim of obstructing and impeding our free, spontaneous, immediate, and aggressive activity, substituting therefore a regulated, methodical, and social form.

*   *   *   *   *

Shyness in a man corresponds to modesty in a woman, since it is shown and manifested first of all and especially in the sphere of sexual relations, thus having as a particular result that of the inhibition of amorous action.

To be more exact, it is first of all the knowledge of an obstacle, and then it becomes both by itself and by its conscient value a force of inhibition. An excess of the restraining influences of education in the formation of character is one of the causes, the most noted cause, of shyness. Education by all the means which it employs is a diminution of vital manifestations (we may recollect, for example, the discipline of bodily pain, the habit of quietness and sedateness, the obligation of silence, etc.). It may therefore be easily understood how an excess of education is shown in a deficiency of personal energies and of strength in general. The result of an excess of education is that when any particular work has to be carried out, especially any act which necessitates the employment of the more conspicuous faculties, such as judgment or selection, or when any complicated work has to be done, its fulfilment is accomplished with some trouble, with inadaptability and a want of energy.

The restrictions of inhibition, instead of preventing the deviation of activities in wrong directions, threatens to decrease and abolish these activities entirely. The more or less visible result of this state is shyness.

This, however, becomes more evident at puberty, when it is manifested as sexual shyness, which is its most apparent form. In its ordinary manifestations it indicates a spirit of instinct which is still poor, that is, which has not yet reached the point of being able to break the obstacles set by custom and by spiritualistic ideology in the way of love. And this aspect of poor strength it still possesses even at a more advanced age.

Shyness is a proof—at least originarily, that is, when it is not complicated by voluntary reactions on itself which may in time transform a character into the perversity of a Julien Sorel or a Robert Greslou[40]—it is a proof, I repeat, of the force which moral ideas, the spirit of respect for authority, and the feeling of duty exercise on a given individual. It is thus that the greater number of shy people come from those places where education is practised by severe and rigid means; from families, from provincial colleges, from institutes of religious education. To this also is due the fact that those skilled in teaching have to apportion the weight of coercive means—even when purely moral—to the vitality of the child, not only for his physical good, but also for his future moral and intellectual development. It is certain that an over-severe education sterilises a child, because it destroys the germs of initiative and personality.

A shyness which is protracted beyond the time of puberty, or rather which lasts all one's life, is always the indication of a great lesion of vitality suffered in infancy that even youth and manhood cannot cause to disappear. It therefore happens that many shy men have been sickly and delicate children, suffering from hereditary illnesses, or from illnesses acquired in early childhood.

This is quite in accord with what we have said in regard to the physical conditions from which intelligence is developed;

---

[40] Protagonists of Stendhal's *The Red and the Black* and Paul Bourget's *The Disciple*, respectively.

but it is even more worthy of our attention when we know that shyness has been a characteristic of many great men; it was even so conspicuous in some of the greatest as to make them be classified psychologically as "shy." This fact, then, in its turn is in entire agreement with what I shall say as to the mode of conceiving genial personality.

This meaning which we have given to shyness as an obscure and vague consciousness of insufficient strength is truly and properly applicable only to its first phases, whilst the shyness of an adult takes a character which is apparently that of autosuggestion: because the repetition of attacks of shyness engenders a facility of reaction whenever the circumstances in which the individual must *payer de sa personne* are renewed.

A shy man is preoccupied with himself, and with the judgments which others are forming of him; he almost feels himself as it were on a stage, and his unnaturalness comes from this continual preoccupation. Like all other unhealthy personalities, he is somewhat vain, and, moreover, suspicious and diffident: like all those who have not grown up properly, he is full of care for himself, and refers everything to himself: like weak people in general, he examines and scrutinises his surroundings, and puts every event that happens in relation to his own person, habituated as he is to fear hostile influences. From this arises the continual attitude of defence of the shy man, who always seems to stand on the alert, and in a warlike and pugnacious attitude. On the other hand, shyness in its more enduring forms is revealed as an exuberance of inner force, mental life, and psychical activity, which act on the individual who happens to possess them, for want of something else: at this time it appears as a disease of the intelligence.

But on account of this characteristic, when it succeeds in directing its strength externally—in making the individual forget the *ego*—then we may hope for a splendid victory.

That is to say, a shy man is often so merely because he has a bad opinion of himself; he is often an optimist for others and a pessimist for himself; if he even sometimes succeeds in conquering himself and appearing boastful and proud, he is certainly not so practically. Moreover, pride, in so far as it is neglect of others, has often its origin in shyness, and this constitutes a reaction in the sense of one's own solitude.

Shyness is a circumlocution, a pause, a *détour* of the intelligence. It is a companion of all spiritual progress, of every ascent towards superiority. It is the pain of everyone who feels differently from others, but who has respect for truth and the sense of the difficulty of establishing it; the anguish of him who feels a new world in himself, but who also feels that it is a too different world.

It is a significant observation, already made by others, that many of the greatest artists and poets were shy. To give only a few names, we may mention for example Virgil, Ovid, Horace, Tibullus, amongst the ancients; Correggio, Michelet, Beethoven, Lamartine, Wagner, Chopin, among the moderns. Almost all the great thinkers, the greatest minds, were afflicted with this malady; from Newton, whose shyness was proverbial, to Montesquieu, Rousseau, Kant, and Hegel. Even men of action, and of the greatest action of all—government—suffered from it; for example, Napoleon, who, even when he had reached the height of his power, could never free himself from all that self-consciousness made him suffer as a boy in the college at Brienne, and later in his love for Josephine. I think the reason is, perhaps, that a mind which wishes to rise to great heights is exquisitely sensitive, and hence susceptible in a much greater degree than others to be *froissé*.[41]

Richness and grandeur of sentiment, the capacity for *sympathising*, which amounts to saying the capacity for understanding men (this magnificent and sovereign quality to

---

[41] ruffled, offended, resentful

which all the varied forms of truly superior intelligence converge), and the exquisiteness of moral sensitiveness, closely depend on a certain diminution of brutal and physical energy, on a certain *affaissement*[42] of brutality—of healthy animalness in man. On the other hand, action has its *optimum* of existence in a healthy and robust vitality. Furthermore, diminution of vitality has in the very nature of things a limit, and this limit is the physical degeneration of the race.

There must therefore exist for every epoch, for every social group in any epoch, and finally for every individuality in the midst of any group, a certain relationship between the means and the degrees of the two opposite tendencies mentioned above; this relationship constitutes the average of the qualities of the epoch of the group and of the individuality.

When the anti-vital influences, which, however, favour the development of social characteristics in mankind, prevail, we meet with degeneration. The vague and obscure indirect relationship which comes between the conditions of the development of the intelligence and physical degeneration has often been perceived; but the merit of more recent conceptions is that of having cancelled this stamp of condemnation and fatality which existed in some of its formulations, and which the unilateralness and superficiality of the Lombrosian school had impressed upon it.

For the rest, Venturi was more acute than all the Lombrosians when he stated the great laws of the utilisation by society of divergent characters who, according to him, are almost always degenerative. With this discovery, however incomplete, Venturi perceived one of the greatest rules of human development.

But to those who with loud voices and a solemn manner deem extraordinary sensitiveness, continued disquietude and discontent, and the continued arising of new desires, to be

---

[42] subsidence, lessening

signs of degeneration, we must reply that they do not know mankind, or that at the most they only know a very coarse type of man, which they wish to pass off as his most perfect image.

Certainly, a great sensitiveness by itself is not a very useful requisite, inasmuch as its possessor runs all the risks of being kept bound down, petty, and inert, if he is placed by circumstances in unfavourable conditions and brought into contact with coarse, rough and brutally egoistic men. Besides, by its own nature, an exquisite sensitiveness is always dissatisfied with itself even more than with others, and it is also exposed to suffering the usurpations and pretensions of others. A spirit with a tendency to rise, which seeks its nobleness, is profoundly sincere, that is, it recognises that it does not possess what it desires; and this afflicts it and gives it a "bad conscience" and a discontent with itself; it suffers from not receiving what it feels is owing to it, but which conditions of reality deny it, whether from a moral or a material point of view; hence, becoming ashamed of its own poverty and obscurity, it remains in its solitude and does not come out into life. If every new acquirement gives new strength and boldness, every new desire in a spirit which is always striving after a higher aim produces, in the mind of a dreamer, discontent and uncertainty. But is not the man who is always rising higher and higher he who has always some new desire, who is not content with his present status, and who forgets and despises that which yesterday seemed to him the very highest point of his desire?

These people, if they feel that they lack a single thing, forget all the wealth they possess, and believe themselves to be poor. But of such material are made those who advance and do not stand still. Who knows that the secret of properly attaining superiority may not lie in this double illusion: that is, believing one's self inferior and always trying to reach something higher, which is very much above common surrounding lowness? Who knows whether some people would have any incitement to work if they had not this wrong perception of reality? Might it not be that many celebrated men came to have a definite and just idea of themselves, not by their mere work itself, but by their success, the admiration of others, that is, by purely external and not internal means?

In certain cases, some great men were revealed to themselves only by the intervention of public opinion, and in this manner may be explained certain unexpected changes in personality after a first success.

We must, however, add to what we have said above that, if confidence and ease are elements of success in small contingencies of life, and for common men, they are for the most part, and especially in a youth, the indication of a certain coarseness and limitation of ideas, and especially the sign of a limited possibility of development, that is, of a certain want of plasticity.

Shyness is accompanied with an exaggerated criticism of ourselves, which makes us, as it were, confront ourselves with an ideal and almost unattainable model. This disposition, however, is in the main beneficial when it is not irremediably overwhelmed with the crushing superiority of the ideal itself; the shy man's want of confidence thus comes from the height of his desire rather than from his limited ardour.

Shyness is a psychological species more diffused in countries of average moral temperature. We may note its correspondence with the Catholic *"bad conscience"* and the state of *"sin"*: delicate blendings which are peculiar to the Latin countries. In the countries of the north—except England, which for very many reasons we cannot class among what are generally called the northern countries—we do not see a real and proper shyness, but a sort of coarse embarrassment: the fine emotion of the south is scarcely perceptible.

I have often, however, had occasion to make a strange observation: Germans, Danes, and Norwegians, who were perfectly at their ease in the company of their compatriots, were greatly embarrassed and shy when they happened to be in the company of southrons, becoming even all the more so the greater knowledge they had of the customs, habits, languages, and the spirit of the southern countries.

Richness of imagination, easy development of ideas, and prevalence of interior life, are conditions which produce an easy rising of this emotion when a man who has thought or meditated too much wishes to enter into life. The emotive tendency arises from the perception of the difference between the life of our imagination and real life, the difficulty of realising even a small part of what lives in our minds. Thus a shy man is the first victim of his imagination, which subsequently gives him a too high and ideal opinion of persons and things; and hence after his first experiences of life makes him see in the world difficulties and obstacles which in reality do not exist.

Against these difficulties—in a great measure illusory—the shy man directs all his energies, and this naturally increases the emotive disposition, which is still further augmented by the consequences of continued imaginative work and the tension which he puts forth to overcome his emotion. The shy man is therefore always straining his attention; thus, in his contacts with men he seems to be always on the watch to discern the physiognomy, the mind, of the speaker, behind his words. This condition has justly been thought favourable for psychological penetration; the two greatest psychologists perhaps who have ever existed—Stendhal and Nietzsche—owed their perspicacity to this characteristic of their minds; but the shy man often goes too far, and in his diffidence comes to see in others what is not in them.

He becomes, so to speak, physically and morally benumbed by reacting on this tendency, forgetting that the greater number of our actions are done unconsciously and do not require any mental tension; when anything distracts him and he ceases to *se creuser la cervelle*,[43] and acts instinctively, he does everything gracefully and successfully. His morbid disposition may be shown by saying that *it seems as if he were not persuaded* that the most interesting thing is not to have an exact opinion on any subject, to perform any just action, but to possess confidence of action. With this uncertainty—in fact, with this eternal doubtfulness—other people become suspicious that we do not know what we are doing, that we are not acquainted with our subject, whilst on the contrary it is the knowledge of too many points of view which perplexes the shy man, and it is the complication of his thought which squanders and dissipates it.

For an opportune action may be carried out by chance or instinct, or else it presupposes a wide knowledge multiplied by many different points of view, and by a choice of the most likely solutions. The first is a happy and even a divine gift, but one which is becoming more and more rare, not to say impossible, in modern life, with its infinite number of new and unexpected combinations. The second constitutes true greatness, but is realised with much difficulty, and, if perfect balance of knowing and doing be an ideal goal, all men are for the most part merely degrees, more or less realisations of it—attempts. The immense greatness of Napoleon, the factor that made him the most complete man of genius who ever lived, lay in this capacity and power of realisation of thought; that is, on the one hand, his fertile imagination which multiplied the aspects of an event or of a thing, and, on the other hand, the intuition with which he rapidly grasped what was most important and essential among these aspects. Rich, complicated, and profound thought draws one away from life because it tends to hegemony in the person who possesses it; when, however, we see it no longer an end in itself, but a means, an instrument of a destroying and creating force, of a

---

[43] to rack his brains

force which exercises its power on man, that plastic material *par excellence*—the most dangerous material however to manage —then we must see in the individual who is so divinely gifted the greatest and strongest extrinsication of the power of being which exists in man.

The passage from the state of knowledge that is many-sided but incapable of action to that of action itself—which presupposes a proper choice of the varied opportunities which present themselves to us—is characterised by want of confidence, and the expression of this latter is shyness. This, however, far from appearing to others as the indication of a broader comprehension and of a finer and more complex appreciation of things, conduces to a result contrary to the more evident and positive interests of the individual, of leading others to doubt his value and what his abilities are; and it must be remembered that such an action is not entirely involuntary.

Every imperfect, hybrid, unhealthy, or deviating form of knowledge has a power of seduction and corruption, whether upon its possessor or upon others with whom he comes in contact. Even though they may be healthy, this power of seduction influences them if they are in a period of plasticity. Thus the emotion under discussion, of which the sometimes morbid character cannot be disputed, comes by frequent repetition to have a corrupting action upon him who suffers from it; who comes in certain cases to the point of seeing the error of others originated by the consequence of his emotion as to their judgment in regard to himself; but, so to speak, he delights in this error, and sometimes even encourages it and increases it by his behaviour, as if he had the intention of deceiving others into the belief in his inferiority, which amounts to saying that he encourages them to profit by himself.

What a number of these subtle and almost incomprehensible aspects in their moral relations among men have yet to be explained! We have still another example of them in shyness, which, deviating still further from normal processes, may become the means of deceiving others in order to overcome them. In French literature we may remember as analogous to this the very fine type of Cherubim, in whom this deviation was shown by a man's using in seduction those arts which are peculiar to women.

The shy man, as we have seen, does not take an exact view of reality even with the overpowering work of his imagination. A cure for shyness, however, may begin (note that I say only *begin)* with the acquirement of the conviction of one's own illusions, and with an intellectual and impartial search for the errors of one's own judgment.

If the shy man, for example, can only convince himself that those who are around him are not intent, as he supposes, upon scrutinising and examining him, but that he is rather only a passing object for their attention, he would soon become cooler in his behaviour.

To have a confident manner we must act as if no one were taking any notice of us—which is really most often the case—although the shy man cannot easily be persuaded that it is so, because of the vivacity and ardour of his imagination, on account of which a voluntary forgetfulness, and a kind of distraction, *of mental abstention,* are the first steps towards the conquest of confidence in one's self. When he who suffers from the disease of hesitation has *persuaded* himself that all the working of his brain over little things is useless, since men do not reason much, for example, when they are going into a shop, or taking a seat in a dining-room, he will then instinctively assume an exterior aspect of coldness and composure, the impassibility of a facial mask, the *éloigné*[44] behaviour (is it not, by the way, just this fear of emotion which accounts for the extreme correctness of English people in their

---

[44] distant

habits and customs, and their standing on guard towards one another, which has given them their manner of contempt and haughtiness—a manner which is otherwise perfect?).

In this way he will conserve his energies, he will be like an engine at low pressure, whilst a shy man usually assumes a feeling of numbness or exaltation in endeavouring to overcome his emotion and to attain to some state of drunken enthusiasm which will sweep away his embarrassment. It is certainly true that much practice in the behaviour outlined above will pave the way for the possibility of a freer and more spontaneous attitude; but, I must add, this is not the way to real freedom. Shyness is not cured voluntarily, or by psychological reaction, it disappears when strength and vigour increase. It is therefore better to try to remove it by means of plain and nourishing food, by long and violent exercise, and by the use of strength, than by any purely and simple moral advice. As it has its origin in a diminution of vitality, it is cured as one's vitality increases.

Therefore Stendhal's famous *Consultation de Banti*[45] is of no use for the acquirement of confidence in one's self, and of amorous power—not nearly so much as a substantial supper, with a little champagne, and a well-heated room! and that is well known to certain ladies who are acquainted with the mechanism and the physics ... of love ... and despise its psychology: and I cannot contradict them, especially when I consider their wide experience of mankind!

Whilst we may speak of a true and real protective social function of modesty, we cannot say as much for shyness, although we cannot altogether exclude it. This particular emotive susceptibility is, in fact, so common *and especially so frequent in the very highest personalities* that the doubt arises whether

---

[45] A fragment described by Horace Samuel as "a piece of methodical deliberation on the pressing question. 'Should I or should I not have the duchess?' written with all the documentary coldness of a Government report."

it has not a real function, even if only in a small way, and limited by the imprescindible necessity of action for man.

It is more natural at a certain age, and indicates the transition from the youthful to the adult phase of human life: it is a form of transition, but, as we have seen, it may cover the whole course of one's personality. We cannot therefore say absolutely that it has no other value than that of a symptom, and that it represents purely a psychological *caput mortuum*, or is, speaking frankly, a vice—an imperfection. In a way it preserves the individual from physical and moral dissipation, isolating him, and making him *inaccessible*. At any rate, it is not *by itself and in itself* an obstacle, although it is the *sign* of an inner obstacle. Only when the emotion has acquired a certain amount of assurance, i.e. the consciousness of being timid, can it constitute a new barrier. With this reflection and complication the emotion passes into an anomaly. Only in extreme and morbid cases, which occur especially in certain speculative and meditative geniuses, in Newtons or Spinozas or in Kants, whose shyness in isolating the individual favoured the development of some of his qualities, and in certain sexual anomalies, in which the shyness that accompanies them necessarily impedes their propagation, can we speak in a certain sense of the beneficent and protective function of shyness.

Shyness is a state of mind highly interesting for the psychologist: because it is a sign of character, and because its function increases with sociality. Its study would seem even more important if this were a place to show its intimate relations with a form of mental decadence, paranoia; but this is not the best place to discuss the question. The depressive tendencies developed by and for sociality, of which we have examined two specimens, are the highest forms of inhibition, conscious inhibition. In the excess of its restraining action it is one of the causes of sexual anomalies. Platonic love, ideal love between persons of the same sex, onanism, Lesbian love,

incest, pederasty, bestiality, owe their existence to a great
extent to the social restriction of sexuality. These are always
the expression of an uncertain, weak, and immature instinct,
which, not knowing how to overcome the obstacles created by
custom, withdraws itself by divergent ways, the ways of least
resistance.

These two emotions, modesty and shyness, make
themselves felt respectively when a woman is in the presence
of a man, or a man in the presence of a woman. A very
modest woman and a very shy man are quite at their ease
when in the company of their friends, and here on the lines of
least resistance we see the great current of love flowing, a
current which, once drawn out of its bed, it would be difficult
to set once more in the proper channel.

Let it not be said that this is inevitable, and that the taking
of certain roads in preference to others is the indication of an
organic fatality. It is just the most intelligent youths and the
most sensitive women who are most inclined to take such
aberrant directions, and so to lose the advantages of the more
restorative and vivifying action which exists in normal love, an
action on which I think I have thrown some light. We need not
then make such light use of the words degeneration, perversity,
and so on; such phenomena are going in the very direction in
which progress in general is moving, so it is true that they are
more frequent where the bonds of sociality are drawn most
tightly, and where sensual love is least vigorous—in the
countries of the north.

Such conceptions of love are the most remarkable result
which has been generated by the contrast that I have several
times mentioned, a contrast which, as we see, has come to
produce forms of thought incompatible with the highest rights
of life ... and we must bear this well in mind if a social ideal
does not smile upon us, an ideal of which the dawn may
already be seen in certain nations, but which ... will *necessarily*

be the last twilight ... *not,* however, the golden twilight ... of humanity.

CHAPTER VI

STENDHAL

One more mask, another mask!

NIETZSCHE

Six years have now elapsed since the spirited and bellicose high priest of contemporary French criticism, René Doumic, surrounded with all the glory and dazzling splendours of his two-world review, hurled from the famous pulpit of *La Revue des deux Mondes* his bull of excommunication against the brilliant and smiling epicurean, Henri Beyle, and sought to bury the slowly rising fame of this writer under the weight of his inexorable accusations.

According to Doumic, Stendhal was vain, ambitious, sensual, and—what is even more terrible in France, that land of democracy, revolution, and *jacquerie*—he was *grossier* and plebeian.

Not long ago Jean Carrère in a great political Italian paper, paraphrasing and psalmodising some of his dog-Latin, already intoned in the choir of the *Revue hebdomadaire* in a series entitled *Mauvais Maîtres* (of modern French literature), accused Stendhal of vanity, impurity, egoism, and, worse than all, of instilling immorality and corruption into the minds of young men desirous of experiencing the emotions of modern literary sensitiveness.

The lively and witty Dauphinois, I imagine, would have smiled as a reply, and congratulated himself that posterity, this posterity of 1880 and of 1900, which he invoked in his lifetime, should still understand him so little: since, for him, the pleasure of being admired as an author would assuredly have given way to his satisfaction at seeing that men still believed of him those things which he when alive would have wished to make himself believe.

The fate of Stendhal has been indeed strange.

The accusations, the calumnies of his enemies, the snarling rancour, the petty spite, the puffed-up and badly dissimulated contempt of those mawkish people whose modesty he had offended, the cordial execration of those whom he stung and even wounded with his darts, the aversion sprung from the fear of those whom he had perturbed with his *choquant* spirit, the weak beatitude or the flaccid debility—in short, all the anger, the enmities which he had rekindled—must have appeared to him uncommonly gratifying, inasmuch as they constituted in his eyes a proof that he was very *différent* from an ordinary man, or that at all events his *mascarade* was a good one.

Where I have succeeded (I do not say with much assurance that I have) in bringing a gleam of light to bear upon his true and deep personality, do I not perform an unfortunate service for the Master, whose greatest pleasure was that of appearing different from what he really was?

But the Master, with his calm smile, cannot surely see any ill in this bad joke which his follower is playing on him—he loved too much to play such jokes on others! And would not this be a fresh disguise for him? Would not this be a new exterior which would hide his mysterious and indecipherable nature still more?

And, since I am sure of His pardon, there is nothing left for me but, as usual, to ask my friend the reader to give a cordial welcome to the Stendhal which I shall put before him.

Never, perhaps, did any other author meet with the fate of Ours. He who worked among his contemporaries unknown and almost unperceived, he who had only one moment of *infâme* fame at the time of the publication of his *Rouge et Noir,* for fifty years and more after his death has interested an international although somewhat restricted public in regard to his life, his works, and his enigmatic figure; and established for himself a group of elect students who love and revere his memory, among whom are counted the names of two great living novelists: a group which has no object of diffusion or of propaganda, but only of aesthetic pleasure and admiration of the Master.

Through the exertions of many Beylists, and especially of Casimir Stryienski,[46] a real Stendhalian literature is gradually being formed; and from his best-known works, and from those works of his which were published after his death, there is now sufficient material for an attempt to give a more certain interpretation of this fantastic personality.

Paul Bourget, in one of his essays, which, among the great number written about Beyle, comes nearer than any other in my opinion to giving an exact representation of this singular mind; an essay, however, which, like everything else by the author of *André Cornelis*, goes wrong here and there by giving us unexpected illuminations which, as it were, afterwards voluntarily bring back the darkness; Paul Bourget, I repeat, affirms in this essay how the sensualistic and ideological philosophy of Condillac and De Tracy, together with the poetry of Italy and the poetry of the war, gave the first form to and afterwards developed Beyle's mind.

Evidently a large number of his maxims and aphorisms on different characteristics and on love (for such they may certainly be called, since his chiselled but unpretentious phrases have often a neatness and elegance of Hippocratic maxims, or of those of the Salernian school), and certainly a great number of his brilliant *aperçus* on the causes of human passions and actions, show the influence of Cabanis.

But where did he obtain this happy penetration, this profundity of discernment, this intimate sense of truth, which we find gathered like an indefinable perfume in his short,

---

[46] A Franco-Polish professor and writer who is responsible for publishing many posthumous pieces by Stendhal.

concise phrases: these phrases as clear and as brilliant as precious stones?

This question puts us in the right direction, and shows us that we cannot find the true nature and sure origin of his mind either in formal intellectualism or in the severe and rigid lines of the ideological thinker.

The criticism which fastens on ideas as they have been left by their creators, the criticism which tries to combat them with opposite ones already established, and, so to speak, crystallised; intellectualistic criticism, in a word, is the useless inheritance of a superficial age, of a classicism which is dead, and rigid in its stereotyped forms.

The criticism of the present age, and still more of the future, the criticism of which the first promising signs were seen in Sainte-Beuve, fulfils, and will fulfil, a very different, truer, and higher mission—dare we say so?—in separating, in artistic works, and in systems of philosophy, those sentimental, affective, personal, and human elements which the author makes use of (often, certainly, without knowing it), those elements which, afterwards transformed and fused into a liquid metal of which the different components are no longer visible, come to form an artistic and philosophical work.

This criticism, it is well known, may be said to be a derivation from romantic criticism.

*   *   *   *   *

Imagine a nature inclined to melancholy, perhaps through having been kept down and unnaturalised in infancy, and perhaps also by reasons of temperament, a mind which a precocious experience (by the fact of its first sincere nature or other reasons) has been made to feel all the aesthetic lowness and brutalness of anguish, all its bitterness and baseness; the spirit of an ardour hidden like fire among cinders, which feels through an infallible intuition that grief is alien to feminine nature and that a woman withdraws it from herself and from man—of whom therefore she is called the comfort by reason of her inward inadaptability to grieve; imagine further a heart which was soon to know the illusory opinions of woman held by man, the errors of the eternal masculine idealism, which seems to be undeceived only to fall again into the opposite error of pessimism, a heart which contains all the sickness and misery of *goodness*, the imperfectness of the weapons of the good man in a fight against a bad man: and you will understand the juvenile phase of the mind of Stendhal.

This phase, among the natural oscillations and outside adventures of youth, was prolonged long after its proper time, even beyond the time of his amours with Mélanie Guilbert; but, I must add, it was more intuitive and immediate than reflective and profound.

His real nature appears, as we shall see later, to recover its rights little by little during all his life, and he, very much more intuitive and rapid than "his great neighbour" Nietzsche, and certainly more sure and instinctive, soon cast himself into the sea of action.

His life was decided at the time when he came to Paris to enter the Polytechnic School, where his brilliant studies of mathematics, begun in the academy at Grenoble, seemed to promise him an excellent success, which he renounced after many doubts.

This is, in my opinion, the nodal point of his existence, the keystone of his moral edifice, the moment in which the inversion of values, to use Nietzsche's phrase, took place.

Contrarily to what the courtesan Julie had said to Jean Jacques Rousseau in a delicate contingency: "Let women alone and devote yourself to mathematics!" he, as he often loved to repeat to his friends, said to himself, "Let mathematics alone and devote yourself to women!"

Thus all his activities, all his desires, all his habits, voluntarily found their own level from now onwards according to this latter directing formula, to which he remained true all his life: "Not to do anything which could seem low and brutal to a woman who is truly—i.e. dangerously—a woman."

From hence proceed all his tastes, all his love for art, for beautiful things, for a free and easy life, his disdain for the German heaviness, for the lymphatic and torpid sentimentalism, the inelegance and materialness of that race, and thus his admiration for the Italians.

But he knew himself only very imperfectly in the early stages of his life. When he travelled into Italy, and many times later, he thought only of living; of enjoying an existence like that of those youths who have not yet acquired a correct knowledge of their ideal energies or undergone their sentimental experiences. Perhaps he gave himself up to a kind of trifling dreaming, an imperfect knowledge of that wider and clearer future which awaited him, a vague premonition of what he was yet to be.

He began to be preoccupied with himself; he began to undergo his first experiences of grief, perhaps on the occasion of his amours with Adelaide Rebuffet, or Victorine Mounier, but certainly and above all with Mélanie Guilbert.

To his love for this corrupt and astute actress he owed the first *renseignements* of his mind, and to this also is due the beginning of his power of observation. May I recall that on the occasion of his love for Louason he even went so far as to act as a clerk for a druggist of Marseilles, where he had flown with this facile singer?

Love, I think, is generally the adventure through which a man comes to know himself, and it is, as I have said, the best reagent and the most delicate sign to assay the different characters of individuals. But must it be finally said that one woman more than another was the first origin of the magnificent development of that analysing capacity which Stendhal possessed in a remarkable degree? These are the foolish questions of a very learned man or a pedant. One particular woman, or this special woman, is only the pretext from which that magnificent bloom appears to the sun and is raised to the heavens. For the most part, great men in love do not love the women, but they live in and enjoy their own love. And what is woman often but the pretext for our capacities, our inclinations, and our needs to enter into a free life? As his introspective power gradually became amplified, and showed him all his deficiencies and wants, he endeavoured by action and life to bring himself nearer to that ideal of perfection and of integral personality which was gradually being formed in him.

In this way, and by this science, we must note particularly, he wished especially to re-create himself, that is, to make for himself a new mind, or rather to destroy that mind which he felt was cramped and falsified by his past education and moral super-stratifications; he wished above all to cure this illness, and he subjected himself to a violent regime, to the regime of amorous action, seduction.

In his mind, therefore, he appears to grasp contrarieties, and certainly his mind was the union of incompatible things, the dwelling-place of whatever things were most contradictory; has not the case of "Armance" been felt by him in his imagination as real? The doubt is verisimilar.

But the cold, lucid analyser who said: "Pour être un bon philosophe il faut être sec, clair, sans illusion. Un banquier qui a fait fortune a une partie du caractère requis pour faire des découvertes en philosophie, c'est-à-dire pour voir clair dans ce qui est,"[47] on another occasion, referring to love, said with an ineffable grace, with a sweetness of which we cannot speak without awakening the most secret and profound feelings: "Je fais tous les efforts possibles pour être sec. Je veux imposer silence à mon coeur, qui croit avoir beaucoup à dire. Je tremble

---

[47] "To be a good philosopher one must be dry, clear, without illusion. A banker who has made a fortune has part of the character required to make discoveries in philosophy, that is to say to see clearly in what is"

toujours de n'avoir écrit qu'un soupir, quand je crois avoir noté une verité."[48]

What is notable in the whole book *De l'Amour,* which he justly regarded as his masterpiece, is on the one hand the preoccupation of being *sec, clair,* and on the other the continued repetition of the words *tendre, tendresse,* by which he means an easy predisposition of the mind to pleasant and suave emotions.

When I speak of his attitudinising, his change of personality, and his mask, I do not mean to convey that Stendhal simply wished to pass from a state of sadness and depression to one of gaiety, or that he wished to dominate his melancholic character and impose upon it a state of joy. That would be a comparatively common fact, and one insufficient to give him any special aspect. What Stendhal endeavoured to attain was a complete and integral transformation of his person which he could present to his deeply psychological mind. Very little therefore is said when it is affirmed that he is the father of analysers; he is much more than a simple analyst.

Knowledge of ourselves, perhaps because it is sought after by a special class of men possessing certain particular inclinations and temperaments, is sterile, painful, and bitter; this must be admitted. But once our eyes have become accustomed to this underground light, once we have become habituated to the scent of mustiness and mouldiness in these grottos, in the awesome tenebrosities of our minds, we cannot in general by a mere act of conventional and artificial will resolutely abandon this exploration and make up our minds for the future to care only for that light which is enjoyed by all: we cannot resist the pleasure—which we yet feel to be of a low and morbid kind—of passing through our own caverns, and the wisest advice is to satisfy one's curiosity to the utmost, and

---

[48] "I make every effort to be dry. I want to silence my heart, which believes it has much to say. I always tremble at having written only a sigh, when I believe I have noted down a truth."

thus to exhaust that desire for what is horrid and brutal, which we all have in our minds, apart from what is beautiful and splendid in them. We cannot prevail upon ourselves once more to love the sun that appears in the heavens; it is necessary that this renewed love should arise from the necessities of a mind which has examined itself. In this knowledge of ourselves we must find some motives for turning our minds in an outward direction; to the study of all things; to interest ourselves in what lies on the surface. Like all other kinds of love, that of self-consciousness can end only by fatigue and exhaustion.

Now this period of observation and analysis—which constitutes a serious danger for many people because they remain in it for ever, as happened to Amiel and to Nietzsche— was not such for Stendhal, for whom analysis was only an extra instrument and weapon for action: it was only another power by which he increased his will.

Through the perennial aspiration of his mind to an ideal of freedom, ease, and grace, he wished to make, and did make, a unique joy of all his grief, of the gloomy castellated dwelling-place of the man who examines and knows himself, a dwelling-place of pleasure and gaiety, an open shelter for those who always keep smiling. And so well and so continually did he know how to will that his mask became a truly living one by the miracle of his magic power.

The bitterness of the man who hides his feelings and endeavours to seem different, as did Nietzsche, never appeared in Stendhal at all; but there did appear in him the joy of a man who has found something which he thought he had lost for ever; there no longer resounded through his clear sky an echo of the thunder of some far-off tempest: but a luminous and profound azure extended itself everywhere, and a heat breathing with life pervaded the entire space.

His smile has something Dionysiac about it, something of the fascination of the smile of the Bacco Giovine, of the Gioconda, or of the other gay and impenetrable heroes of

Leonardo da Vinci.[49] If in his irony there sometimes appears an aggressiveness and a bitter taste which make one suspect that he wished to avenge some of his own inner defects on others, it must be recognised that this is not his habitual manner. From the words of his contemporaries we see their admiration for the treasures of his fine, subtle, intoxicating mind which he poured out in his conversation, and it must be agreed that, if he wished to appear superficial, he had at least an attractive and adorable superficiality.

Thus we see him pass through life like Fabrizio Del Dongo, his favourite hero, going from one love to another, a fascinating conqueror of women; but, how differently from his hero, how well he accepts defeat!

Only too often did his heart—that heart which he wished to keep quiet—make him the victim of its meshes; and how often, to cure himself of a love which he thought was getting dangerous for him, did he fall into another even more dangerous?

"Je ne l'ai jamais su," said Mérimée, "qu'amoureux ou croyant l'être."[50] And, apropos of amorous conquests, he himself said: "La chose réussit une fois sur dix, et elle vaut bien la peine de subir neuf rebuffades."[51] And yet this man, who made love "l'affaire principale de la vie," confessed that from 1821, the year in which he returned from Milan to Paris with his heart full of love for Matilde Dembowski, until 1824, not one single woman could draw him from this passion:—

"Je n'ai eu une maîtraisse que par hasard en 1824, trois ans après; alors seulement le souvenir de Matilde ne fut plus déchirant. Elle devint pour moi comme un fantôme tendre,

---

[49] The Bacco Giovine is a painting of Bacchus which had originally been of John the Baptist. Gioconda is more commonly known as the Mona Lisa.

[50] "I never knew him except when he was in love or thought he was."

[51] "The thing succeeds once in ten times, and is well worth enduring nine rebuffs."

profondement triste, et qui, par son apparition, me disposait souverainement aux idées tendres, bonnes, justes, indulgentes."[52]

* * * * *

There exists in all higher men, apart from a more or less notable intelligence, an excess of sensitiveness, or rather of emotiveness.

All the different blendings of character which appear in them—so often curious, anomalous, and original—depend upon a variable adjustment which our intelligence devises, so as in some way to remedy the deep perturbations caused to a thinking being by the least little shock to this excess of sensitiveness. This suffering sensitiveness, which is perhaps the secret fount of all moral greatness, is the gift which human misery and unhappiness bestow upon the genius. When his sensitiveness is spent and worn out through contact with the world and with fortune, the genius has fulfilled his mission, and has evaporated the energy which thrust him upwards to a high intellectual position.

The greater number of artistic works, and very many superb and formidable philosophical constructions, in their logical aspects, appear to the careful examiner as simply means by which the so-called higher man endeavours to calm the torment within him, the anguish which his Protean emotiveness causes him under a thousand aspects and in a thousand contingencies.

This painful, ever-present, and powerful sensitiveness was also the continual state of Stendhal, and the contrast between it and his intelligence settled down from time to time, as I shall show, into special forms—a kind of compromise, a *modus*

---

[52] "I only had a mistress by chance in 1824, three years later; only then was the memory of Matilde no longer heartbreaking. She became for me like a tender ghost, deeply sad, and who, by her appearance, sovereignly disposed me to tender, good, just, indulgent ideas."

vivendi. These truces between the two powers of his mind were in him irony, wit, the cult of energy, and finally the apotheosis of the desire for what is bad. In another man this antagonism would find its conciliation, apparently at least, in pride; in a third in ascetic resignation and renunciation; in a fourth in a withdrawal from the world and in solitude.

So, again, every thinking man must in his youth overcome a Promethean period, a period of tension, and of effort to free himself from something which oppresses him; a period of oscillation and anxiety, of want of energy and of reckless daring at the same time, of pauses and advances; something which resembles the myth of Prometheus chained to the rock, the period of melancholy and exaltation, the romantic period of "Sturm und Drang."

Everyone, after having become a mature man, comes out of this battle more or less complete; that is to say, according to the different potentialities which were in him, he becomes a being complete in every respect, an individual perfectly sufficient unto himself and to the circumstances in which he is placed, or else an individual with some defect which may or may not be compensated for by other advantages.

What man more than the divine Goethe was the incarnation of the first species? He came out of the romantic period with the most complete, harmonious, and eurhythmically beautiful personality that has ever been seen. It seems almost impossible that there should ever have come on this earth such a perfect genius, such a *man* in the widest and most magnificent sense of the word; and above all, it seems incredible that he should have been a German. If the argument of the descendants of the kind-hearted and perfidious Arminius deceives us, if the specious syllogism of those who claim for Dante and Garibaldi a Lombard (and hence Teutonic) origin, on account of their names, appeals to us, I shall feel myself just a little inclined to find in the name of Goethe some subtle and ingenious Italian derivation.

But, coming back to our Author, it seems to me that Stendhal was an incomplete though a great personality; and besides, if he showed certain defects he knew how to remedy them with something great and noble, something worthy of himself. This something is his grief, which he turned into laughter by an effort of his will, his grief which he transformed to the divine flame of art and action in a serene, free, and victorious conception of life.

Whatever was in the moralistic experience of France for fully two centuries: the noble moral scepticism of La Rochefoucauld, the force of mind which concealed the sorrowing sadness of Vauvenargues, the devouring passion of La Bruyère, the smiling and veiled cynicism of Chamfort, were finally changed in him into a new power which overcame all evasions, doubts, and painful moral oscillation.

Thus he, if he did not absolutely desire what was bad, wished at least to have the appearance of it, and he armed himself with that quality which in our gentle modern society continues to a certain extent the tradition of ancient cruelty: irony.

Irony and its younger brother, wit, were to several great minds the only consoling company of their inner solitude. "Irony is the last libation which great geniuses make to the infernal gods," wrote Carducci.[53]

Wit served many people as a hiding-place, a disguise; for example, that wit which is bitter and turned against itself, like a new strength endeavouring to test its power, like a baby which takes its first steps; that sweet and smiling wit of Sterne which is like an ostentatious juvenile haughtiness that conceals the modesty of a fine sentimentalism, that sour and bitter wit which is Heine's revenge on the weakness of the human heart.

Stendhal's wit was often aggressive and violent, it served him as an arm of offence more often than of defence, at least

---

[53] Giosuè Carducci (1835-1907) was an Italian poet and literary critic.

in those years of his life spent in the *salon* and in diplomacy. But this new acquisition by which his figure assumes a special aspect has a profoundly psychological cause which could not escape from Stendhal.

The admiration which all feel for wit, and the pleasure which a person really gifted with wit gives in a conversation, certainly come from the fact that it is the equivalent, so to speak, of man's first character; it is a kind of ancient pride and cruelty, restored and adapted to social use. That it is so is shown by the fact that it is only possible in those in whom work —the heavy burden imposed by society—has not oppressed the best and most primitive energies of the race, since it is a luxury, a voluptuary expenditure of our intelligence. "Ma foi," said Stendhal in fact, "l'esprit manque, chacun reserve toutes ses forces pour un métier qui lui donne un rang dans le monde."[54]

But let us hear what he himself says in his *Souvenirs d'Egotisme*, in speaking of the time when he returned to Paris from Milan, where he had left her who was the object of his greatest love, Matilde:—

"Le pire des malheurs, m'écriai-je, serait que ces hommes si secs, mes amis, au milieu desquels je vais vivre, devinassent ma passion et pour une femme que je n'ai pas eu !! je me dis cela en juin 1821, et je vois en juin 1832, pour la première fois en écrivant ceci, que cette peur, mille fois répétée, a été dans le fait, le principe dirigeant de ma vie pendant dix ans." "C'est par là que je suis venu à avoir de l'esprit, chose qui était le

---

[54] "My faith, the spirit is lacking, everyone reserves all his strength for a job which gives him a rank in the world."

bloc, la butte de mes mépris à Milan en 1818, quand j'aimais Métilde."[55]

"J'entrai dans Paris, que je trouvai pire que laid, insultant pour ma douleur, avec une seule idée, n'être pas deviné."[56]

And still better in a letter which he wrote to a friend two years before:—

"Ma sensibilité est devenue trop vive. Ce qui ne fait qu'effleurer les autres me blesse jusq'au sang. Tel j'étais en 1789, tel je suis encore en 1840. Mais j'ai appris à cacher tout cela sous de l'ironie imperceptible au vulgaire."[57]

And again by reason of this suffering sensitiveness he had, as he loved to repeat, "le goût de la mascarade."[58]

His mask is very agreeable, roguish: it is a weapon of seduction, and at the same time a noble modesty of mind which will not give way to the first comer; it is a desire not to be a *dupe* of one's self or of others; it is a stratagem which must serve to satisfy a certain strange and impertinent curiosity of hearts which delights in seeing unseen the mechanism of the sentiments of others; it is the hiding-place of him who can observe, without awakening suspicions, the ingenuous trust which men repose in the sincerity of that purely superficial mechanism which we know as physiognomy, which surveys

---

[55] "The worst misfortune, I cried, would be that these dry men, my friends, among whom I am going to live, should guess my passion and for a woman I have not had!! I said this to myself in June 1821, and I see in June 1832, for the first time in writing this, that this fear, repeated a thousand times, has been in fact the guiding principle of my life for ten years." "It is through this that I came to have spirit, something which was the block, the mound of my contempt in Milan in 1818, when I loved Métilde."

[56] "I entered Paris, which I found worse than ugly, insulting to my pain, with only one idea, not to be guessed."

[57] "My sensitivity has become too keen. What only touches others wounds me until I bleed. As I was in 1789, so I am still in 1840. But I have learned to hide all this under an irony imperceptible to the vulgar."

[58] "the taste of masquerade"

their trouble and emotion by reason of this foolish and fallacious exterior, and which permits the observer to smile at it moderately. It is, in short, a defence against the low and contemptible vulgarity and maliciousness of mankind.

This uncertainty, this moral oscillation between the two opposite principles of good and evil, which is the common and secret charm of that wonderful series of French moralists of the seventeenth and eighteenth centuries, is felt very much more in these modern times, and, since life and action are becoming more and more intensified, it is but natural that some great mind of our present age would have wished, with an act of energy, to cut the Gordian knot.

Friedrich Nietzsche was another who, in *Beyond Good and Evil*, frankly took the side of evil.

For the rest, egotism, egoarchy, superhumanism, imperialism, are really rebellions, reactions, liberations; they are often perhaps also the bright guiding stars by which we navigate our ship; the clothes which we put on, the companions of that startling and poetic fantasy by means of which we flee to our desolate solitude; we deceive the bitterness of our thoughts; we get away from that hateful self-consciousness; we delude our sight, occupied with the continual and painful spectacle of ourselves.

Is it possible that the ancients were acquainted with such complications and antitheses of the mind?

In my opinion they were not: they had often a violent and even a raging passion, the battle of man against fate, which is the principal character of the highest forms of Greek tragedy. They knew strength, vehemence, sincerity, and they showed it in a gesture, in an attitude; but they did not know the fierce inner battles, the battles of opposite principles, of the spirit of sacrifice and mastery, of lamentation and contempt, of commiseration and laughter, of good and evil.

It is a boast, but a sad boast, of modern minds, this moral problem, with the presence of the opposition in it of two irreducible terms. The ancients had not such doubts, such anguish, such anxious and tormenting questions; and, firm and whole in themselves, so to speak, either they knew one only of the two principles, or they took up an intermediate position, without oscillation and without propounding themselves questions.

Carducci in this regard says: "Antithesis, this rhetorical figure which is so prominent in contemporary literature, and which is wanting in Greek literature, or in the literature of the best age of Rome, or of Dante, is the proper and true manifestation of the discord of our present age, of the age which began in 1789. On the one hand, Maximilian Robespierre likes flowers, birds, and society verses, and Saint-Just writes voluptuous poems; on the other hand, Byron passes from *Childe Harold* to *Don Juan*, Leopardi from the *Songs of Italy* and *Dante's Monument* to the *Continuation of the Battle of the Frogs and Mice*."

It will be permitted to me to observe that this word "antithesis" is too vague and formal, and does not go far enough into the root of the matter. No! great poets do not give us this antithesis merely from a certain spirit of individuality, or a modern invention, or literary device, as Carducci appears to believe; or, still worse, as others hold, from an attitudinising or an affectation; but this painful antithesis is felt in the main by all modern minds, still more by the highest minds: hence the greatest poets and geniuses feel it and show it in their works.

Thus it is, I think, that Heine well represents another example of the psychological contrast of which I am going to speak. But he is not so demonstrative as the personality of Stendhal, and, even more and better, that of Nietzsche. The sentimental type of the mechanism of action and reaction is clearer and more evident in them, and is almost shown in their style, since their intention is more openly a moral documentation, and the substance of their works is, to a great extent, introspective and psychological. In Heine, however, the artistic object still remains, and the abundance of *motifs* and rhythms, the richness and charm of images, and the dazzling, laughing, many-shaded, and transitory succession of impressions lessen the value of moral opposition, using it only as an artistic means. Nevertheless it exists, and it is not difficult to discover.

In Stendhal, however, at least in the Stendhal shown by his last works, this contrast is mastered and overcome, and those few traces of the battle which was waged in the silence of his heart would be observed in these works (in the *Rouge et Noir* for example) only by readers already advised of and alive to the fact.

I may, however, add that if some of these traces survive in the *Rouge et Noir* nothing whatever of so much stormy agitation is observable in the *Chartreuse*, where a victorious and equal serenity, the serenity of an Attic sky, is found in all the characters: they seem to be children of spontaneity and grace; Fabricious, Mosca, Sanseverina, are nimble, quick, and ideally beautiful wild animals in their natural freedom and in the simple and instinctive elegance of their movements. The creature man reappears to us in all his terrible and beautiful naturalness.

Arthur Chuquet, to whom we must be grateful for his admirable and patient work on Beyle, but who in several parts of his book appears to have badly or not at all understood the fine and precursive spirit of Beyle (at which, indeed, we must not be surprised, for it is something that often happens to learned men of the most praiseworthy group to which he belongs), speaks of "quelques ressemblances" of Stendhal to Rossini.

The comparison would perhaps have pleased Stendhal greatly, for he loved to be misunderstood; but the apparent resemblance is only very superficial.

The far more simple spirit of the gastronomer-musician; his cunning, kind-hearted smile; his character, transparent in his unclouded and thoughtless youth, his joviality of an emeritus glutton and an amiable table companion, cannot be compared with Stendhal's complicated mind, bristling with points and crowned with roses of the Dauphinois, a man of passion and of war, a psychologist and a diplomatist, a man of letters and a *causeur*.

To my mind he has much more in common with his predecessor, the ineffable abbé Galiani, and with his successor, Friedrich Nietzsche.

*   *   *   *   *

My admiration for the genius of Beyle does not prevent me from seeing that the character of Julien Sorel in *Rouge et Noir* is defective in composition.

Owing to this defect, I believe, he has in general been somewhat misunderstood, especially by those who do not like to think, who do not like to look beyond the common horizon, who from some indolence or other cannot read the deep thoughts between the lines, and who do not feel a shudder of sorrow and voluptuousness when they glance into the depths of an abyss.

Julien's perversity, it seems to me, is only reconcilable with his sensitiveness by a chain of successive experiences of life which have led him as a necessary consequence, and as the only way to salvation, to the doctrine of the practice of evil for itself. In other words, Stendhal imbues the mind of Julien Sorel with what was in his own mind in infancy, and also with thoughts that he had matured afterwards in his vigorous manhood.

It may be remembered that he wrote his novel in the year 1830, after many other books which were a sharpening of weapons, as it were, and therefore when his mind must have been more complicated than it was in his youth.

He brought this taste for *mephistophelising* on himself, and shows it to us even in his *Vie de Henri Brulard*, in which he takes an extraordinary pleasure in making us believe atrocious things of himself when a boy, which, for the rest, are belied by many other particulars. It is but natural that the unknowing and ingenuous reader should be somewhat disconcerted, and see in Julien Sorel nothing but an abominable and infamous monster.

We may, however, recall that Taine, the orthodox, illustrious Taine, the great official critic of the France of the latter half of the nineteenth century, admitted having read this Stendhalian masterpiece no less than eighty-two times; and we may also recall that all the works of Stendhal exercised an extraordinary influence on him!

In this regard it would be curious to find out the real reason why his celebrated essay on the *Rouge et Noir* was omitted from the second and succeeding editions of his works, and has reappeared only recently in the posthumous and definitive edition of the *Nouveaux Essais*.

It must be remembered that Sainte-Beuve said of Duvergier de Hauranne, and of Victor Jacquemont: "Ils avaient été mordus par Beyle, et ceux que Beyle mordait sont restés mordus."[59] Is it possible that Taine wished to hide the traces of the "bite" which he carried? That would be as much as to say that the "bite" was a deep one!

Bourget affirmed that the special merit of the *Rouge et Noir* is that it contains some sound truths on the France of the nineteenth century. He also tries to show that the social conditions of France at the beginning of the century were the general and indirect causes of the manner in which Julien Sorel's mind and conduct were developed.

It seems to me that those causes mentioned by Bourget are the most visible and apparent causes; but that beyond these

---

[59] "They had been bitten by Beyle, and those whom Beyle bit remained bitten."

contingent and transitory motives—which nevertheless give his character a special colouring of time and place—there is something more efficaciously determinative.

Let me try to make myself clearer.

There are certainly very great differences between Chateaubriand, Constant, Beyle, Bourget, and Barrès, whether by their special characteristics or the degrees of their talents; but it seems to me that among their masterpieces—the *René*, the *Adolphe*, the *Rouge et Noir*, the *Disciple*, and the ideological trilogy of Barrès—there is a family resemblance, and that one can follow the development of a like spirit, of a similar primitive nucleus, of modes of feeling and desiring.

But it seems superfluous to say that if two successive terms of this ideal series show conspicuous and undeniable resemblances, the extremes show very great differences.

The imaginary or real incapacity for life and action, the irreducible incommunicability, and the sense of ineffable inner torment which accompanies it, the passion for solitude and for self-observation, and the desire, together with the ineptitude to enjoy love as all others enjoy it, the deep and sincere goodness, and the sad temperament which are all peculiar to the mind of René, are likewise the remote depth of mind of the other characters: they have suffered in infancy from the same illness as René, and if they go forward to other states of mind and diverse psychological complications, it is because their blood has been enriched with new energies; but René nevertheless remains the ancestor from whom they received such a great part of their mind.

René suffers from his disposition; but only approximately takes into account the reasons for his sufferings, he even finds a morbid pleasure in them; and, in exaggerating their entity, and in contemplating their singularity, he finds cause for satisfaction and pride: on this account he never reacts upon them.

In Adolphe the knowledge of the causes of his grief is more advanced; but he draws no profit from his knowledge, which is even turned to his disadvantage; his will has not yet armed itself against the insufficiencies in and the defects of his character, and from this his behaviour suffers greatly; he goes forward by leaps, or jumps, according to whether the momentary impulse of his clairvoyance or the reasoning of his heart prevails; from which there results an incoherent movement, an inconsistency in his behaviour, with a most painful vacillation in his feelings, a perpetual doing and undoing, an eternal uncertainty which, in the end, only serves to make him lose the good and angelic Ellénore, and finally results in her death.

Julien Sorel, on the other hand, whilst continuing to possess an extraordinary sensitiveness, a sensitiveness which often, against his wish, and in spite of himself, betrays him, has armed his heart with hardness and malignity before entering into life.

Here, I must say, begins the falsifying of personality and the deviation of the moral individual; but who would maintain that this is not closely, unavoidably natural, considering the fact that it is necessary to overcome an excessive and exuberant emotiveness, or at least to hide and to neutralise its effects? Considering this sensitiveness, and given also a will to live, which crosses the thousand uncertainties and clouds of manhood, breaking the involucre which it offers to a virile mind that is just finding itself, is it not only too natural that it should incline towards the opposite extreme?

This want of equilibrium did not escape Stendhal, who, not finding this too artificial and violently malignant power human and capable of living, ended his hero's existence on the gallows.

But how much piety, grandeur, and poetry do we find in this extreme fate!

In Robert Greslou the quest of the bad for itself, the dissimulation and transformation of his own character, the reaction and voluntary change of his own tendencies, is most complete, and he succeeds better in evil; his end even comes unexpectedly: perhaps the author had other designs in view in giving him such an end, rather than allowing him to reach the necessary and fatal consequences of the acts of the protagonist.

Finally, in the Barresian trilogy the victory over one's own temperament is clearer and more certain, but there is also in it a less conspicuous anti-social tendency, one might even say that the egotism of his hero is very little removed from common egoism. In the work of Barrès this deviation from normal personality, begun with René, returns as it were to the ordinary course, at least in its results, although perhaps the means by which such results are attained—the so-called *culture of the ego*—may be somewhat irregular.

*   *   *   *   *

There is an evident affinity between the formulas which Stendhal proposed and gave to himself and to his friends for practical use, and the entire Nietzschean moral system. This latter is only a system for imposing action, and, in a particular degree, the greatest and most brilliant kind of action: dominion.

Both, however, deceive themselves in believing that men can come out of themselves solely by means of intellectualism and logic, or rather the formulas of Stendhal, even more than the systems of Nietzsche, showed the first traces of the rise of something more sure and irresistible because more profound and organic.

It often happens to us in various circumstances to have the feeling that we are separated from some things towards which we feel ourselves attracted, by a supposition and objection of our own, that is, by a creation of our morbidly magnifying and deforming imagination, and then in a trice we recognise that the supposed difficulty was only an illusion, or a thin and transparent veil spread between our tendencies and the things themselves.

And then we seek to overcome this obstacle by pure reason, but in vain, for it is of the same nature as, and is even a part of, such reason.

How and why should this be so?

It is often because our intellect, in its ignorance, is called upon to give our defects a different appearance, and to offer ourselves a justification which does not wound our self-love so much, and to create an exterior and objective difficulty, where, on the contrary, there may be only a deficiency of our desires, which are not sufficiently strong, vital, or entire.

But stranger still is the fact that we use up our energies in what is, generally speaking, a useless battle, and we look for the satisfaction of our tendencies only in an entirely rational victory over those difficulties, in formulating which we have made idols of them in the Baconian sense of the word.

Sooner or later we perceive by chance that the growing impetus of our appetites crushes and overcomes all the barriers of the theorising *ego*, neglecting all formulae and systems, and passing naturally and spontaneously to the possession of the things.

This force comes from the depths of our sentiment; in other words, it is not an intelligent, discriminating and rational activity; but a more animal-like and primitive force: it is our nature itself in its most instinctive and profound shape.

Notwithstanding that, these formulae and systems which have, so to speak, an exhortative function, are highly significant for the psychologist.

What Stendhal fulfilled in himself was a work of disintegration, even of disorganisation, because he sought to withdraw himself from the ideal and real bonds and chains which society has imposed on man by a moral and positive law: and he sought to destroy all that mechanism of the inhibition of action, whether sexual, destructive, or dominating, which, by means of its prolonged action in the course of centuries, has made the animal man a social being, and one adapted to work, i.e. often only a domestic animal, and hence a brutal, miserable, and vile being.

He sought to break, and he effectively broke, those chains which had weighed down man for centuries and made him almost everywhere, to use Nietzsche's expression, "a herded animal."

But what does all this signify? What we have said is perhaps only superficial proof, and we must inquire into the matter more closely.

An idea, an aspiration, a desire for freedom, systems of exhortation, are all signs of an important transformation, because it is organic and connected with temperament; they are the first signs of a future complete victory.

Would the idea in this precede the fact, would the mind transcend the body, according to the Platonic hypothesis; or would they be the conscious equivalent of an organic transformation already begun?

I think that the second supposition is the true one.

The certain fact is, however, that when we have become ready for and adapted to action, these formulae and systems, by which we sought to galvanise our will, disappear and are forgotten.

But our mind goes beyond all this. What is still further proved by those other observations which we have made?

They only show that something primitive, originary, strong, grand, daring, and virile, has been long compressed and held a prisoner in man by a blind and obscure necessity, which, in his view, has sought to kill whatever good was in human nature.

Thus the Stendhalian intuition of the impoverishment and brutalising of the primitive nature of man through society becomes one of Nietzsche's theories, based upon introspective analysis, of whom, indeed, it constitutes the principal discovery.

My conclusion, the consequence of what has been said, can be expounded on two different planes of truth.

For those who like depth, the dissection of the muscles, nerves, and bones of corporeal unity, Stendhal shows us the magnificent case of a progressive change of personality, of a slow recovery of the true and originary *ego*.

In the book he has left us that is most suggestive and fecund in ideas, he says: "Comme on ne choisit pas un tempérament, c'est-à-dire une âme, l'on ne se donne pas un rôle supérieur. J. J. Rousseau et le duc de Richelieu auraient eu beau faire; malgré tout leur esprit, ils n'auraient pu changer de carrière auprès des femmes."[60]

If, therefore, with the example of his own life Stendhal *appears* to show that such a thing is possible, we must suppose, in order to explain the fact, a change of temperament.

But, remaining in the clear domain of psychology, and without advancing physiological hypotheses, Stendhal's person is most interesting, for he offers us—analysed and examined by himself with the minuteness and precision of a mathematical demonstration—a splendid example of one of those transformations of personality, and the chronicle, perhaps, of the process by which a grand, genial artist—a Goethe, a Shakespeare, or a Balzac—may embrace the entire wide circle of the human mind.

For those amiable minds who seek the "surface of things," for the "light and ignorant minds," for those who sweetly "live and let live," Stendhal was the man who united many destinies in himself, who knew the pure and sublime ecstasies of the

---

[60] "As one does not choose a temperament, that is to say a soul, one does not give oneself a superior role. J. J. Rousseau and the Duke of Richelieu could have done whatever they wanted; despite all their spirit, they could not have changed their career with women." — *On Love*, chapter 59

thinker and the contemplator, and the easy and joyous intoxication of the seducer; who realised the Leonardine aspiration for universal and integral life, who incarnated the wondering and curious mind of Faust.

He enlarged the limits of the human mind, and felt living and moving within himself in all his vastness, entirety and beauty, a true *man*.

CHAPTER VII

NIETZSCHE

From what we know of the private life of Nietzsche, we may certainly affirm that there must have been a strong and profound contrast between his real mind, his most intimate ways of thinking and feeling—those ways that shape the practical action of every individual and determine the acts of his daily life—and the substance of his theories, of what he wrote and published.

He has, in all his works, exalted a type of activity and being, which, while not perhaps quite the contrary of what he felt in his mind, is certainly very far removed from it, and is a form of existence and sentimentality very different from his own.

In affirming this, I do not wish my words to be taken in a depreciatory or condemnatory sense, for I think we cannot find the beginning of any error in all this, nor can we say that it is the vulnerable point where criticism can show Nietzsche's doctrines to be in the wrong.

An acute perception of one's own weak points, a sincere drawing up of one's defects in a particular regard, is already a step forward, even considerable progress, in the direction of freedom and amelioration, if, indeed, such have not thereby been attained. To hold up an ideal contrary to what we feel to be our present reality as a means of recovery, as an expedient to arrive at strength and superiority, is a characteristic only of strong and great men. Such a manner of acting represents a case of pragmatism in vast proportions, an experiment to transform our entire character, for the modification of conscious conditions would precede the transformation of our sentimental and affective nature, so intimately connected as it is with our physical nature. And, further, is it not possible that this is a rudimentary example, an initial attempt to cultivate those unknown psychical forces which we are now but beginning to catch a glimpse of, and which were so largely employed by the Indians, our forerunners in the matter of psychological experience, whose level we have not yet been able to reach?

For the rest, I have in the preceding essay laid stress upon the different suppositions which we can make in this regard, and I need not further insist on them here.

All Nietzsche's work is penetrated through and through by self-observation. His originality lies entirely in his feeling, in the richness of his inner life, which he developed to a great extent. When, for example, he speaks of circumstances favourable or otherwise to the rise and growth of the higher man, he goes out from his inward experience, from the consideration of his own case; throws himself out of himself, so to speak. So, again, the battle against morals, which forms so large a part of his works, is a battle in which he himself lived, and, in this direction above all, he felt everything he wrote. This is why his writings are lacking in facts, in visions, in what we call outward and plastic imagination.

Urged on in this way by his passion for analysing, for finding out the true causes of human action, for scrutinising the inmost recesses of his mind, he lost sight of concrete facts, particulars, events; he pulverised his experience, so to speak, and reduced all his impressions to pure logical mechanism, to their demonstrative and rational value.

This tendency is dangerous for a writer, as it may result in the death of every kind of beauty and variety, as happened to that unfeeling analyst, Amiel. Nietzsche, indeed, has much in common with him; but, whilst in Amiel the will was condemned, by the powerfulness of his analysing instinct, to consume itself, it succeeded, in Nietzsche, in rising up, and finally made that inner world, in which it was at first a prisoner, the object of its action. In other words, Nietzsche came to *avail himself* of this *mental world* to make of it a system of psychological suggestion and transformation.

The power of his analysis, and the excess of his critical faculty, together with his impatience to achieve results, and his enormous, boundless ambition for success, induced him to give up his philological studies, with which he had begun his career, and which always were for him an objective reality: thus he left the world of exterior for that of inner reality.

For the rest, those who are possessed with such destructive power, together with such a desire for renown, cannot take pleasure in minute details, in the little world of the savant or the specialist. Their desire for intellectual mastery, being unable to obtain results with sufficient rapidity in the scientific field, is turned to their own moral life (if they have not a decided leaning towards poetical creation), and in this way arose the moralists: those who devise the human mind.

We have already observed how we may note in Nietzsche a great difference between his manner of feeling and his demeanour in private life and in society. This latter aspect of a person is always the expression of how far he is firm, traditional, and profound; and it is thus very difficult, as regards the greater number of men, to change the habits of life of the classes among whom they were born, of their birthplaces, and their epoch.

Nietzsche's mind, entirely absorbed in the production of ideas, was not incited to action in an equal degree, which, in fact, remained in a fragmentary state for him, if it were not altogether alien to his being; so that, whilst his thought was a reaction on his sentimental life, as we shall see, it nevertheless remained in a purely theoretical region, and had no influence whatsoever on his practical life.

Thus, what has already been said about the great theoretical daring and the insufficient practice of the German mind is confirmed once more in him.

But to stop at this conclusion would be unjust, since we must always bear in mind that his thought broke barriers in pieces and cast down idols, which, previously to him, no one had been able even to shake; and moreover his formidable criticism is, and will be even more in the future, the incitement for others who are better trained for war to a wider, greater, and more real activity.

In every page, in every line of his writings, we may remark his passionate longing after a beautiful past, which he cherishes the hope of renewing, and of thus being able to restore man to his ancient vigour; there arises a hymn of glory for all things beautiful, free, and unrestrained, which made of life an apotheosis and a funeral pyre for the rekindled lust and ardent cupidities of men. Yet he showed by his goodness, his generosity, his affection for his sister, and his deep sincere devotion to his friends, that he was very different from this; but above all he showed his profound morality by sexual coldness.

From this contrast between thought and action, theory and practice, which was shown by both Stendhal and Nietzsche—but which, let us hasten to add, was exhibited by the latter in a much greater degree by reason of his race, his native land, and his studies—sprang another aspect which was common to both.

Both Stendhal and Nietzsche spoke of a certain intimate secret of theirs; they affected to be the bearers of a hidden treasure, both visibly pleased themselves by putting a mask on their faces, and both did their best not to be *discovered;* with this object they put forth all their strength; and if, in spite of Stendhal's intention, some of his autobiographical notes and diaries had not come to light, and if certain preferences and tastes which reveal Nietzsche's character had not been observed, criticism would certainly not have been able to investigate what human material was contained in their works.

Those critics who would sincerely pause, and accept in good faith the exaltation which Stendhal and Nietzsche made of their heroes, of the preferable type of man which they fashioned *out of their dissimilitude*, according to the ideal form which they eagerly sought to attain, would be discreetly superficial and far from perspicacious.

Hence, then, a factor that may be called new, at least in appearance, is clearly visible in contemporary literary and philosophical knowledge: the preoccupation of action. Intellectualism has reached, in its development, the point of denying itself in the magnifying of action. The most modern criticism considers philosophy, which was once held to be an almost divine art, as the most anti-vital form of human activity, and its followers as the most absurd specimens, and the least animated, of the human race. Our knowledge of the antinomy between the two activities, more or less confused in the past, has now been securely established, and testifies in many ways to the excellence of action.

Now, Stendhal and Nietzsche, especially the latter, are two thinking men who renounce their past, and who proclaim and magnify action: they are two apostates of intellectualism.

A recent critic, Papini,[61] in a collection of essays on different philosophers, which has at least the merit of being impartial in their universal extermination, holds that the origin of Nietzsche's *philosophy* is weakness. Plausible arguments and a certain appearance of truth are not wanting for such a statement, which however, to the dispassionate inquirer, appears to be merely the confusion and obscurity of a truth.

I maintain, indeed, that Papini himself is not quite convinced of the truth of his idea, and that he has put it forward more for the sake of appearing original than for any well-founded reasons: if this be not so, so much the worse, for

---

[61] Giovanni Papini (1881-1956) was an Italian writer and philosopher who was associated with Futurism and other avant garde movements. He was a convert to Catholicism and also a proponent of Fascism during World War II. The book referred to here is *Il crepuscolo dei filosofi* (The Twilight of the Philosophers) from 1906.

then his argument will be like an arrow shot so far as to be lost to view. I mean that he has had a certain obscure intuition, and that, instead of developing and clarifying it, he has exaggerated a simple aspect and turned his thoughts in the wrong direction, destroying the few germs of truth which his theory contained.

Papini's argument in regard to productions of the intelligence is, generally speaking, of no value. It cannot be contended that with flabby muscles, a weak heart, and an overfed stomach, a man can think and write well. Therefore the weakness or the strength of the writer says nothing in regard to the merits of his work.

In a particular instance, however—and Papini has laid special stress upon this—he tells us that Nietzsche, with his ideas, endeavoured to deceive himself, and, to a certain extent, to make suggestions to himself; that he, being flabby and delicate, wished to believe himself strong and healthy; and, finally, that Nietzsche showed "his weakness once more in not succeeding in truly and concretely doing in action, and in the world, those things which he theoretically believed to be superior."

This accusation of not having known how to realise his own ideas will not stand. To each one is given his work in the world. From a thinking man we cannot expect more than a useful discovery, a magnificent conception, an increase of knowledge. The happy application by ingenious inventors of physical and mathematical principles, discovered by others, to problems of practical utility is considered by intelligent persons as of no more merit than is due to those students who first established such principles by long and hard work. The masses are far too much inclined to esteem practical application and the success of material enterprises too highly, for such tendencies may be thereby encouraged.

Coming back, however, to the accusation specifically directed by Papini against the work of Nietzsche, is it not possible that this weakness, if we may continue to call it so, that this sense of limitation, insufficiency, and inhibition—as it would be more just to say—which is the sentimental form of which Nietzschean thought constitutes the intellectual reaction, may be only the greater knowledge, verified in him, of a state which is more diffused in modern minds, and of which he himself has been the illuminator?

This weakness—let us call it so for the moment— seems to be the consequence, and, at the same time, the condition of progress, as I have already said in my chapter on work; it should seem that our complicated and refined civil life is only rendered possible after the extinction of ancient virtue, primitive ferocity and strength. Humanity could not acquire the advantages which came to it from social existence without renouncing other advantages which always constitute the eternal aspiration of the human mind.

The painful sense of this loss, the indefinite aspiration towards the renewal of a joyous and entire life, the nostalgic desire for declining virtues and beauties, constitute, it may be said, the sentimental basis where the creative imagination of Nietzsche found its inspiration and dreams. Such a mode of feeling, however, remains hidden and mistaken by the intellectualistic development of his theories; and the coarse thread of his sentiment disappears beneath the rich and pompous embroidery of his thought.

This sentimental state, which, to a certain extent, Nietzsche rose out of, we see depicted with all the majestic colours on the palette of a great artist, Anatole France. In almost all his novels we feel the air of a tepid atmosphere, an atmosphere of secret sorrows and hidden sighs: not a heart-breaking sadness; but nevertheless a full resignation, a smile of sweetness of mind and of knowledge rather than a frank, self-satisfied mirth.

Such a state of mind, almost indefinable in his first works, is matured and concreted in his *Histoire contemporaine*. I should here like to quote this extract from the *Mannequin d'Osier* :—

"Ce reproche (d'avoir été nommé 'méchant' par sa servante) ne fâcha pas M. Bergeret. Il feignit de ne point l'entendre, ayant trop d'esprit pour ne pas excuser les libertés d'une fille ignorante. Et il sourit au dedans de lui même, car il gardait dans le fond obscur de son âme, sous l'appareil des sages pensées et des belles maximes, l'instinct primitif, qui subsiste chez les hommes modernes de l'esprit le plus civil, le plus doux, et qui les porte à se réjouir quand ils voient qu'on les prend pour des êtres féroces comme si la capacité de nuire et de détruire était la première force des vivants, leur vertu essentielle et leur bonté supérieure, ce qui à la réflexion se trouve véritable, puisque, la vie ne se soutenant, ne s'accroissant que dans le meurtre, les meilleurs sont ceux qui font le plus de carnages, et puisque ceux qui, par instigation de race et de nourriture, donnent les plus grands coups, sont nommés généreux et plaisent aux femmes, naturellement intéresées à choisir les plus forts et incapables de séparer dans leur esprit la force fécondante de la force destructive, qui sont en effet indissolublement unies dans la nature."[62]

---

[62] "This reproach (of having been called 'wicked' by his servant) did not anger M. Bergeret. He pretended not to hear it, having too much spirit not to excuse the liberties of an ignorant girl. And he smiled within himself, for he kept in the dark depths of his soul, under the guise of wise thoughts and beautiful maxims, the primitive instinct which subsists in modern men of the most civil and gentle spirit, and which leads them to rejoice when they see that they are taken for ferocious beings, as if the capacity to harm and destroy were the first strength of the living, their essential virtue and their superior goodness, which on reflection is found to be true, since, life being sustained and increased only by murder, the best are those who cause the most carnage, and since those who, by instigation of race and food, deal the greatest blows, are called generous and please women, who are naturally interested in choosing the strongest and are incapable of separating in their minds the fertilizing force from the destructive force, which are in fact indissolubly united in nature."

And also this from the *Anneau d'amethiste,* in which Bergeret turns to his dog Riquet which had taken fright when a pigeon rose suddenly from the ground and flew away:—

"Mon pauvre Riquet, cet oiseau, que tes ancêtres auraient croqué vif, t'effraie. Tu n'as pas faim comme eux. Une culture raffinée t'a rendu poltron. C'est une grande question de savoir si la civilisation n'affaiblit pas chez hommes le courage, en même temps que la férocité. Mais les hommes cultivés affectent le courage par respect humain et ils se font une vertu artificielle plus belle peut-être que la naturelle."[63]

Whilst, however, in Anatole France we see a careless abandonment to the fatality which accompanies progress, a gentle serenity, like the quietening of a melancholy desire, the smile of a meditative wisdom, in Nietzsche, on the contrary, we perceive an inexpressible disquietude inciting him to search for the cause of his feeling, and we see his intelligence coming to the help of the latter, fortifying it, and making his will austere and combative. While the one lets himself be carried along in the muddy current of common thought, the other combats it, and makes every endeavour to work his way towards the broad, pure sea of life and strength.

Thus the philosophy of Nietzsche is the last and most recent insurrection of the fine ancient mind against its expansion and liberation. Will his deeds have been performed in vain; will they be like a warlike threat, which, in our epoch of peace and immobility, can startle no one, and must they therefore be considered as a single isolated attempt without the hope of their having any effect on man? I do not think so. I believe at any rate that Papini—who has perhaps the merit of having understood, even if only confusedly, a part of the

---

[63] "My poor Riquet, this bird, which your ancestors would have eaten alive, frightens you. You are not hungry like them. A refined culture has made you cowardly. It is a great question if civilization does not weaken courage in men, at the same time as ferocity. But cultivated men affect courage out of human respect and they make for themselves an artificial virtue perhaps more beautiful than the natural one."

mechanism of our author's mind—and other critics have been entirely wrong in neglecting the investigation of what Nietzsche represents for modern culture, and especially for the German mind.

There are also, however, special causes of a purely psychological order, by means of which what Papini calls the weakness of Nietzsche—which is only the clear knowledge of a modern state of mind—constitutes on the other hand the imperative condition of his power as an analyst and searcher of the human heart.

The knowledge of a state of mind, and the possibility of reproducing it literally, are based upon the existence of a state of transition or evolution, from this into another, and from this again into a third. Thus, for example, the psychology of a strong man will not be made up by a strong man, since the knowledge of his state is, for him, something entire and existing by itself, incomparable with another state; but it may be made up by a weak man who has become strong. Similarly, the knowledge of a single passion or of a special character—in a word, psychological ability—is not a feature of those who have felt one passion only, or who have a particular, decisive, and well-defined form of character: but of those who pass from one state to another with ease, and who possess a kind of instability. This particular quality of being, so to speak, on the bridge which joins two different states, enables us to perceive exactly all those traits which delineate the figure of the two opposite conditions and modes of being, which is the base of literary temperament—the temperament of the creator and of the poet.

As regards the question at issue, we may add that an exact knowledge of the attributes of strong and weak men is not so easy in the case of a passage from the state of a strong man to that of a weak man, as, on the other hand, from the state of a weak man to that of a strong man. The case of Nietzsche may be generally and approximately referred to this latter category.

In this regard I remember having had a particular impression when I saw for the first time a series of portraits of Nietzsche, taken at different times in his life. In the very first, those taken in infancy, we may observe a certain lethargy and a heaviness of lines, which seem indecisive and puffed-up as if by excessive lymphatism; the eyes are confused and inexpressive. In later portraits we notice the gradual manifestation of a neatness of contour and a decision of lines which continue to increase until we come to the very latest portrait, in which we see a face with bold and energetic lines, incisive and sharp: a fine aristocratic face, showing strong will-power.

We see in Nietzsche the case of a slow recovery, of a continual progress towards conditions of health from, perhaps, a congenital state of illness. I wish to anticipate an objection here, and to state that even if he finally went mad, this does not by any means signify that his physiological conditions did not continue to improve: for, as has already been shown by others, his insanity was of exogenous origin, and was not the fatal outcome of an initially abnormal physical constitution.

*   *   *   *   *

Imperialism, superhumanism, egotism, considered as theories, as systems of conduct, art, and philosophy, are the indication of a growing life. In this connection we may invert Nietzsche's celebrated proposition on the significance of the ascetic ideal: "The ascetic ideal has its origin in the prophylactic instinct of a degenerating life," and say that the ideal of the higher man has its origin in the expansive instinct of a growing vitality, of a vitality which, having been compressed and diminished, returns to primitive grandeur and strength. The practical life of Nietzsche, and his physiological history, are exactly parallel to the development of his thought, and his work might be defined as "A moral and intellectual Recovery." In this sense, Nietzsche's thought is only the generalisation elaborated by the knowledge of the conditions and the circumstances which facilitated his recovery, together with the enlargement, the ideal magnifying, of the sense of expansion and increase which it underwent. Better still, his propositions are transpositions, translations into psychological language of what was most favourable to his physical life.

Nietzsche's works form as it were an ascending series, a series which is interrupted by an unexpected outburst of madness. It is a slow and gradual transformation from certain valuations and judgments to almost contrary valuations and judgments. But even in the first works we note a few ideas which are maintained almost unchanged in the complete evolution of his thought.

The nodal points, the most important points of this series are, in my opinion, marked by *Human, All-Too Human, The Gay Science,* and the *Genealogy of Morals.* It may be said that these works are the principal stages of his progressive journey; and in them, I may remark, especially in the second, he has achieved what is best in his thought, and which will certainly live. A few pages of *Human, All-Too Human,* those, for example, referring to thinkers and writers, contain germs of thought which will be the subject of further development and discoveries by future psychologists. In the *Genealogy of Morals* he has scientifically established the reasons for the changing of moral values, and has shown how morality is the objectivation, the theoretical and intellectual justification of a special form, a concrete mode of life.

I set little value upon *The Birth of Tragedy,* and the *Untimely Meditations.* When writing these he was under the influence of the ideas of others, the philosophic system of Schopenhauer, and the aesthetico-philosophic system of Wagner. We feel that these works show a deviation of his mind, which seems to be making an effort to convince itself of something repugnant to it. Thus his conceptions of a Dionysiac and Apollonian state are quite fantastic, and correspond to no reality whatever.

Human, All-Too Human shows some advance, and even a change in direction. Nietzsche finds his path, the way to the natural and personal development of his mind, which he had lost, and he proceeds in this way with *The Wanderer and his Shadow,* and with *The Dawn.*

The Gay Science is the beginning of a new period, and shows the high ascension of his mind, which in *Thus Spake Zarathustra* and in *Beyond Good and Evil* reaches its culminating point.

With the *Genealogy of Morals* his artistic fire dies down, and his scientific, systematic, and explicatory preoccupation arises, which has its finest expression in this work. Insanity, unfortunately, interrupted the author's proposal to publish a synthetic work of his complete system, which, however, I believe, would have contained nothing more that was essential to it, even if it would have been enriched by the value of practical explanation and propaganda.

And now we can at last begin our examination of the substance and general value of Nietzsche's works.

The fundamental problem which all social Utopias and all moral philosophies assume to be answered one way or another is the following: Does the most desirable and highest advantage of society consist of well-being assured to all—the greatest happiness of the greatest number—in the tendency to mediocritise all abilities; or in opposing and confirming the differences, in widening the gap between rich and poor, between exploiters and exploited?

Those who accept the first solution are democrats in all the different senses of the word; those who accept the second are aristocrats: and those who accept the first agree to accept for humanity a future resembling a deep, low-lying bog. It is a psychologically ascertained fact that genius flourishes best in periods of social dissolution, of scattering of wealth, and of sexual dissipation. Genius springs up wherever there is accumulated wealth of labour and power, which is displayed in works of magnificence and beauty.

Now democrats themselves must admit, at least from a utilitarian standpoint—which is the only standpoint upon which it is possible for us to come to an understanding with them—that genius confers great practical advantages upon society itself (not to speak of the value which it gives to life, increasing its seduction and attractiveness). Democrats should persuade themselves that inventive, mechanical genius—which they naturally try to show is of the highest importance—is born in such conditions; and a society which is so stupid as to suppress the special circumstances of the existence of the higher man does not deserve to live, and stands self-condemned to death, or at least to the obscurity and barbarism that form the death of a nation; its historical death.

Now it was just this problem of the higher man—the conditions of his being, the circumstances favourable to his development—which was, one might say, the constant work of Nietzsche's mind.

"Humanity should constantly propose to itself the production of men of genius." This is one of the propositions contained in the first organic and mature writing of Nietzsche, *The Birth of Tragedy*, and from several indications we may say that his succeeding work is nothing but volumes of precepts for those who feel in themselves the power of this higher development, and a solution, developed at length, of this problem.

To this special characteristic of his thought is due the importance of the moral problem. Current morality is the morality which is suited to the greater number, it is the conscient form of the conditions of existence of the majority. Thus the morality of goodness is the law of the least strong; the law that suits the masses, who have no function other than that of accumulating energies in the assimilative form of work and production. The higher man evidently takes his starting-point from common conditions; but, precisely because he is a higher man, he is obliged to separate himself from them, and it is here that we see the necessity for another morality, that is to say, of another involucre which will protect and facilitate his development. This is why he discards his former morality, and also why it is abjured the more as the individual is greater in intelligence, his aims higher, and his views broader, combined with the difficulties of his conditions of existence. This separation, however, is not easy; the more profound and delicate his sensitiveness, the more he will feel the force of attraction of his feelings, his ideas, and his emotions, rather than the newly rising strength: the strength of his own superiority and the inspiration of his genius which urge him to the separation.

From this comes all that sense of nostalgia, all the profound regret which we observe in the most violent invectives of Nietzsche. We find in his most daring and destructive criticisms a sense of melancholy desire and of secret sympathy for the things he opposes, for the men against whom he is darting his most terrible epigrams and most ironical definitions, as if with his words he were killing something very dear to him, so that he finally suppressed himself. For this reason even his fiercest stabs do not wound us, for we can see the life-blood flowing of the man who offends us so much. The very violence of his attack seems to be only the dissimulation of a vacillating will, of a heart which still feels a very great love for what it is abandoning.

And again, there is in all his works, especially in his last, a feeling as of one who is continually endeavouring to conquer himself, who desires—without a truce, without failure, with a terrible hardness and fierceness of will—to thrust forward his own thoughts to the extreme limit, to bend the bow of his own feelings to the utmost: an arduous and contentious sense of growth, of constant transformation, which gives a bitter and magnificent voluptuousness to the sensation of omnipotence. This aspect of his thought, which I fear I have not expressed in a manner worthy of him, is common to him and Emerson;

and it may be said to be almost entirely peculiar to the English and the American mind. We shall later see its value and significance so far as the Germans are concerned.

The preoccupation of the existence and the final victory of the higher man over the difficulties of life is always occupying his attention and becoming more and more grave. Read what he says in this connection in *Beyond Good and Evil*:—

"The more a psychologist—a born psychologist, a diviner of characters—gives himself up to the study of the most select cases and men, the greater is the risk he runs of being overcome by pity: he has more necessity for insensitiveness and good-humour than any other man.

"The corruption and the ruin of the highest-placed men, of those minds most unlike ordinary minds, is the rule; it is terrible to have such a rule always before one's eyes. The manifold martyrdom of the psychologist who has discovered such a waste of material, who for the first time—and afterwards, as it were, always anew—perceives the entire 'incurability' of the higher man, the eternal 'too late' in all the senses of the phrase, in the course of history may one fine day be the cause of his becoming exasperated and revolting against his own fortune; finally trying to destroy himself so that he also may become wasted material."[64]

By the very law of the struggle for existence, the higher man is the object of more active, more eager cupidity: the eyes of those who wish to overpower and impoverish are turned towards him as to a specially rich piece of plunder, rather than to others, and he, for this reason and on account of his own nature, is very likely to perish, as has been so well outlined by Nietzsche on pages remarkable for their ardour and inspiration.

The most dangerous seduction, the seduction of goodness, of noble and tender sentiments, operates upon him on a vast

---

[64] *Beyond Good and Evil*, sec. 269

scale, and he continually runs the risk of being its victim. Woman, a humanitarian idea, a conception, a profession, are all different forms of the perils which the higher man may meet with; but the first is especially common and grave.

It is strange that Nietzsche has not specially referred to this; but in his works his decision not to occupy himself with sex, woman, and love, is too evident to be without significance.

His silence on these subjects, which would have provided him with so many examples of different developments, is very strange indeed.

Is it not marvellous, in fact, that the most enraged accuser of all the defects and decadences of mankind should have observed such a scrupulous silence on this side of the question?

I do not mean to exaggerate when I say that I think it is Nietzsche's greatest weakness, all the more as he has not had the courage to confess it and to analyse it. The charitable justification put forth by his sister must not deceive us. If the sexual life of Nietzsche were known, the information would, in my opinion, bring much light to bear on his entire personality.[65]

Was it a real organic deficiency, or was it a timorous presentiment of fear, and a voluntary flight to preserve himself from it? Or was it perhaps a means for concentrating all the strength of his genius upon his beloved ideas? Who knows? Perhaps all these things together.

In addition to woman, however, who is the most personal and vulgar enemy of all superiority, there is a mass of entities and aspects of life which may mislead the rising force. The complication of these interests, these inimical forces, attaches itself to and operates upon the higher man by means of morality. Morality is the abstraction, the generalisation, the

---

[65] Nietzsche himself wrote, "The degree and kind of a man's sexuality reach up into the ultimate pinnacle of his spirit." (*Beyond Good and Evil*, sec. 75) [Ed.]

evaporation of these activities, which have in morality their most perfect and seductive instrument of power and impoverishment: and hence arises the necessity for breaking through this net so as to acquire a perfect command over one's self; to be able to affirm and bring to completion one's own thought and one's own ideal.

Every creation, every invention, which is of more than ordinary commercial merit, judged by its amount of greatest practical utility, every work which is above the petty interests of trade, is produced in comparative leisure: which is always, at least at the actual moment, an oppression of others, a usurpation of their property. The higher man must, however, submit to this law, which is almost a law of nature, constituting the *sole condition* of perfecting his own capacities and activities.

Great men of science, art, or letters are constantly made the objects of the reproof that they are guilty of the most ferocious egoism in regard to their friends and acquaintances, and to those who are even dearer to them: mothers, sisters, wives, lovers.

This accusation is unjust. The egoism of those who are called praiseworthy by humanity is a maternal egoism. As a mother who suckles her child eats and drinks the best that the table bears, not for herself, but for her baby, so the genius is often insatiable, overbearing, and wrapped up in himself, in view of his work. And is not this work often quite different from its author? How often has a work not done harm to its author especially, like a newborn child which causes the death of its mother?

To mediocre interests, mediocre circumstances; to exceptional interests, exceptional circumstances.

Thus, again, we often hear the corruption and immorality of the higher man spoken of.

Let it be so. We must remember, however, that this corruption is generally turned to the advantage of society; for creation, the work of the higher man, possesses the virtue of the seven loaves and the seven fishes which were multiplied so as to satisfy the hunger of all.

And that is the justification of the immorality (if we may call it so) of the higher man in view of his higher interest for society, of which he is the benefactor.

Nietzsche's work, from *The Gay Science* onwards, is wholly hortatory, a combination of practical rules and formulae, seductive propositions, incitements, and suggestions to the end of securing an entire change in one's moral personality, and of obtaining a practical knowledge of one's self: things which, on one hand, are necessary for us to pass on to the psychology of the higher man, and which, on the other hand, likewise express his conditions of existence.

This is the practical signification which the work of Nietzsche has for an ordinary individual, and this is the reason why it has become so popular among young men, ambitious men, and thinkers. It is, in a certain sense, a guide, a stimulant, alcohol; and it is but natural that these people should make an apology for it, as for a benefit which reaches them at an opportune moment.

Nietzsche's morality is a stimulating morality; it is not for those who, whether in a high or low position in life, rest themselves or stand still; but for those who desire to make, and do make, progress. His is a dynamics of morality rather than a statics, and in this fact lies its value.

If, restrained by a stratification of theories, counsels, commands, and rules during the period of education, with coercive methods and limitations, the beginnings of one's real personality are unable to develop, to come to light and break their chains, a hortatory work of this kind would be incomprehensible and useless. Hence this philosophy is for those who wish to find themselves, for those who wish to develop a decisive character, who wish really to live. It is the manifestation of a newly arisen vital force, which, having undergone a painful experience of reality, tends to oppress, in order not to be oppressed.

That this, and nothing else, is the origin of Nietzsche's morals is obvious when it is remembered that strong men have a very great interest in the propagation of the so-called morals of slaves, while they look with some disfavour on an increase in their own ranks: if, indeed, it can be said that morals of any kind have any influence upon human nature.

Truly great works have always many aims and significations, particular and general; and this is even a proof of their greatness. An interpretation of Nietzsche's work would therefore be incomplete if it did not explain the position and value of this work in relation to the form of civilisation and national conditions among which it originated.

The philosophy of Nietzsche, considered from this point of view, appears like the splendid dawn of a magnificent day for the mind and soul of Germany. The Germans will, it is safe to prophesy, give up that torpor, that heaviness, that sentimentalism, that inertia and passiveness of will, of which some writers accuse them—too lightly, it must be said, for such writers do not perceive that closely connected with these defects are the highest virtues which constitute the immense strength of the German people, giving them, together with a character inclined to sacrifice, a spirit of solidarity, steadiness in work, patience and pertinacity, the means of obtaining an enormous store of mental and economic acquisitions. The German mind, freed from a certain slowness and obtuseness, will become lighter and more artistic; and, preserving the more essential of its primitive virtues, will take to itself other virtues as a complement. Then it will have arrived at the summit of its greatness and power, and will shine brilliantly in the magnificent noon of its life.

This, of course, will not be the work of a few years; but perhaps of many centuries. What I say need not cause any astonishment: we may remember, for example, the coarseness and barbarity of the early epochs of France and England, and their succeeding greatness.

Nietzsche has, in my opinion, the historical merit of having shaken off this heaviness, this enormous, confused organism of his country, and of having felt within himself—and afterwards marvellously objectised in his works—the disease which opposed the affirmation of his will, and of having also set forth the remedy for curing this disease.

The German nation is in preparation: immense energies, as yet shapeless, incongruous and partly contradictory among themselves, smoulder in the glowing crucible of its social life. Nietzsche saw with the clear eye of a prophet and a soothsayer what was required to make these forces unite in a sublime apotheosis of human power and genius. Surely the German nation should feel grateful to the man who suffered for himself and for others, who had such a powerful vision of a future full of beauty, who desired and who knew how to show his fellow-men the means by which it could be attained!

Nietzsche's "philosophy," therefore, is not the "philosophy" of a weakness that wishes to appear strong, not a deceiving "philosophy"; but a liberating doctrine, a propaganda of transformation. The Nietzschean predication is an effort to show us how to go out of ourselves and to overcome ourselves; it is not a deception, a mask, except at a first cursory examination, for two reasons: the one methodical, for the man who wishes to adopt new habits, to change his conduct, and hence his sentiments and ideas, must have these sentiments and ideas always before him; the other general, even philosophical, because making for one's self a new conception of the world, forming an exhortation of force and mystery, may be the indication of something more essential and material which is being changed.

And what does it matter if a single individual does not realise his own ideal; what does it matter if the huge strength whereby he bends the bow of his will shakes the whole foundation of his life and finally leads him to the obscure realms of madness? He was a man of his age, he was the representative of a state of mind much more widespread and important for the psychologist than the existence of an individual.

Every nation has the task of enlarging the human mind, and of making it more beautiful and splendid in its patrimony of feelings, affections, and thoughts: we may even say that different nations or races—or, if it be preferred, different historical groups—whether by elaborating the material which comes to them from the cosmopolitan market of ideas, or by their own making of new discoveries and adding these to others, are *inventing* the new mind of the future.

Thus, for example, we do not as a rule conceive how much we moderns are indebted to the moral and psychological experience of France, of which country the discoveries in this field constitute the warp and woof of our European psyche.

A great part of our moral wealth—as will be observed by the careful reader who has had some experience of ideas—is derived from the works of Pascal, La Rochefoucauld, La Bruyère, Montaigne, and Rousseau.

Every nation, however, bringing its contribution to the history of the life of humanity, does not bring it all at once; but follows a well-determined law of development. Every fresh increase is preceded by a period of study and research—something dim and shadowy, and yet important at the same time; something like what takes place in biological evolution, where coarse, rough forms of colossal dimensions, but with undefined functions, precede forms of a much better mould, more adapted to surroundings, although smaller and more fragile.

Thus the modern Germanic mind, inasmuch as it is cloudy, indistinct, and uncertain, is, to use a word of our author's, in a crude state, and is but the prelude to a magnificent moral development, of which, indeed, we may already see the first traces.

And, while the English mind, after having given all it could to the world's knowledge, is now in a stagnant condition, far different acquisitions, far different victories, are promised us as a result of German knowledge; but, in this Teutonic mind, whatever is *unfermented*, heavy, and coarse must be entirely changed.

Now, Nietzsche was the precurser of this transformation; he is the first moralist of Germany: a country which, in this respect, is very backward as compared with her neighbour and her elder sister: it was Nietzsche who gave the first impulse to the great work of refinement and perfection.

Madame de Staël said: "Les auteurs français de l'ancien temps ont en général plus de rapports avec les Allemands que les écrivains du siècle de Louis XIV, car c'est depuis ce temps que là littérature française a pris une direction classique."[66]

In the same way Nietzsche particularly resembles the moralists of the sixteenth and seventeenth centuries more than any other writers; but whatever in them still remains confused, indefinite, and intuitive, what in them is still undeveloped, is by Nietzsche brought forth and elucidated. The law of the successive development of different forms of human activity in different civilisations, by which these repeat their first *motif* in developing on a broader scale, still applies here.

I compare the magnificent exaltation of Nietzsche's works to the ancient ardour with which his forefathers, the rude barbarians, descended into the south: and is not all his work a thirst for light, for air, for the south? His doctrines are the aspiration of the north for the south, of the mind of countries deprived of sun and life for light, for heat, for the blue of the

---

[66] "The French authors of the old days generally have more connections with the Germans than the writers of the century of Louis XIV, because it is since that time that French literature has taken a classical direction."

southern sky. And for this reason Nietzsche's works may be called the moral and aphoristic, translation of the *aperçus* and the aesthetic predilections of Stendhal for Italy.

Nietzsche's work is a *southernisation* of the northern mind, its refinement, its embellishment.

It used to be said that Nietzsche borrowed from La Rochefoucauld, Chamfort, Taine, and Renan, and certainly the ideas, the emotions, of contemporary sensitiveness are common to both him and them; but his merit lies in having widened knowledge to a greater extent, in having thrown light on obscure moral relationships. Every advance in knowledge is an advance in self-consciousness, in knowledge of ourselves; but it must be followed by an eccentric wave, by a return to periphery and to exteriority, in order that it may be truly called a new and efficacious conquest of universal knowledge.

Besides these fundamentals, however, we have a number of other results which Nietzsche's work offers us liberally, and owing to which it is of so much importance, especially what he has written as critic and psychologist.

The continual occupation of Nietzsche's thought was religion, in which he saw the great corruptress, the most dangerous deceiver, the origin of all the seductions that menace man. So firmly was he impressed with this thought that he desired to compose his last work (which was not completed) especially against religion.

Much has been said in regard to the anti-religious criticism of Nietzsche and his hatred for Christianity, and I have no wish to repeat what is already well known. I shall make only one observation, which I do not think is out of place. Was it Christianity as a positive and exterior religion, having its culminating point in Roman Catholicism, or the Christian spirit in its original pureness and its restoration as carried out by the reformers, that Nietzsche had in mind when he spoke of Christianity as being the religion of the conquered, of the weak?

In my opinion he had Protestantism specially in view, that hard, abstractive, and rationalist movement; that mind, fierce and bitter in its unreal aspirations, which banished the beautiful images of Christ and of the Virgin, which banished solemn architecture and magnificent temples, and which permitted only music, the most abstract and least sensual of arts, to accompany religious feeling. It was not Roman Catholicism that he accused, with its altars, sometimes odd-looking, but more often ornamented with masterpieces of art; not Catholicism, with its memory of smoking sacrifices in the censers, with its solemn rites in which candles blazed and rich chasubles, precious, many-coloured pluvials, and bejewelled chalices glittered; but what he did accuse was the bitter, dry, and fanatic Reformation, with its hatred for art and for anything attractive to the senses, and with its rationalistic and democratic foundation.

Roman Catholicism was an adaptation of primitive Christianity to the spirit of peoples who, by race, the climate in which they lived, and for other reasons, had remained pagans, and it was therefore a radical transformation of it. The primitive Christian spirit was for Catholicism the rough but solid foundation upon which the latter erected its splendid palace, and constituted the nucleus of belief for the people and for its most humble priests, that is to say, for the inferior minds; but for the higher minds the Church was gradually separated from its original design, and this primitive Christian spirit lost ground to make way for the ancient dominating spirit of the Latin race. This is why this religious sentiment had its palingenesis in Germany and the northern races, in which, sociality having been more developed, there is likewise a greater vigour of interior life, a greater development of altruistic tendencies, of emotions, of sympathy, pity, and solidarity.

We must here however note another point which characterised the Reformation: the hatred with which it persecuted the manifestations of sexual life was a true hatred of the North towards the South, one of those many historical aspects in which was once more revealed that ever-present antagonism between northerns and southrons.

* * * * *

Was Nietzsche a philosopher, at all events in the more limited sense of the word?

I do not think so; he was a psychologist, and this word must be taken in a sense which I would indicate by the expression psychologo-moralist.

For there are two different fields of psychological inquiry: the one reserved for pure savants and bordering on physiology, which is occupied with research into the elements of our inner life, and their manner of associating with what were at one time known as faculties (such as memory, judgment, the perception of time); the other field bordering on morality, and cultivated by men of letters and artists, who seek to throw light upon the causes of human action, the true nature of social sentiments; to reveal the dynamics of the *"heart."* This moral psychology, in which so many talented men make a figure (including all literary geniuses), may be treated systematically, and then we have works like the maxims of La Rochefoucauld, Pascal, Chamfort, and Nietzsche, who, in more than one respect, may be said to continue and develop more widely and deeply the thought of his predecessors.

One of his best merits as a psychologist is that of having understood the great importance of the psychology of North and South.

The psychology of North and South—as a base for the knowledge and distinction of temperaments and characters, as an aggrandising of the normal individual differences which are presented to us in a human group, *as an incomparable natural experience*—began with Stendhal: he inspired Nietzsche, and Nietzsche borrowed from him, in many places. It is noteworthy that both showed a conspicuous liking for the mind of the south: the continual admiration which Stendhal expresses for the more strongly passionate Italy, the Italy of the Renaissance, coincides with the heroification by Nietzsche of Cesare Borgia and of Napoleon, both, be it noted, Italians. This is quite the contrary of what some modern sociologists affirm in regard to the superiority of the northern peoples over those of the south; but the reasons for the preferences of Stendhal and Nietzsche would hardly be understood by these modern sociologists, for they are too wide in range and, above all, they are not prevailingly ... democratic.

Nietzsche's great merit, however, as a psychologo-moralist is that of having gone some way towards solving the moral problem with his great genial intuition, which, unfortunately, he did not develop to its latest and final consequences.

So far, in fact, there have been no moralistic philosophers or psychologists; but only makers of precepts, catechisers, propagandists. Nietzsche perceived that the question of morals, far from being discussed, was not even put forward, and that we had only had apophthegms or apologies; no doctrine given us by reason. In truth, he himself only followed its development from a certain epoch down to his own time; but he did not investigate the conditions of its origin.

Nietzsche makes us see that our present form of morals could not necessarily have been different from what it is; and it is the same in all moralists, *for it is the condition of existence of moralists themselves as workmen,* that is, limited, restricted, and specialised beings. The formulators of morality express only their own peculiarities, their personal conditions of existence, i.e. the conditions of existence of a group. Nietzsche affirmed the right of an existence not only practical but also doctrinal, of an entirely opposite morality, the morality of those who usually do not write ... of morality, being men of action and mastery.

There was thus formulated and written for the first time the law of those whose only law is their own good, their own expansion, in contrast to the utility of the masses, the morality of parasitical and aristocratic beings, which, although never before outlined, was not on that account the less lively and warlike.

Nietzsche in this way notably extended the limits of thought; since, if it is necessary to admit a community of mind in a wide sense among such different human individuals, we cannot but recognise nevertheless that this very man of thought, the intelligent man, the writer, even, must necessarily fail to perceive the blendings of sentimental colouring and states of mind which belong to different species of men: to those of action pure and simple.

Now, of these states, that of the master and the strong man was most alien to the condition of the thinker, especially in our present democratic age; but Nietzsche, with a great effort, was able to bring back thought to the point of view, the visual angle, of primitive strength and completeness; he carried out, in other words, the aristocratisation of knowledge.

But to do that did he truly put himself, as he says, *beyond good and evil?* No: his point of view was *immoralistic,* antisocial; not *amoral* and natural.

This is the higher point of view, because it is the synthesis and reconciliation of both tendencies or both principles, democratic and aristocratic.

Such a task I think I have perhaps with some success performed, in pointing out the relationship between morality and sociality on one hand, and sexuality on the other, and in establishing the physiological value of the word *aristocratic.*

I have looked at the matter resolutely from the point of view of the species, that is, the biological point of view, and I have defined morality as a necessity and a consequence of society, which implies a diminishing process of life.

Nietzsche's work, however, has still another value for us. The phenomenon presented to us by him gives us highly valuable explanations in regard to geniality.

The development of genial personality, as it is better expressed, is a kind of return to a full life; a species of *recovery* or renovation; in it contrary things seem to come into harmony with one another; we observe a broadening of the mind, a spiritualisation of man, together with a fresh increase of strength. So, again, Nietzsche's life, his doctrine, all the slow evolution of his personality, if profoundly analysed, are found to be a document for the psychologist on the nature of the most obscure and sublime human fact: genius, a nature which may certainly be revealed here and there in some higher men; but which in Nietzsche, by the particular aim of his work, and his eminently introspective character, is illumined with a dazzling light.

CHAPTER VIII

NORTH AND SOUTH

It is a great mistake that the moral and physical differences which separate different peoples from one another should have hitherto been almost completely neglected; and especially the differences between the peoples of the north and those of the south. The characteristics which distinguish them from each other are to some extent of the same kind as those which distinguish one individual from another of the same race: so that differences between peoples are the same as the differences between individuals, multiplied and enlarged, so to speak, through a magnifying-glass.

Differences between social groups can be much better remarked than those between individuals, whence it comes that knowledge of peoples lends the greatest assistance to an exact understanding of man for a future scientific doctrine of characters and temperaments. The psychology of peoples, however, in spite of what is affirmed to the contrary, has yet to be formed, or rather gathered together and established, since it is at present in a crude state; in particular literatures which represent only their own peculiar thoughts.

Some would wish laws, customs, and traditions to be even more important elements for the formation of this science; but I think they will serve rather to call the attention of the psychologist to certain factors, such as that in literature, as the comprehensive translation and summary of a state of mind produced by manifold causes, such thoughts are no longer manifest as particular instances; but that, in general, literature is the best fount from which to draw.

A special consideration makes me insist upon an opinion which I hold, viz. that to literature more properly so called, i.e. inventive literature, poetry, tales, and novels, is entrusted the element which I hold to be the central element of every form of character: the mode of feeling and conceiving love.

This characteristic, so simple in appearance, and yet so complicated by various tints and blendings, tells us more than anything else about an individual's personality; and hence, even if there were no other reasons, this alone would be sufficient to explain why the principal, not to say the only, theme of literature is love. So, again, this trait individualises, and gives its own physiognomy to each of those two accumulations of tendencies, sentiments, and activities which I symbolically indicate by the names north and south.

Some writers, giving a too concrete and material reality to this twofold conception, prejudice whatever amount of indisputable truth it contains; and, taking this alone as their starting-point, they draw a series of deductions which border on the inverisimilar and the ridiculous. This happens because they do not bear in mind that such a conception is an abstraction of numerous and particular data and facts, which in this generalisation must necessarily sacrifice something of themselves in order to fit into the unanimity of the law. I have nevertheless always believed that such a formula, if properly applied, would show the cause of innumerable human facts, and that it would serve to explain the principal facts of civilisation better than all the theories that have been put forward in regard to superior and inferior races, aristocratic and plebeian, Aryan or otherwise.

These differences in the manner of conceiving life, in morality, in activity—to which corresponding physical differences (which we may observe even between the northerners and southrons of our own nation) form a comparison—are observable, at least in essence, in every people.

It would be very easy to demonstrate this, and the objection generally made—that such differences are due to an intermixture of northern blood in the more southern people of the group—does not give us the true reason, because it may be asked why and how such new ethnic elements possess such singular properties.

I think, then, the best that can be done is, the existence of such distinctions being admitted, to deduce the manner of their formation, from which we may infer highly interesting consequences.

The psychologist is often the pioneer who prepares the way for the physiologist; but the psychologist must partake of the nature of the physiologist if he would arrive at an exact understanding of certain human facts. And this applies in the case of the question under discussion. For example, to be able to understand the cause of certain particular specifications of the northern character and temperament, one must bear in mind the general conditions of climatic surroundings, and the somatic conditions of the primitive bands who, so far as can be ascertained, emigrated.

The first fundamental exigency in an unfavourable climate, if man desires to survive, and, what is of even more concern, if he wishes to survive in a state of health and resistance, is that of combating the cold; the second is working continuously and constantly to overcome those difficulties arising from the sterility of the soil. Both these causes operate in the same way in causing an increase of alimentation. Cold surroundings and a strong muscular activity engender the production of a large amount of animal heat, and make the greater number of organic processes take place in order to achieve results that, in general, are of an inferior value as compared with others that might accrue, such as nervous activity, intelligence, generation.

This necessity is turned into an organic habit, into a *constant direction* taken by the phenomena of nutrition, which are subject to the same laws of inertia as psychologists, taking their inferences from physical facts, have applied to the currents of the nervous channels. The inner exchanges and activities of physical elements tend to assume a certain new balance, in which some given activities prevail over others in proportion to the adaptation of interior to exterior conditions.

In other words, in order to make up for considerable losses, some functions augment more than others. In this way the production of subcutaneous fat and of animal heat is increased; but the organs of nutrition especially take predominance over all other systems, in the first place, by the greater quantity of food, and in the second by the greater potency of digestive capacity which is required of them, the quality of the nutriment being inferior. The very sterility of the soil, in fact, prevents its productions from having a great nutritive capacity, and hence it becomes necessary to increase the quantity of food. From this complexity of conditions arises the necessity for an alimentation based especially upon hydrates of carbon of vegetable or animal origin, as being the most economical productions, and also those which maintain life in a state of least activity, that is to say, as a state of pure and simple resistance to anti-vital causes.

At one extreme of the direction I have referred to we find the peoples of the farthest north, the poor Eskimo, whose usual food is the fat of seals, of which they swallow quantities that we should think appalling.

This characteristic, however, is also to be met with, though in a less pronounced form, in the food of central and northern European peoples, especially the Germans, who take an enormous quantity of hydrates of carbon, as is shown by the infinite number of sauces, cakes, and soups for which the German kitchen is famous. The northern drink—beer— possesses qualities more nutritive than stimulating, at least in Germany, for English beer is generally much more alcoholic than German, and corresponds to the greater use in England of different kinds of flesh, that is, of nitrated foods.

These influences, then, many in number, yet acting in the same direction, determine the functional prevalences of some systems, naturally to the detriment of others, and especially of the nervous system, and to this is due a certain obtuseness, difficulty, or slowness of nervous and psychical phenomena.

For the rest, we may observe similar facts in the peasants of our own land, who, living in conditions analogous to those described, at least as regards the difficulty of existence, reproduce to a certain extent modes of being which are more common and diffused in other nations. This is the case to such a degree that the anthropological characteristics of different peoples are much less different in the lower classes, *especially the rural lower classes*, than in the upper classes, especially in the towns.

These causes which I have endeavoured briefly to point out were the more easily able to impress themselves on an organic constitution in proportion as they acted on those groups which, being weaker, had been driven out of the more favourable regions. In this way, in the course of centuries, they determined the form of temperament which prevails in the countries of the north, the phlegmatic temperament of the ancients and the lymphatic of the moderns, the clearest type of which is seen in the Eskimo.

I may be accused of drawing conclusions too boldly. A fashion that has lately been brought about by a reasonable and justifiable reaction against the excesses of materialism—fortified with the old religious rancour against every natural explanation, swollen by an insipid, literary-spiritualistic rhetoric—at once condemns ideas that take their origin from a far-off source of thought. The principal defect of these ideas is their vagueness, and their character, which partakes more of intuition than of induction; but we may recollect that more than one Hippocratic idea had to wait century after century for its documentary and strictly scientific confirmation, which, after having been given, only showed us another proof, if such were wanting, of the genius of the author of the *De Aere, Locis, et Aquis.*

Thus the doctrine of temperaments, of such high importance to ancient medical men, has gradually been abandoned by science, and has become the property of philosophers rather than of doctors; and has sometimes even passed into the possession of artists. The indeterminateness and imprecision of these ideas prejudiced this doctrine in the minds of scientists (for the scientific spirit is, on the other hand, one of distinction, delimitation, and analysis). They, however, depended only upon an imperfect and crude state of the means at the disposal of science, which did not yet possess such sensitive instruments for appraising the value of that doctrine, and for translating the exact amount of intuition which it contained, and contains, into positive terms of measure and datum. The fact nevertheless remains that the greatest doctors, those who had a practical and first-hand acquaintance with medicine united to a positive understanding, regarded the knowledge of temperaments as the basis of treatment for their patients.

Those who see only the classifying and crystallising aspect of science have always been pleased to look upon the doctrine of temperament as a pure fantasy; but scientists gifted with broader minds perceive its great susceptibility of development.

The temperament which we have seen is most frequent in the north is that which is best adapted to the fundamental exigency of continuous, methodical, and uniform work; ill adapted, or not adapted at all, to the activity of intellectual creation in general and artistic creation in particular. The northern organism has very slow but uniform exchanges—i.e. without notable oscillations, so that it can provide a constant supply of energy, whilst the physical conditions of artistic creation and production are those of a very shaky balance. After this digression we shall return to the subject under discussion, which is prevailingly psychological.

The people of the south are more fascinating, more handsome, more harmonious, for in them the individual is complete, perfect, full-grown. A great deal has been said in recent times in regard to individualism, and it has been considered as almost entirely a characteristic of the northern peoples. This is completely erroneous. The individualism of the northern races is a social individualism; that of the southrons is a natural individualism. The one is reflexive, recent, formal; the other spontaneous, primitive, real. The first —which, it may be mentioned, is more peculiar to the English people, who are in many respects the most developed of northern races—arose out of the spirit of solidarity which preceded it, at a time when, conditions of existence having become somewhat milder, it was permitted to detached individuals to distinguish themselves and to feel as individuals. Among the peoples of the south the individual is weak because he is separate, fragmentary; among the peoples of the north he is strong because he affirms himself, so to speak, in segregating himself in the compact mass of the social group. The individualism of the English is a *return* (using the word in the partially atavic sense I have mentioned in chapter IX.), not a primitive fact.

The amount of the average personality of an individual among us southrons is small; his personality is superficial and brilliant, but not very deep or extensive; his inner life is poor, to say the least; his store of feelings and ideas is poor and mediocre; his intellectual life is showy and weak. His exteriority is, however, perfect; he lives completely and directly outwardly what he feels inwardly; he brings his whole mind to expression; he does not suffer from *great illness of the north: incommunicability,* that is, the feeling of a gap between the thought and the deed, the disproportion between the interior and the exterior life, the clear knowledge of which we have seen in Nietzsche's philosophy, together with a heroic attempt to escape from it. Sometimes the awesome shadow of his thought does not overpower the individual, and he appears more beautiful because more animal-like.

The northern races, on the other hand, often give one the impression of people still in their infancy; their moral ideas and feelings almost correspond to the conditions of a perpetual youthfulness which struggles and fights with itself in an endeavour to attain manhood. Out of such a state as this comes that Romanticism which colours the northern mind and literature. Personality in the north is much wider; but its development is as a rule only partial and fragmentary, or it even deviates in aberrant directions through excess of social constraint. From hence comes the morbid impression which we Latins feel in reading almost any portion of northern literature. We may recollect the drama of Ibsen, or the novels and works in general of Björnson, Strindberg, and Geiyerstam, in which we are struck, more than anything else, by their strange and fantastic conception of love.

I should like to describe all the different aspects which in social life, public and private activity, morality and love, are peculiar to the northern mind. This, however, has been done by others, especially in Italy, where, ten years or so ago, we had a group of writers whose best representative was Ferrero,[67] who gave us an apology for, and what amounted to almost an apotheosis of, northern virtues: with much temperateness and success on Ferrero's part; with but little logic, no criticism whatever, and with most exaggerated and false deductions on the part of others. For the rest, when I spoke of morals, I alluded to those particular specifications and aspects which it took in the northern countries by reason of the greater impulse of social necessity; and, on the other hand, what the characteristics of the German mind are—which is usually accepted, but wrongly, as the representative of the northern spirit—was told long ago, and very well, by Madame de Staël in her classic *De l'Allemagne*, which the majority of authors borrow from without acknowledgment, and of which they

---

[67] Guglielmo Ferrero (1871-1942) was an Italian historian and novelist who is best known for his five-volume *The Greatness and Decline of Rome.*

reproduce the ideas at second or third hand without knowing their source.

This youthfulness and what I am tempted to call the immaturity of the German spirit are manifested in many ways.

The writers whom I have spoken of above have brought several of these indications into evidence, although they have not by any means interpreted them justly, and they have confined themselves to the most apparent and common.

I will here pause to consider three facts which I think of great significance, as they belong to the intellectual life, properly so called, of the German people, although none of them has been previously commented upon or has had due prominence given to it.

These are: the absence of a sense of humour or comedy in their literature; the poor development of the plastic arts or the art of drawing; and the great development of music.

The importance of this triple order of manifestations will appear greater when it is considered that their development is quite the reverse of what it is in the English nation, which has nevertheless much affinity with the German.

Generally speaking, in the historical development of literary forms, comedy is one of the last to appear. The faculty of laughing at things and men is an indication of the attainment of perfection, of the greatest extension of mental power; and laughter conveys the knowledge, obscure or not, of superiority over others. Seriousness of every kind indicates that excessive attention and importance is given to things which happen to occupy one's mind, and reveals the tension and gravity which every beginner gives to his work. Humour appears when the mind has acquired a certain autonomy and *aisance*. The *vis comica* is exercised first of all on ourselves, and then on others; it springs from a refined sentimentalism, from a profound knowledge of ourselves, and from this it often took in the beginning a veil of light melancholy: as progress is made, it becomes more joyous, open, and aggressive. The first stages of its formation, very light and frail, we see typically represented in Sterne. After him the humorous spirit in England loses that stamp of gentle spiritual sensitiveness, that trace of personality, and becomes more outward and vivacious.

In German classical literature comedy is almost altogether wanting, or, to be more exact, those examples which remain of it have only a historical, and not an intrinsic value. To this want we may compare that of the spirit of *moquerie* and caricature, which last, however, to tell the truth, is not absolutely alien to the German mind.

It is not necessary to insist here on the absence of the plastic arts; but I shall consider the value of this fact later on: at present I should rather like to make some observations on the great German musical production.

Why is it that of all arts music is the only one which receives all the suffrages and preferences of Germans; and that literature, which is nevertheless fairly well advanced, appears, as compared with music, in a very backward state? Why is it that Germany alone has a larger number of great composers than all other countries combined, some of whom are the greatest musicians who have ever lived; for among them are reckoned a Bach, a Haydn, a Beethoven, a Mozart, and a Wagner, and, coming down by way of Weber, Schumann, Liszt, Schubert, and Mendelssohn, we arrive at the Meyerbeers, the Brahms, and the Hofmanns?

The reason I will give will explain more than the reason why one art should be in a more flourishing state than another: it involves the nature of the German mind.

In music the gap between imagination and expression, between thought and feeling, is not wide; a close connection even unites the two. A sound is, in fact, thought and expressed immediately in its physical characters, and the means of execution is not complicated; there are no complex technicalities about music, and this art permits of the direct expression of the most involved combinations. It is capable of expressing all the indefiniteness and complexity of the German mind to a greater extent and better than any other art. In music the German mind does not feel its impotence of expression so much, and with music it affirms its aversion for what is clear and concise, for what, in their opinion, disables and mutilates inner life. And on account of its immediateness, and the close connection between a mental image and its expression, music is genetically the first of arts, whilst the plastic arts are the sign of a later evolution.

As the psychology of north and south shows, in an exaggerated form, certain aspects of the development of personality, it may help us to understand this better, and to study it in its entirety. The defects of the southern character are: poverty of mental knowledge, a stereotypedness of forms which is hidden by specious imitations of a classical ideal, exaggeration of expression which does not correspond to a real inner feeling, and sexual dissipation; the defects of the north are the reverse; obscurity of thought, indecision of will when met with alternatives, poorness of expression and action, deviations in the conception and practice of love.

From what has been said arises a conception of personality which makes its complete evolution consist of a double phase, a rhythm. The first phase is one of assimilation, of acquirement of experience, of scrutiny and examination; it is characterised in its last stages by a profound movement of thought, which is sufficient for itself and does not seek an outlet: it is, as it were, a laying aside of materials without considering where they should be placed. This phase of interior anabolic activity is the scientific phase, the phase of mental acquisition, and is marked by the most austere traditional morality, both the morality of work and anti-sexual morality. The end of this state is evidenced by the first appearance of tendencies towards action and expression, which almost coincide in point of time with the awakening of sexual impulses. Such a coinciding is another proof of the value of the latter in regard to all other activities.

After a period of study, battle, and indecision, a romantic period, the second phase of personality begins, the active, catabolic, creative and artistic phase. What was previously indistinct and obscure is exteriorised in language, in work; what was merely a proposition becomes a fact and aspires to that perfection and maturity of action: beauty. *With this latter, by which complete harmony and the exact balance between interiority and exteriority are expressed, this rhythm is closed.*

Thus in the ancient conception of beauty as being the end of all things is contained the psychological truth which I have tried to explain.

It should seem that every broadening of the human mind, as regards its stock of ideas and sentiments, is accomplished with a loss of entirety and fineness of personality, at least for the majority of men. If we represent the course of this by a circle, and if we assume the first half of this circle to indicate the first phase, and the second half the second phase, we can thus represent this fact, recollecting that many men develop to the first half of the curve which every one is destined to reach, but stop at a point more or less distant from their goal. In such a way the line forming the circle would never be closed.

This is the defect of the northern spirit, which so often shows us great personalities, which, however, appear as if they had been interrupted half-way in their course, and remained neither aesthetic nor beautiful: vice versa, the southron almost always comes to the second phase; but the length of his curve, the radius of his circle, is short. The physical and moral precocity of the southron is merely the expression of the facility with which he passes to the second phase.

By means of this conception of the phases of personality and its circular course, it is possible to make a comparison between different individuals, and to express a judgment upon their value. That is to say, in order to determine individual hierarchy, we must know not only the extent of the brutal mental patrimony, but also the capacity for and power of making use of it, that is, of passing to the creative, active, aesthetic phase, which is, if we so desire, what determines the social value of an individual in public consideration and the economical payment for work. To mention an example of judgment in which mistakes are often made, if an Italian twenty years old has given signs of certain positive qualities, whilst a German of the same age is still "in the clouds," we are not therefore at liberty to say at once that the latter is inferior to the former; but, if he is unable to overcome the phase of indeterminism, then we may say so by all means. It is for this reason that it is so difficult to predict what a young man will be able to do, and to make definite statements as to the future of a youth of his actual qualities is the most dangerous exercise of the art of divination: an art, however, never out of favour with mankind.

By far the larger number of human beings do not attain the complete evolution of personality, or at least they only partly attain some particular divisions of it, some activities or tendencies: in some rare, happy moments of their existence; at some fleeting instants which often constitute their single greatness, and of which they have an indelible recollection, whenever a retrograde step does not make them look back upon that moment as a sin and a weakness for which they should feel penitent.

It may be easily inferred from what precedes that enthusiasm for northern nations is somewhat illogical, for, if these nations are promising, and highly promising, they are still merely in process of formation; and it is especially thoughtless to extol certain particular aspects of their social life which are perhaps merely transitory.

Morasso, partly from a reaction to the ideas of Anglo-Saxonising sociologists, and partly by reason of his own tendencies and affinities, apologises for the Latin ideal of sexual dissipation and pleasure. Both, however, are contrary to truth, and contradict both life and the teaching of history.

The integrative phase of work, with its companion phenomena of the spirit of solidarity, a narrow sexual morality, and all the psychological fringe of sentiments and modes of affectiveness, which Ferrero has described as attributes of the German mind, does not represent the ideal perfection of a social group; but represents its youthful stage. The northern sexual morality is subordinate to special circumstances of temperament, of climate, and especially of social development, which are, perhaps, quite transitory. On the other hand, Morasso has not observed that what he says is contradictory, since he has failed to note that sexuality is clearly antisocial, and that this characteristic necessitates a decidedly anti-sexual preparatory phase.

In the nations of the south, the greater amount of sexuality, and the easier and more complete passage to the second phase of personality, correspond to a lesser social necessity, as one's few wants of life can be procured with comparative ease.

In this connection it may be remembered that whole groups of people in Italy live during the summer on a few varieties of fruit. It is exactly on this account, however, that our people have remained in a backward state of civilisation—backward, at least, in comparison with the standard of civilisation that I have endeavoured to set up, which is based upon that of richer and more cultured nations; hence it is not right to accept the Latin ideal without further examination.

The truth which reconciles the two opposite views is not a mean between the two extremes, as is usually lightly said; but is found in a higher point of view which we may sum up as follows :—

The necessity, due to economic conditions, for a social bond has during the course of many centuries given rise to transformations and adaptations of physical and psychical personality, and especially to the inhibition of the amorous action. At the time when society attains its end, which is that of assuring a large production and accumulating a wealth of energy, human personality is reintegrated, and once more assumes those forms that the southern nations show in simpler, and yet more conspicuous, ways; but reintegrated personality, in its aristocratic form, is wider, more spiritual; in a word, more human, on account of the action of the preceding period of sociality.

Let us now see what the mechanism is by which the continual evolution of personality takes place, the passage from one phase to another. The knowledge of the forms of this passage will be most useful in letting us see some psychological characteristics, some aspects proper to those nations of the north which are at present in process of changing, as social groups show phenomena of development similar to that of individuals.

Every fresh addition to personality, it may be said, is acquired pragmatistically; that is, the prevision of the advantages which we may obtain from a particular quality makes us complete the series of acts which are due to that quality, until the quality itself is developed. In other words, it is the process of imitation which is at the base of all moral progress. Imitation is the repetition of certain exterior acts, an almost physical fact, bringing in its train the true and positive addition of moral qualities. Thus, sexual imitation urges a youth to the premature fulfilment of sexual acts before he finds a real enjoyment in them; and this causes a precocious development.

Every more evolved form of personality, even if more narrow and restricted, exercises a more or less strong fascination on other forms that have not attained such a degree of maturity. The seduction of woman on man, naturally making an abstraction of sexual attraction, falls within the scope of this law, for, in every social group, woman has a much smaller personality than man; but one which is more finished and complete.

Whenever two human beings come into the presence of each other, there is a reciprocal appreciation; a reciprocal intuitive judgment, which is in most cases fairly exact, although it is only instinctive, and composed of elements which are not readily susceptible of analysis: this determines the manner of being and acting of the one in the presence of the other, and, in particular, the emotive state of each. Like two bodies that exercise a double attraction on each other, established by ascertained laws, so also the relationship which determines the behaviour and action of each is regulated by a fixed law, which is an attenuated form of the law in force in the animal kingdom. There, almost every meeting of two units is a struggle which leads to a *modus vivendi*, by means of which the victor assures his preponderance, and the loser admits his inferiority. Custom has modified this primitive roughness, suppressed the real fight, and reached the point of being able to arrive immediately, by means of simple *signs*, at the factor which puts an end to the struggle, viz. the acknowledgment of the stronger. The modern equivalents of this struggle remain, and in a look, a smile, a sign of embarrassment, the psychologist can perceive the originary state of things, as it truly exists in essence even now; and from the emotive expression, the looks, and other almost imperceptible signs, he can easily determine in every case on which side the sense of superiority lies.

I do not wish it to be inferred from what I have said that this unequal relationship corresponds to the real value of the individual; on the contrary, through the delicate and complex nature of psychological actions and reactions, through the intervention of a greater emotiveness with either individual, the relationship indicated above may be quite false. But what is of special consequence is, in the first place, that this is not the equivalent of a relationship of simple contiguity or equality;

but of a true and real dynamism between superior and inferior; and in the second place that what determines it is not the sense of the extension of one's own personality, but *the sense of power*, which is exactly parallel to the range attained by the evolution of one's own personality. For this reason, a learned encyclopaedist may be embarrassed in the presence of a most ignorant politician, and the greatest philosopher before the most fatuous coxcomb.

The sense of power, the security of one's self, is the most exact measure of the degree of evolution of personality; but not, it must be said, of the value of personality; and it is the most prominent characteristic of the aristocratic mind. There are men whose very look imposes dread, and who have the gift of overpowering the most intractable: such men are born masters, and are the champions of the species man, the individuals who manifest the boldest forms of human life. The sense of power has an entirely organic basis; it is the knowledge of vigour and purity of descent. It is quite a different thing, however, from the sense of physical force; to which it is related as organic vigour is to muscular vigour, in accordance with what we have said previously. The evolution of the sense of power seems occasionally to run parallel to the development of sexuality and to accompany its oscillations; when it is fully established, however, it is maintained like an autonomous psychological fact. The sense of power is independent of one's social position, of intelligence, of culture; it may often be found even in opposition to all the conditions which determine the social value of a person. The poor and miserable Spaniards have a personal pride and conception of themselves not possessed by even an American millionaire. Individually the sense of power is more developed among the southern peoples, aristocratic by nature, as it is the outcome of happy surroundings and a distinguished race. The sense of power attains a maximum in the life of an individual: among those nations where sociality has made itself felt, the age at which, in general, this maximum is reached is continually tending to become later, in accordance with that aspect of the northern temperament by which all vital phenomena are retarded. Moreover, numerous varieties are seen in the same race.

And now I shall briefly describe the mechanism of the passage from one phase to the other.

Every meeting between two men gives rise to an instantaneous and unconscious comparison, a valuation from which comes an indelible, invincible impression:

The sense of difference. This impression produces in the one who feels himself inferior, whether or not he has a clear knowledge of it, a feeling of grief, of depression, of discouragement. Thus the perception of the distance between his own interior world and the exterior world, between potentiality and power, gives way to scepticism in regard to his own nature. But, as the force of personality increases, the grief felt is exchanged for something more active—hatred and envy. *"Différence engendre haine."*[68] This is one of the greatest psychological discoveries made by Stendhal, for it explains a large number of facts concerning morality and aesthetics which had previously been very unsuccessfully accounted for. If this axiom holds good for two persons who feel themselves to be different from each other, it is even more true for the inferior individual. This hatred, however, may be the principal impulse towards perfection, when one considers the possibility of acquiring the desired quality by effort, as it may eventually imprison the individual in an iron cage, so to speak, where he will pine away as if he were in a perpetual dungeon.

Superior natures pass beyond this; for them this period is only a transient meteor; but for the others it is not so. It is incredible with how much dissimulation, with how many little

[68] "Difference engenders hate"

stratagems, people endeavour to hide this hatred, which is really unconscious admiration.

At this point a large number of examples taken from the psychology of the democratic mind could be brought forward, if it were worth while.

I cannot, however, help saying something in regard to the aversion for art and works of beauty, which is one of the most frequent vices of vulgar minds, when, indeed, a snobbish, artificial, and insincere sentiment of admiration does not take the place of this vice.

An obscure instinct makes certain natures feel a manifestation of superior life in works of art, something nobler and stronger; but their shallow minds prevent them from admitting this, as it would be contrary to the conditions of their being; and then the intelligence seeks the most plausible reasons for diminishing it, drawing the most captious reasonings from morality, politics, and practical life, of which they make a conviction to impose upon themselves first and then on others.

This is the only origin of the fantasies—to tell the truth, not by any means grandiose fantasies—of those who predict a future devoid of art, and with the supremacy of science, or the Utopias of the ideologists who dream of a scientific society where every one will go to bed at the same given hour, to be determined by a committee of hygienists; and will have sexual intercourse to a certain degree, up to a certain fixed standard, and no further.

This special anti-aesthetic crystallisation of ideas may even determine an entire life completely apart from a sentiment of beauty, and may render it incapable of true elevation. And this, I may remark, may often be observed even in persons who are fairly intelligent.

Hatred, then, may sometimes be of value; but it is always a danger. A careful observer will see that it indicates a force which knows itself and desires to increase; but woe to the man who remains in this state! for it is a most unhappy and arid condition, and permits of neither the unconsciousness of humility nor the serene virtue of superiority.

Beyond this, when progress has been made, we have voluntarism, tension, action, which follow the attainment of the thing or quality wished for, the satisfaction of the desire, together with the sense of power and ease.

I have thus decided that the apology for and the philosophy of action are proper to the period of tension and the romantic stage, as also to the latter belong the aristocratic state of mind, the classical spirit, and the "Olympic state" of Goethe.

CHAPTER IX

SOCIAL RHYTHMS

In the fantastic intricacy of social facts, the thinkers of every age have endeavoured to discover fundamental *motifs* and principles, whether with the object of establishing laws of a scientific character, or with the more practical aim of finding a guide for political movements. In this way we have the philosophy, or rather the numerous philosophies, of history, which were the application of metaphysical systems to social facts. Against these, towards the middle of the nineteenth century, arose sociology, which made many promises, but which has not so far been able, and will very probably never be able, to carry any of them out, since it cannot be said, even at the present time, to be in a very active condition.

Sociology was an artificial attempt, even an error, of thought. The defect underlying it is shown by its having a name previously to its having a substance; and, whilst other sciences had a wealth of facts before having a systematisation and a delimitation, sociology was born as an entire scheme in the mind of Comte, a scheme which his followers sought to amplify by their individual researches, but which nevertheless remains little more than a skeleton. In fact, the majority of so-called sociologists only made florid speeches and drew up vast programmes, professions of faith, and anti-religious and anti-metaphysical invectives. Personally, I am more modest, and I do not think that with what follows I am creating a new science; but I seek merely to put forward a few ideas somewhat out of the common.

In the examination of any given social phenomenon—the development of a class, the rise of an industry, or a change in the activity of a people—it often happens, when we think we perceive the characteristic lineaments, the distinguishing features, of a law, that, in studying more minutely the collateral circumstances of the fact, it appears to us significative of another order of generalisations, that is to say, as if bordering upon another law. And then it occurs to us to ask if it is truly possible and scientific to think of inferring absolute principles to which we may adapt social facts. A more mature consideration, however, and a comparison of different data which are historically and geographically more remote, will often cause analogies to flash across our minds, and will enable us to feel deep and unexpected harmonies. We seem to recognise, under the various disguises of notes, variations, and flourishes, the same fundamental theme.

Still further analysing the substance of these analogies, we find it to be purely psychological; we perceive that it is a transformation, a repetition, of our individual psychical experience.

Now I think this is the only way in which we can give a legitimate explanation of social facts; but it must also be recognised that very little has been done in this direction, although a sufficient justification for such a state of things would be the recollection that a clear vision of these facts is very difficult to obtain on account of the disturbing influence of our moral values and of our sentimental life.

In this chapter I shall speak of some phenomena of social dynamics which I shall call "rhythms," and which may be observed either in every society—both in its entirety and in its comparison with others—or in each of the different classes which compose it.

Work, and all the social and moral formations which depend upon it, in so far as they constitute its conditions of existence and all that favour its development, are not, as some hold, fixed and established models for our society, nor the ideal principles which we should propose to ourselves. Whoever holds this opinion will have but a confused conception of social life, and will not understand what is most essential in it;

and he will even less understand the mechanics of those human facts which are found in the aggregate.

Society of a productive and working type is a stage, a kind of passage; but it is not the final point of the cycle which regulates all social developments. Moralists may say that that is unfortunate, that it should not be so, but I am bound not only to state these facts, but to add that a form of society in the absolute and complete sense of the word, such as these people dream of, would be the heaviest blow which could fall upon humanity. In the preceding chapters I have treated this idea at length, so I will not deal further with it here.

I have already remarked in the proper place that society was developed by the weaker individuals' being compelled to emigrate to more barren districts in a northerly direction, and that the necessity for combating contrary and unfavourable influences developed some qualities which enabled them to withstand such influences, and to increase their own numbers. For this reason the northern nations may be considered as reactive, reflexive, and resisting peoples.

These successive emigrations towards the north constitute, in my opinion, the essential condition of all human development, although naturally I should not give an equally uniform importance to this fact in explaining other particular questions concerning different peoples, since social facts arise from so large a number of confused causes that it is difficult to trace with certainty what is really most important in connection with whichever question one may be called upon to treat. Closely connected with this fact, however, and forming a further indubitable proof of it, is the law of the emigration of civilisations towards the north, the great law established by Hegel, which was, in reality, only an empirical fact of observation that was still waiting to be explained. Now it seems to me that, in my hypotheses on the origin of society and the psychological mechanism which controls the relations between workmen and masters, will be found the explanation of this law.

I will not take into account the emigration of past civilisations, that is to say, pre-Hellenic civilisations, for these correspond in part to other types, although they had elements in them common to ours, and although there was always shown in them the fundamental relationship which unites all the possible developments of humanity. If, however, we consider merely the direction taken by European civilisation, we may see that its course was fairly regular: it began in Greek society, and then passed to the Latin world, where it made a long pause: Italy had a new rise of culture, and an event took place through Italy which has very rarely been paralleled in history: that of three great and important forms of civilisation in the same region. From the Italy of the Renaissance the great tide of European civilisation passed onwards to Spain in the reigns of Charles V and of Philip II, from this, by an apparent exception to the rule, to England in the time of Elizabeth, and finally to France in the glorious period of Louis XIV.

It will of course be understood that with the names of these sovereigns I merely indicate the greatest point attained in the time of a particular civilisation, but that periods of splendour likewise preceded and followed.

In this extension the greatest progress of European civilisation followed the direction of the coast-line towards the north. Two factors, therefore, seem to have had some influence in the development of civilisation: the sea, and latitude. Inland countries have never possessed great civilisations, that is, original and creative civilisations.

Austria itself, although it had short intervals of real political greatness, cannot be said to have given rise to an autonomous civilisation, for Austrian culture did not possess any particular distinguishing characteristics, as was the case with that of other nations. Germany long remained—perhaps from its inland and northern position—in a very backward state as regards the development of culture. Sweden and Norway are still so, but these countries are very different from Germany, and it would be a mistake to class them together, for Scandinavians differ greatly from Germans, both as regards psychological characteristics and physical conditions.

The apparent exception to the law of the emigration of civilisations towards the north seen in the early development of England (which preceded that of France by about a century) is explained by its special geographical position, with the presence and prevalence of a factor which, for both economic and physiological progress, is so powerful an element: the sea. Physically the sea is a factor which aids the refinement and strengthening of a race, and socially it is an element of wealth and development. To this fact is due the precedence of England to France in the matter of social evolution, and still more to Germany, which latter is the nation now in process of development, and where the change from one mode of life to another is most observable.

It must further be observed that the German state which has taken the lead, and, let us say, assumed the sovereign authority, viz. Prussia, is the only state of Germany bordering on the sea, and also the most northern. The Prussian character —incisive, energetic, quick to act, with tendencies towards business and diplomacy—is different from that of other Germans, and bears the closest resemblance to the English character.

The reason why the work of later development is entrusted to the more northern peoples may be found in what I have said in regard to the psychology of the northern spirit and the double phase of personality. We must, in other words, remember that principles and laws which are suited to individuals are even more suited to a society, and that the succession of the two phases which we find in individuals is also applicable to the political and social organisation of a group.

Dwelling briefly upon this subject, we may say that, at the present time, and even in Europe itself, we may find examples of the rule of phases.

Thus there are nations almost without a history, although possessing an inner intellectual life and a strict morality. They may, indeed, be preparing a great future for themselves, although they are now in an undeveloped state: consider, for example, the present condition of Finland and Scandinavia. There are others which are passing from one phase to another, Germany being the finest example. Others, again, have reached the height of their splendour, and have now entered upon a period of stagnancy, if not of actual retrogression, England, for instance; others which are almost performing miracles in order to preserve their greatness, but which, in doing so, absorb all their energies in the battle of life, such as France; others which have for some time been in a decadent condition without the hope of early recovery—Spain and Greece; and, finally, others in which we may note the first signs of a new period of youth—Italy.

Every nation, in short, may at a given epoch be found to be in a period of development, at a certain point of the cycle which it must pass through. It is therefore very unwise to make comparisons, and to condemn or exalt this or that nation without taking these circumstances into account.

The burden imposed by the ever-increasing complication of civilisation upon every nation which is entering into life makes us think that the possibility of undertaking such a mission is subject to an important condition. The store of ideas, facts, knowledge, and activities which, in the early ages of mankind, was so small, has gradually attained enormous dimensions.

New peoples who, in the darkness and solitude of the north, in a torpid and prevailingly inactive life which calls for but little exertion of organic energies, have acquired a greater capacity for physical and intellectual work and a greater amount of resistance, are entering on the stage of history to give rise to fresh cycles of wider and still more comprehensive culture, for every period of a particular type utilises all the knowledge of the preceding period.

From one type of civilisation to another there is probably no direct transmission; between Oriental and Hellenic civilisation there was not, for example, much intercourse, and it may even be said that only a few foreign elements entered into the initial formation of the latter, so that Hellenic civilisation is perhaps the most original and uninfluenced that ever existed. Among individuals of the same succession, however, among forms of the same type, there is a continuity of transmission. What follows will be the explanation of the mechanism by which such transmission takes place.

The phenomenon of the double phase which we see in any passage of any type of civilisation may be noticed especially in the history of the revival of Italian culture in the period known as the Renaissance.

The obscure and little-known phase which preceded this glorious period—the luminous and conscient phase of a single rhythm—was the epoch of the tenth, eleventh, and twelfth centuries, which may boast of having prepared the way for the real originality of Italian culture.

The phases which every civilisation passes through are:

(1) The phase of accumulative work, productive activity, a scientific and learned aspect of intellectual life. (This latter proper only to modern civilisation.)

(2) The phase of political expansion, artistic creation, and scientific discovery.

The passage from one phase to another is indicated by a most interesting phenomenon: militarism. I can here only allude to this rather than explain it, for I must settle a few points. During the second phase, the phenomena which characterise the first continue their development, but assume a different aspect corresponding to their mode of being in the second phase. To be more exact, science in this second period assumes a more active and ready aspect, and true discovery and invention attain their maximum; whilst, on the other hand, science in the first period is characterised by description, the development of already established ideas, by delimitation, and exactitude. It may thus be said that, whilst militarism in the first phase has a real *raison d'être*, during the second phase it degenerates into mere parades and reviews.

Our habitual conception of civilisation—which I will call *historical*, because only those groups which are deemed worthy of mention under this conception are taken into consideration by history—comprehends those indications which, in my opinion, characterise the second phase. They are, in fact, the most apparent and exterior phenomena of the life of a group, and form for the most part the matter treated of by history, and there are nations who may now perhaps be preparing within themselves the means for carrying on still further the great progress of civilisation, and who are as yet without a history, although living a profound and energetic life.

When a social group, either by the rigorous discipline of certain individuals in it, or by the apportionment of individual assessments for the public good, or by the limitation and restriction of all free and spontaneous acts, has reached its culminating point, the catabolic or disseminating phase begins, whether in economical production or in thought; and then those magnificent deeds are performed by which history may be said to exist; the usual accompaniments of a rising culture make their appearance, science contributes new inventions and discoveries, art produces its marvellous masterpieces, philosophy puts forth its most daring conceptions; the plant man luxuriates in all his opulence and vigour. It is in this way that we should explain the splendours of the Roman Empire following upon the intellectual darkness and prudent domestic economy of the Republic; the Italian Renaissance after the Middle Ages; and the pompous grandeur of the French monarchy in the reign of Louis XIV, after the feudal barbarism of the Carolingians and the first Capets.

In the periods mentioned men gave themselves up without restraint to voluptuousness and sexual intercourse, and this is, in my opinion, the most significant phenomenon of the phase. It is natural that social lethargy and death should have followed these periods, as it is also logical and inevitable that the phenomena accompanying the greatest amount of power should be interwoven with the first signs of decadence.

We must, however, come to an understanding as to the meaning of this word "decadence." I wish it to be understood as meaning that all the functions of this mechanism which we call "state" are, during these periods, gradually deteriorating and vanishing; but that yet at the same time they help to increase the value of the individual.

It is my belief that, in order that the higher ends of the race may be served—to which the ends of society are subordinate—returns to a primitive state are necessary from time to time, and that sexual license in periods of "decadence" is the expression of this necessity, as the enriching and expansive action of love on the individual helps to revive him to a certain extent, and to withdraw him from the excessive action of sociality, putting him once more in that state of independence and incoercibleness upon which every social formation is based. When, however, large groups or classes in society have abandoned work, that is to say, when primitive conditions have been renewed, those conditions of disproportion between the number of individuals and their food supply are also renewed, to remedy which society came into being: and then follow terrible social crises which completely subvert and overthrow the ancient order of things. Then come periods of scarcity, of anarchy, and of revolts, out of which fresh adaptations to the exigencies of sociality are gradually formed, a work which sometimes occupies many centuries.

The decadence, therefore, of the forms of organisation of a state, enriched, however, with the fresh energies without which no manifestation of life is possible, is hence of real and actual benefit to humanity.

This "return," therefore, which has just been mentioned, is general, and comprehends the progress of civilisation itself; but I shall here have to deal with more restricted themes.

In the advance of civilisation towards the north in a determined type—e.g. that of the so-called western civilisation which began with Hellenic culture—every previous stage was adopted as a model for the following stage, which the latter sometimes consciously, but more often unconsciously, endeavoured to imitate and attain. This imitation thus occurs when the second phase of the cycle has begun, the expansive, artistic, and creative phase. Thus the successive forms of the type have tended to widen and develop what was at first invented by the Greeks.

I must emphasise the fact that every form of civilisation, in its first phase, is entirely original and personal; at most, it elaborates and transforms the elements of moral life common to all humanity, so that to this extent it may be called truly original; but, when it begins to exteriorise and objectise, then begins the *imitation of the forms* of the preceding stage. Thus, Roman culture, holding itself proudly and austerely isolated under the Republic, was influenced by Grecian principles in its imperial development, *Graecia capta ferum victorem cepit:*[69] and both changes were separated by the change of the Republic into a warlike Empire, and by the conquest of almost the whole of the then known world.

After what is now commonly called the long night of the middle ages, which should at all events be called the night full

---

[69] "Captured Greece has conquered its savage captor"

of premonitory dreams, the Italian Renaissance took its principles from the Graeco-Latin world; but especially from the latter.

All the mental and moral refuse saved from the wreck of the empire, with mystico-Christian tendencies, and fresh elements cast by invaders into the crucible of the mediaeval mind, gave rise to the real matter which formed the Italian mind; *but the study and investigation of antiquity gave it its format, and humanism was the outcome of this fact.* The humanist was merely the intermediary between the past and the present; and of the hundreds of humanists who lived in the fourteenth and fifteenth centuries very few could properly be called original thinkers; with their gaze continually fixed on their model, they lost sight of their actual work, and would not deign to occupy their minds with anything but antiquity. On the other hand, the truly great poets and artists of this epoch, even if they did admire the classics, were not oppressed by them; if they accepted the rules laid down in the classics, they did not seek their inspiration in them.

This identical state of things was repeated in Spain, in France, and in England: thus, in their respective periods of transition, Spain more directly imitated Italy; England and France—which, moreover, often exercised a reciprocal influence on one another—imitated Spain and Italy.

This imitation took place, of course, only at the beginning of early periods; it often disappeared, leaving but few traces behind, and gave place to national characteristics, when national personality was firmly established. If France afterwards developed into a great nation as a result of fighting against both England and Spain, that fact does not detract from the force of my argument. English culture, although in early times it was influenced by the culture which immediately preceded—especially in regard to literature—soon shook off these influences; but, notwithstanding this, no modern nation has by its own unaided strength made greater progress than

England towards the forms of antiquity, whence it follows that, of all northern nations, England is the one which to the greatest extent reproduces the purity of the Hellenic type physically, and the Roman character morally.

This passage from one phase to another is generally a process of *southernising*, if the use of such a barbarous word will be permitted me, of quickening the progress of life.

As large social groups pass into the second phase of existence, we may observe two great phenomena which are their principal factors.

The first is a process of refining and reinvigorating the will-power, which loses its characteristics of torpor and passiveness that made it almost an inert force, and which assumes a greater character of personality and incision.

Rest, quiet habits, and regular and methodical work, a patriarchal tenor of life in one's domestic circle, together with, perhaps, a special diet, have the effect of blunting and deadening the organism, although they fortify it and prepare it for great efforts. Nothing in life is lost, and even the idler and the wastrel have a beneficial mission. An increase in the *capacity* of activity, however, is always obtained by tension, a strong preceding stimulation of the nervous system: a very painful effort for a man who is accustomed to a kind of drowsy carelessness. Only by such means is it possible for accumulated energies to show themselves, and it is therefore necessary that *voluntaristic* periods should interpose between the two eras of a society.

We find in these periods an apotheosis of energy and activity, all men seem to try to use them as external agents, and to employ all their own inner forces in the battle of life. Latent and potential energies, gradually accumulated during many centuries, are liberated, and new ways are opened up in the lowest segments of the nervous system. By the continual impulse of the will-power, the physiognomy itself, the anthropological type, becomes modified, and its coarse, heavy lines are rendered more incisive and expressive. Thus the English countenance, originally more like the German, has in the female sex assumed an aspect of beauty and grace, and in the male sex an aspect of vigour and strength, which makes this nation one of the most superior types of northern races.

The second general process of transformation is the growing desire for amorous pleasure. This may, to some, seem surprising; but its truth is undeniable if we consider the history of periods of great culture. The physiological cause of the effect of such pleasure on physical constitution and on character has already been explained at length in an earlier chapter, and I may therefore be excused from once more dealing with the matter. This influence may be applied here on a larger scale.

When what I have already said is borne in mind, one may conceive the immense value of the social phenomenon in question, and how the pursuit of voluptuousness may be an element of progress, irrespective of what certain catholicising moralists may declare to the contrary.

The centralisation of individuals in great cities is the most efficacious means of carrying out both these processes, because the proximity of so many individuals incites, kindles, and sharpens competition and develops the will; and, again, in large cities facilities and opportunities for meetings of the sexes are numerous.

In this respect even modern Germany provides both a noteworthy example and a certain proof. Before speaking of this specially, however, we had better take a comprehensive look at some aspects of modern German life, for Germany is the finest ground for observation that can well be imagined, because she is now in a period of transition, and also because states of passage are, in biology and psychology, most interesting.

I have already had occasion to mention the particular qualities which are characteristic of the northern mind in its general tendency, but even with these we have seen only one side of its character, the traditional side of Germanic thought, and it would be a great mistake to think that there was nothing more to take into consideration.

The German mind is proteiform, and full of snares, said Nietzsche, and he knew his countrymen; it is susceptible of infinite development. We must therefore see another part of it, what I should call its dawning part, which has already been faintly perceived and is full of promise: we must, in a word, see what I may be permitted to call its dynamic side.

This is the side which Ferrero, who has so justly appreciated the first, has not observed: overcome, perhaps, by his theoretical point of view, and by his politico-sentimental prejudices.

This aspect of the German mind is, however, very important, for it is the repetition of a fundamental *motif* which was manifested in the evolution of possibly every people, and which may serve to make us understand certain states that, being merely transitory and sensitive, were not deemed of sufficient importance to be taken into consideration by historians.

In Germany, the development of the learned, assimilative period, initiated by Winckelmann, Lessing, and Müller, has not yet been completed, and even now we can scarcely perceive the signs of something new, original, and creative. The form of life of German society is even at the present day scientific: I mean that the predominating aspect in its intellectual life is science; it is, however, in a preparatory, transitory, and absolutely indefinite state. The proofs of this may be seen in the awakening of certain forms of activity which were almost unknown in the Germany of fifty years ago. German culture is now on the point of entering upon its second phase.

Its militarism, its bold school of energy and will, are symptoms of this. Centuries of meditation and silence have given the German people the benefit of an enormous store of latent energies which are now shown in the organisation of the Government services, industrial production, and scientific activity. The nation, after having overcome immense difficulties, has attained physical well-being, and with this its strength and desires are increasing, as is also the wish to preserve its new acquisitions.

An individual who improves in health feels the force of his passions increasing, and likewise the desire to preserve his own ease and comfort, even to the disadvantage of others, as he also feels the necessity for expansion and development. This is the physiological and psychological truth which is at the basis of the phenomenon of militarism, a truth which all the anti-militant writers do not consider, for certain sociologists are in essence merely good metaphysicians à la J. J. Rousseau, who in their fine reasonings do not treat man as he actually is, but as he ought to be according to them, or as what they imagine him to be.

It must be remembered that there is nothing in the character of modern Germans resembling the warlike spirit of the ancient Germans, the Germans of Arminius who defeated Varus; although, indeed, the warlike spirit of the ancient Germans did not partake of the nature of violence and ferocity which we may observe in truly warlike races; in this regard, at any rate, modern Germans are very far removed from their ancestors, to such an extent that the schools of art and poetry which sought to bring back those memories met with scant sympathy on the part of the public, and no followers tried to continue their efforts.

The Germans, then, are not a warlike nation, and yet they are the premier military people of modern times. How does this come about? Ferrero holds that it was Bismarck who, violating the Prussian nature, first made Germany a military nation. It must, however, be recognised that Prussia, even without Bismarck, would always have been the most military nation of Germany, and it seems to me further that Bismarck, with all his strength and exotism, to use Ferrero's word, would never have been able to make a nation of soldiers out of a nation of poltroons. Words are merely words, and if sometimes one may have the appearance of demonstrating deeds with them, the paradox soon becomes evident, at least to the man who thinks with his own brain. The truth is that Prussia is now the most military nation because it was formerly the most advanced intellectual nation, and, after having given to Germany and to the world its greatest thinkers, it had in the course of things to pass from thoughts to acts.

Militarism is the first step towards a wider field of action and a more noble life, for the first necessity of the man who has reached a higher stage of existence is to defend himself from the greed of others, a necessity which brings with it one's growth and expansion at the cost of others.

Militarism is a phenomenon of growth ; it is manifested (at least in its spontaneous and natural form, not in its imported form) when wealth and general comfort have become more widespread and have strengthened the average personality, making it in some ways more rapacious and more disposed to enter into action: it is likewise produced by the attitude of reaction and defence which must be assumed by a body of men who have become wealthy by means of their own work, if they do not wish their fortunes to be the booty of others. The former motive especially animates the higher classes, and is the mental outlook of those who command; the latter sways the lower and working classes, who live in a more restricted morality, and is the mental outlook of subordinates and of those who obey.

For the rest, the existence of a vigorous and sane militarism is based on this different mental state of superiors and inferiors. The military spirit is made up of two parts, one being that sense of duty and sacrifice, that deep regard for discipline, solidarity, and especially of subordination, which are the fruits of social and democratic development; the other being that spirit of mastery which is at the same time a disposition to command, the will to power, and the sure knowledge of one's own responsibility; and we may add that the spirit of mastery should be found only in the few men who guide the masses, for whom is reserved the heritage of blind obedience. The greatest real distinction between these two tendencies, which must, however, be unknown to the mass of subordinates, constitutes the strength of the armies of the younger nations, such as Germany, for example, or even to a greater extent Russia.

Indeed, the absolute verification by Prussian militarism of these opposite conditions is in perfect agreement with what may be observed in the German nation considered as a whole, where complete, or almost complete, maturity of the superior classes corresponds to a kind of psychological childishness among the masses.

The military spirit, however, as it is based upon such an insecure foundation, is not a lasting factor, however little the proportion of the ingredients may be changed. Thus, for example, given the present historical conditions, a strong military system in the nations of the south is perhaps impossible, for these nations are too naturally and instinctively individualistic. As for us Italians, we all feel ourselves to be rulers, and those ties between man and man which we call solidarity are not very strong. Equally impossible, at least up to the present, but for contrary reasons, is the existence of militarism among the nations of the extreme north, among the Scandinavians, for example, where the gregarious and civil element is strong, but where the directive, active, and aristocratic element is wanting. I am not, however, one of those who believe in an everlasting idyllic civilisation in Scandinavia, or in the somewhat overpraised agreeableness of its customs. Even Germany, less than a century and a half ago, was a peaceful nation, segregated from international life; yet she has now become a most formidable power. To conclude, we must beware of predictions based upon an obvious, common reasoning, that what has been, is now, and always will be the same: a syllogism which greatly pleases a few simple-minded sociologists.

No matter what may be said to the contrary, militarism has morally and physically been of immense benefit to Germany. Under its influence the almost inert, vacillating, and weak German will has been strengthened and rendered more rapid and laborious, changing in its turn the slow, torpid organism of the German people.

The stiffness and automatism of the Prussian soldier, so often joked at, especially by the French, should really be highly esteemed, for this apparent stiffness is, as it were, an effort to overcome a certain coarseness and *gaucherie* peculiar to races just entering into a period of culture.

When an individual of the Latin races sees for the first time a parade of German soldiers, or hears for the first time a body of German troops passing through a street—I say "hears," for the good reason that the sound made by the regular marching is more noticeable to the ear than the troops themselves are to the eye—he is certainly very much surprised, and almost inclined to laugh; but, if he is in the habit of reflecting, he will remain in a meditative mood when he thinks of what all this signifies, and he will end by admiring the more he understands. Then he will no longer imagine that he sees a ridiculous sight; but he will be astonished at such a continued, bold effort of a race to conquer its own nature and to rise out of itself. He will observe that this military demeanour tends to give a certain nobleness of form to a body not too well favoured by nature in this respect, and, although the attempt is just at present very far from attaining its end, it cannot but be recognised that some result has been achieved.

On New Year's Day, 1906, I saw at the Brandenburg Gate in Berlin a curious sight, which appeared to me to be a confirmation of what I had been thinking in my psychological peregrinations through the capital of Germany. The reader need not expect to hear of an adventure: it is only a simple matter.

On that day all the ambassadors and princes had come to pay an official visit to the Emperor, and to wish him the compliments of the season. At the Brandenburg Gate was stationed a little picket of troops, whose duty was to salute the nobles, high officials, and other functionaries. The usually quiet and expressionless eye of the Prussian soldier who happened to be acting as sentinel at the moment I passed seemed to be lighted up as by a flame. His head continually turning from one side to the other to perceive from either entrance of the monumental gate, and from the opposite side of *Unter den Linden,* the arrival of someone in uniform; his arm bent nervously, his hand gripping the butt-end of his rifle, all showed the great exteriorising effort which his decidedly simple task made him employ.

Need I say that this little ingenuous episode made a deep impression on me, standing there as a single discreet spectator? Those who are aware that little things often say more than great things will understand what I thought at that moment: militarism is not the morbid, atavic phenomenon it is generally said to be; it is a normal and healthy phenomenon. All ideologists who have thought differently have not been able to think in a general way, that is to say, they have not been able to make abstractions beyond themselves, which is the first canon of rigorous thought.

What is meant by saying that hard military discipline, the sacrifice of one's personality and criticism, is a terrible state of slavery for those whose life is bound up in thought and intellectual activity? It is right to say that the higher intellects are oppressed by military discipline; but in the first place not all those who exercise their brains more than their muscles are of strong intelligence, and, in the second place, if these latter are injured by such discipline, that is the fault of the spirit of equality which desires for all the same duties and the same importance, and not of military institutions.

The careful inquirer will observe that, undoubtedly connected with what precedes, is one of the most curious facts of modern Germany, and that is the enormous number of books, pamphlets, and reprints, the aim of which is to convert the heavy doctrinal wisdom of classical German science into distinct and clear formulas. We could draw up long catalogues, some of them very curious, of books with titles like the following: "What we should know of Geology," "How should I learn Languages?" "The Elements of Astronomy," and so on.

This practical preoccupation with knowledge is, to tell the truth, an English and American importation; but it is on this account all the more significant; and there is also some signification attached to the enormous diffusion of and the favour extended to a certain kind of literature which teaches how to "Increase One's Own Mental Output," "How to Become Energetic," "How to Strengthen the Memory," "How to Increase the Will-Power," "How to Attain Success," etc.

Whoever has recently travelled through Germany, or has even had dealings with Germans of the more active classes, will have noticed that one word is always on the lips of modern Germans on every occasion and at every moment, "Praktisch!" "Praktisch!" "Praktisch!" ("Practical!" "Practical!" "Practical!"), as if by their continual use of this word they would persuade themselves and others that they were no longer the nation of theoretical speculation and infinite reasonings.

The immense attraction that past civilisations, the two classical cultures in particular, undoubtedly have for the German mind, which enables Germany to boast that she has produced the best connoisseurs in this regard, arises from her profound necessity for models, for *exteriorisings*.

I myself do not doubt this; and I believe in addition that by this need, which corresponds to the deficiency of some qualities, a great many of her sympathies and antipathies may be explained.

Mignon,[70] as well as being the Italian girl who unconsciously wishes for her unknown fatherland, is the symbol of the German mind, anxiously longing for light, for the sun, for the free and serene forms of the south; she is the symbol of the German mind, embarrassed and grave, which aspires to an ideal of freedom, grace, and elegance; she is the key to the secret of the melancholy peculiar to the northern mind, which feels that it has been exiled, as it were, for many centuries.

Thus the painful and obscure feeling of its want of form and elegance is the real cause of the hatred and the antipathies of the German mind.

Why does the German so cordially hate the Frenchman, and, even more, the Englishman, while he is rather sympathetic towards the Italian? It is because the Italian is entirely out of reach of any German imitation; the Italian is like a model for the German; an ideal so far off that he cannot be envied, whilst a secret instinct assures the German of his greater affinity to the Frenchman or the Englishman, who, however, are much further advanced than he in the direction he is following, and who are therefore all the more hateful to him. Then, again, the poverty of the Italian may be balanced against a few of his superiorities, which, however, are found in Englishmen and Frenchmen also, although in a smaller measure, and which are in them accompanied with some qualities possessed by the German also.

We have seen that the conscious or unconscious imitation of the forms of the preceding state of culture is the first step by which every fresh state makes its presence felt in history. This imitation is clearly visible in present-day Germany,

---

[70] A character from Goethe's *Wilhelm Meister's Apprenticeship*, who inspired many subsequent works about her.

especially in regard to English and American models, and even French forms up to a certain point, although Germans naturally do not care to have this pointed out.

For the rest, conscious or unconscious imitation is quite a natural process. We cannot reasonably accuse a nation of altering its nature when it wishes to imitate another, even in some harmful respect. Imitation is the process by which all social advancements take place in customs, habits, thought, and feeling.

The first exterior imitation takes place in the interior of the group itself. In other words, aristocracies have a progressive function for every society: they are the first to realise the forms of life which will afterwards be adopted, through successive infiltrations, by the entire social group. It is noteworthy that this law holds good even for the physical type, the modification of which is begun in the aristocracy. It may easily be believed that this happens by an intermixture of blood, which is easier in the aristocratic classes than in others; but, if this method of transformation exists, and if it is simpler and more direct, that does not necessarily weaken the argument in favour of a slower action proper to one's self.

Madame de Staël is wrong in thinking that the imitation of one nation by another is a grave error on the part of the latter. It is certain that imitation is the first step towards attaining an individual strength and arriving at originality. The imitation of forms of culture is a natural fact of which hundreds of examples could be adduced, and as such *per se* it is neither good nor bad.

To confine our attention to Germany still, we see that this country, previously to having a really national literature, had to pass through a period of coarse and tedious French imitation, represented by Hagedorn and Weiss, for example, and another period, immediately following, of English imitation. We may even add that this last fact, if it seemed a retrogression in view of the object aimed at by writers of the time—classical French art—was really an approach to what they could obtain by their own genius.

Between imitation and originality there are all the other stages of progress, and if the first imitative attempts always show traces of the borrowed forms—awkwardness and discordance—we cannot, on the other hand, omit mentioning that, in more original work, no imitation whatever is to be seen. And this is due to the fact that a real originality does not exist; it is perhaps a revival of older forms, and a widening and development of their substance, rather than a creation *ex novo*.

As the first attempts to imitate the French failed in literature, they failed also in politics, and all the genius of Frederick the Great was not equal to the task of introducing French culture into Germany, a culture which was the final product in the life of a race with a long history.

It must also be recognised, however, that all the designs of Frederick the Great were realised in less than a century after his death.

To make Prussia a military state; to put her at the head of Germany; to make the German nation active rather than speculative; to make Berlin a capital similar to Paris: all that this monarch with so much genius thought out has been realised, and although Germans have still but scant sympathy for the sceptical and smiling ruler, artist, and warrior, he still remains the greatest man, and the man with the keenest insight, whom Germany ever produced.

As we have already said, the deficiency of the German psyche for the sense of form is shown in the poverty of their productions in painting and sculpture as compared with their abundant literary and musical production. Even here, however, we see indubitable signs of a change, and modern Germany may boast of having a school of painters of real value, and of great masters such as Böcklin and Lenbach.[71] The flourishing

---

[71] Arnold Böcklin (who was actually Swiss) and Franz von Lenbach

condition of arts, and especially of the plastic arts, is the highest form in which the perfection of a culture is observed, and it is the expression of its complete maturity as compared with an ideal of development which it is not easy, or perhaps still premature, to decide; but which may nevertheless be perceived. The plastic arts and the art of design should not be overlooked, as they are by historians and sociologists, in judging the merits of any given social form, that is to say, in fixing the stage of evolution which has been attained.

The importance of this historical element results from two series of reasons: from intrinsic reasons, those which depend upon the *vital signification* of the plastic arts, and from extrinsic reasons, from the only conditions in which their development is possible, that is, from their being able to spring up only in societies with large cities, where wealth and power are developed in a splendid and luxurious life. The development of the plastic arts is as it were the integration, the extreme perfection and exteriorising of a culture, and in its methods it follows a course parallel to that of other social phenomena.

Modern Germany, with the enormous and progressive increase of Berlin, has set out upon this road. In Berlin flourishes all this work of fermentation and refinement. There the German mind is being elaborated and transformed, assuming a more nervous and free-and-easy character. In a word, Berlin, a proof of the view of the civilising action of voluptuousness which I have upheld, is becoming a city of pleasure.

Of course, German corruption is still in its infancy; it is somewhat vulgar and coarse, and, if it often has the appearance of brutality, it is really only ingenuous and presumptuous. It rather manifests a desire to show itself for the sake of effect than of actual vice; and it still partakes too much of the nature of intention and artifice to be elegant. Voluptuousness, however, is a school in which scholars soon reach perfection, and it is a teaching which easily spreads; and it may safely be prophesied that Berlin will soon become a city of pleasure, as Paris and Vienna are at present.

Would it be right to prophesy anything else for Germany in wider spheres? There are many facts which would authorise my doing so, nor is the temptation wanting, for the making of forecasts is something that most people eagerly desire to hear. But I have mentioned Germany here merely as an example, as the nation in which a little known social process may be easily observed; and, again, many others have already drawn sketches of its future, and I should gain but little credit by adding yet another to the number.

Again, every brilliant prophecy is set under the Damocles' sword of a probable supposition: that the jealousy of some stronger nation, which perceives its own power being undermined, and its supremacy threatened, will with a supreme effort retard or altogether annihilate the rise of Germany.

I nevertheless think that the aim of this book may be served by the making of a few partial conjectures.

The Germans seem to have the manner of saying: "Laugh at us, make fun of us, of our coarseness and barbarism: you will not disturb us, and we will not hurry on your account, for that would be sacrificing the benefits of our past experience and compromising our future work; but we cherish the unshaken hope that we shall yet attain a greatness, a beauty, far vaster and more glorious than any you have hitherto conceived!" This inmost conviction is at the bottom of the so-called German cordiality. And it does not seem that they are wrong. Other writers have referred to the economic and political expansion of Germany. The supremacy of her science for more than a century is known to everyone, and I need not carry coals to Newcastle. Something which I think more worthy of being mentioned, however, is that I believe we can observe signs of a change in the nature of German intellectuality.

Up to the present, German science, in harmony with the spirit of the people, has been restricted to establishing, completing, developing, perfecting; it has not discovered or invented anything very noteworthy: its gigantic bulk may deceive one as to its real value; but for the man whose work lies in the consideration of ideas it is not difficult to see that the *beginnings*, the *germs*, of modern science are of French, Italian, or English origin. Whilst, however, French, Italian, and English hands have scattered the seeds on the earth, the guardian angel who watched over them, watered them, and beheld them grow, is German. Thus the scientists of most extraordinary genius to whom Germany has given birth cannot be said to have opened up new paths, or disclosed new points of view; in a word, they cannot be called true creators.

It seems to me, however, that the nature, I might almost say the species, of the German mind is changing. A man of infinite genius stands on the threshold of the future of German science—Hermann Helmholtz.[72] This name—the name, perhaps, of the greatest of scientific creators—foreshadows a time when knowledge, having become more active, yet stronger, will have attained the period of its splendid flourishing in the invention of new principles susceptible of wide application and vast development. This period will perhaps witness the predominance of Germanic art, which is at present little more than in its infancy, and perhaps also the greatest expansion of German political power.

But ... I have just caught myself in the act of having recourse to the Sibylline art, so I will stop.

---

[72] Hermann von Helmholtz (1821-1894) was a German physicist, physician and philosopher of science who made significant contributions in several different fields. In his work on thermodynamics and muscle metabolism he argued against some of the then-prevailing vitalist theories of biology as being anti-scientific.

Let us now consider another series of social rhythms which we may call internal, for they belong, properly speaking, to the classes which compose a society itself.

The difference between the classes is of a physiological, constitutional, and nutritive kind; and a moral difference of ideas, sentiments, and knowledge appears above this, as a product of it, or a superstratification, contrarily to what has been affirmed by the ideologists of a social Utopia. We cannot, however, hold with other writers that these are true anthropological differences, differences of race and origin, although we do not deny that this may be so in some cases.

The directing and dominating classes endeavour to keep down all higher and exceptional individualities which may rise up and seem dangerous to their security, or which even seem to be new competitors. Thus, all noble individualities, aristocratic natures in the sense that I have previously given to the word, which spring up here and there, even among the lower classes, must overcome a strong resistance before making themselves felt. This opposition is manifested in many ways: politically, economically, morally; but, above all, physiologically.

A poor and deficient allowance of food, that is to say a dynamogenic supply, while it makes people all the more willing to submit to the yoke of servile labour and organic impoverishment, is likewise an instrument of political oppression, for weak and badly fed individuals are far from desiring liberty and independence, or, if they do sometimes feel such a desire, they do not possess the intellectual power of discovering what means they should employ to attain their object.

A revolt is therefore very often the only way to wealth and comfort for the downtrodden, and it is the sole act of weak and subordinate individuals to which a high value can be attached. It is almost always the last desperate indication of a despairing vitality; but it sometimes also denotes a rising vitality. The fascination which this word exercises on every free spirit, that beautiful and attractive something which it possesses in spite of the contrary suggestions of the morality of the governing classes, is to be attributed to its worth, its sense of something animal and vital which is newly affirmed: for everything vital, strong, and violent has, as we have said, a profound significance for the race, a significance, the indication of which is aesthetic impression, and the seal of which is beauty.

By rigorous social discipline, and by the slowly accumulative influence of work, which, if it does not lead to wealth, fatally deteriorates one's personality, certain groups in a society succeed in reviving and reinvigorating themselves. The conditions which make society possible—the respect for mutual bonds, obedience to moral and positive laws, and especially the partial sexual renunciation which is the nucleus of every sacrifice imposed on the individual—are all based upon a general diminution in the social body of active and aggressive qualities, a diminution which, translated into physiological terminology, signifies a reduction in animal vigour, accompanied perhaps with a diminution in sexuality. When, however, a preceding assimilative period has accumulated a certain power in a group, there comes a moment when personality is reintegrated, reinforced, and completed, and a fresh supply of blood seems to revive the old desire, and with the aristocratic state of mind the ancient psychological animal form is once more established.

Indeed, all great historical phenomena of the rise of classes are merely movements of collective transformation of character and states of mind, beneath which lie physiological changes.

The great historical phenomena of the rise of ecclesiastical power, apart from military power, the formation of the middle class as a directing influence, and the modern proletarian movement, all indicate that ever-increasing groups of human beings who have arisen from an inferior state, and on whom centuries of coercion have impressed the stamp of a deformed psychological and physical structure, are gradually regenerating themselves and coming nearer to the aristocratic state of mind.

Yes! The modern proletarian movement is a movement of which the final aim is the attainment of that perfect state which I call aristocratic—of course, within the limits permitted by the large number of its followers, and by the means at the disposal of present-day culture. This will unwillingly be recognised by those who are taking part in the movement, and who are stimulated in their apostolic and militant activity by what they call their likes or dislikes, which a psychologist, however, must call their envies and cupidities. They do not see that in the contempt and hatred with which they cover the governing classes there is contained merely the desire to resemble them in some way; that their hatred is only longing, and their contempt unconscious admiration. This is the illusion of all those natures which are backward and ill developed, but not without a certain strength when out of the presence of a superior nature.

I must not, however, put forward illusions in my turn, and become the sport of a few words. We must not, I mean, consider hatred from a moral point of view, although it is certainly a force of great importance.

Hatred is for the individual, whatever may be said to the contrary, a necessary state of passage, and it was and is the state of mind of all rising classes: as it is also the psychological state of mind of contemporary socialism. For this reason some noble minds of delicate moral sensitiveness deprecate this feature of the socialistic movement and greatly dislike it.

On reflection it will be seen that this state is purely transitory, the residue, so to speak, of a servile mind, which will gradually disappear. With the victory and acquisition of power, if socialism ever secures it, this state of mind I have mentioned will lose many of the traces which betray its origin, in the same way as the richer members of the modern middle classes continue more and more to resemble born aristocrats.

The inherent fact, then, which forms the rhythm of individual personality, takes place within the group itself through entire groups composing it: the return to primitive forms of being, the reapproach to the eternal type of the race; to the aristocratic state, liberty, and primitive beauty.

The individualistic and aristocratic mind of the south, the animal man in all his pride, is the eternal prototype to which social necessity itself inclines, and which it rhythmically renews in all its phenomena, from the individual to the class; and it even seems that *the maintaining of the race itself in the form of existence represented by society—a form which tends to deteriorate it—is possible only by means of similar periodical returns to unrestrained strength and life.* Love is thus the primal virtue, the virtue of virtues, the clear eternal fountain in which humanity finds fresh energies that, in society, are wasted, or rather changed into means of production.

I should incidentally like to remark that my comparisons of the developments of societies with individual evolution is in no way connected with the organic theory of society; my conception is genetic and dynamic, and does not take into account the correlation of different functions, which latter is a static conception.

The primitive relationships between masters and servants were those which necessitated muscular and brute force, and violent physical superiority, for it was precisely by their physical supremacy and warlike gifts that aristocrats arose. The share of intelligence in mastering men began with the rise to power of the clergy. It may even be said that the clergy were the first thinkers, and as such were at first reviled by the strong men and the warriors: we have for the rest seen what the origin of human intelligence was, and how it was necessary that it should first take root among the weaker men. The clergy, however, with their cunning, their indirect and equivocal manners, and the seduction of their spirituality, knew how to possess themselves of power as well as the fierce aristocrats, by whom, although at first looked upon with suspicion, they were at length considered almost as equals.

The succession of these stages appears to be an inherent rhythm in human society, and the effect of laws which are found to be identically the same almost everywhere, for we observe the same phenomena in the east, and particularly in India. Thus Indian tradition speaks of a terrible battle which took place between the Brahmans—the higher orders of the clergy—and the ancient race of warriors, although both classes sprang from the nation of Aryan conquerors which descended into India and there founded their civilisation. What is even more noteworthy is that this battle between the religious and aristocratic classes ended in the defeat, even in the annihilation, of the latter; but after a short time the priests saw they had committed a grave error, and were compelled to gather together bastard lines of the ancient stock to save Indian society from utter dissolution.

It will thus be seen that the rise of the middle class, as the most intelligent and active section of the working classes, is not by any means a phenomenon of modern times. It is shown, for example, in the history of free Italian communities—a history which it would be very desirable for sociologists to know and to study, recognising at the same time the mind and the passions of the middle ages.

Though the *bourgeoisie* of past ages was based on manufacturing industry, out of which arose the guilds of the so-called *arts*, this does not necessarily imply that it differed from the middle class of the present time, which has sprung from mechanical industrialism; for the production of some form of merchandise is the essential fact which characterises the class, and which shapes its existence.

The exciting, belligerent history of our Italian communities would perhaps make certain idyllic sociologists see to what extent the nature of man essentially repeats itself, even after the lapse of centuries of modern culture, and might convince them of a truth which they do not apparently wish to comprehend, namely:

The period of wars and battles is fortunately not yet at an end; and I say fortunately because, to judge from all appearances, such an end would also mean the end of all progress.

Egoistical motives (personal aspirations towards comfort; the liberation of the individual) are not very evident in socialism; but they exist, and they are the true causes of the movement. The necessity for contingent and opportunistic union (for the single individuals, being at the lowest extreme of the social scale, count for nothing) conceals the true causes of the movement, and gives it an entirely false stamp of altruism and solidarity. I admit that the social spirit has a certain reality, which general strikes, subscriptions to funds, and other generous acts, not at all rare, indubitably show; but the victorious affirmation of the proletariat will be the indication of the complete disappearance of that altruistic spirit, of which, moreover, sociologists are astonishingly far too proud. There will shortly happen what happened to Christianity, which, from its heroic period, specially marked by the magnificent historical phenomenon of martyrology, passed on to pagan and domineering Catholicism.

Every party, every class, in its period of propaganda and conquest, disguises its real aims in ideal motives, which, upon attaining power, it disowns. Mind, I do not say that such a deception is intentional, for then it would be a hypocrisy, and historical hypocrisies, whatever politicians may say, do not exist. It is in the very nature of things that when an individual or a group passes from what I call a democratic state of mind to an aristocratic state of mind, he, or it, respectively denies those principles which he at first affirmed or denied. This results from changed conditions.

It often even happens that the necessity for establishing one's self firmly in a new position makes one go too far in the opposite direction. The first act of a new power is always to declare itself distinct and separate from the people it has left behind. This is how the supposed betrayal of the proletarians by the middle class in 1789 is justified, as the former had fought with, and for, the latter against the Government.

Every new class which attains mastery brings with it a fresh store of ideas, principles, and rules, by means of which it may be said that more justice is done on earth. From the most manifest and scandalous injustice we pass to more mitigated forms of it; it should even seem that the differences between the various classes in society, so great in olden times (we may recall the distance which even at present separates a king from a slave in the pompous and luxurious civilisations of the east), are really lessened in modern times. This double process, by which masses of people tend to raise themselves, whilst the privileges of aristocrats are diminishing, I should call the phenomenon of the aristocratisation of democracies, and the democratisation of aristocracies.

This convergent movement is perhaps the feature which permits a society to be called vital, whilst in the motionless and decadent societies of the east there is either no movement at all or else a divergent movement, that is to say, one which increases the distances between classes instead of lessening it. We may recollect the example of India, where this movement was so strong as to cause, on one hand, the brutalising and the utmost physiological misery of the individual through excess of subjection, and, on the other hand, the degeneration of the aristocratic classes through debauchery and lewdness.

In conclusion, the democratic and the aristocratic spirits are, so far as society is concerned, face to face; philosophically considered, they are in the relative positions of idealism and realism.

The political forms of a human group seem continually to oscillate from one state of mind to the other, as also in philosophy and science these two eternal and opposite currents of thought seem to be predominant in turn, the ultimate victory never resting with either.

Human progress is a continual expansion and amelioration, a continual integration, which is gradually perfected by the light of one or other of these principles, without life itself saying that either is correct.

CHAPTER X

THE CREATION OF GENIUS

Work, as we have seen, while on one hand it deforms and impoverishes the human frame, renders it monotonous, reduces it to the lower level of a pure mechanism, and debases its energies, is on the other hand a process of assimilation and augmentation, since every human phenomenon may be said to oscillate between two opposite poles, and may therefore be regarded from two opposite points of view. Whatever advantage or economic wealth accrues from work in general must be considered as an increase in personality; and our own feelings, in fact, make us look upon the wealth which we possess by reason of our activity as an increase in the space occupied, so to speak, by our *ego*. Intellectual work, then, will bring us an interior mental increase, derived from knowledge, as well as an exterior increase.

To explain this antinomy, we must conceive of work as having the effect of setting in one single direction those energies which are now spread over a wide area and hence of making a man more powerful in this one direction; but with the fatal result of making him less and less capable of living apart. Even this, however, happens only when the wealth he acquires by means of work is more than what he spends upon the mere necessaries of life; and we must add that this is something which does not very often take place.

This twofold characteristic, lowering personality and yet partaking of an accumulative nature, is especially evident in science. Renan held that science was an aristocratic production; against this view Nietzsche, with more acuteness, affirmed its democratic nature. We have innumerable proofs that this latter opinion is nearer the truth, not the least important being the fact that science was never in a more flourishing condition than in our present civilisation of sociality and work. It is well known that the socialistic Utopia, which is the latest expression of the democratic mind, is greatly to the fore in modern science with its dreams of social reconstruction, and has a certain antipathy for art, which is esteemed and loved only by a few of the more intelligent socialists. I do not mean by this that there is no place in modern science for superior and noble minds; for, indeed, the latter are the truly great scientists, that is to say, those who exercise a creative faculty in science.

I think, however, that if it is permissible for low and humble men to enter the realms of science, it is otherwise so far as the world of art is concerned. Every man of good will, without great intelligence, may be of use in the first-mentioned, if he will only be content to perform tasks which, though humble, may be very necessary; but in art good will alone is not enough. True, the proving of a little fact, the description and estimation of the circumstances which surround it, even the discovery of a little truth, may be accomplished by a little man; but a little man can never create even the littlest *beauty*, for the good reason ... that *beauty* cannot be qualified by such an adjective, and that to paint a little portrait such as one of Memling's, or to cover an immense canvas with the colours which form Tintoretto's "Paradise," one must have an equal *power*: and this, at any rate, is not found in a little man!

It is for this reason that a great artist can do without the work of mediocre and small men, who, indeed, are outside of the province of true art, whilst the greatest scientist is the very man to make use of the contributions of others in order to discover newer and wider truths.

Science thus differs from art (I do not now speak of philosophy, for I hold personal views on this subject which I will put forth in another place), and the scientist from the artist, inasmuch as while the first may—and does for the most part—remain for some time in the state of a mere labourer, manual worker, and accumulator of materials, and finally furnishes a crude work, the artist, although necessarily having to pass through the state of technical assimilation, must necessarily ascend above it, otherwise he would not be an artist. The well-known etymology of the word poet—maker, creator—well signifies the aristocratic, personal, and synthetic activity of the artist. The poet, even the novelist, will give the clearest answers to our inquiries, for it is in the mind and work of the literary creator that there is the greatest degree of knowledge, and that the most obscure phenomena of creative activity are illuminated with the brightest light.

As the different development of various branches of literature in historical succession during a period of civilisation is a most important element in enabling us to understand the peculiar character of its literary thought—although *the form of such a succession, being generally able to appear well defined and fixed, almost constitutes a law of thought;* as, in more elevated spheres, analogous observations may be made in regard to the development of particular arts, it follows that we must, from a very high standpoint, regard the relationship between art and science as being subject to a certain law.

The problem of this relationship has always attracted the minds of thinkers, and has occupied the attention of the greatest intellects. The whole life of Leonardo da Vinci was a continual duel between the two fundamental tendencies of thought, and his mind must certainly have been stimulated in endeavouring to grasp the relationship between the two. From the time of this fascinating mind, which, like a Sphinx full of mysterious charms, soars above our mind, eager for knowledge and quick to comprehend, down to the present day, this problem has always been under consideration by human thought.

Art is, in general, harbingering, creative, intuitive. It may be said that the first knowledge of every truth is perceived by art, and is on account of its very greatness difficult of interpretation, dazzling, fleeting, as rapid in its movements as light itself, and, like light, without form and void. The developing process of thought consists in the continued transposition of truths that are scarcely conceived by the creative imagination in forms which are clearer and hence less artistic, and gradually more particularised, minute, and more readily defined, that, is to say, in more scientific forms.

The spirit of science is prevailingly that of studying, defining, distinguishing, and its acts are analysing, classifying, and comparing. In other words, the subordinate faculties or qualities of the mind take the greater share in the formation of science.

These qualities are necessary, but are only instrumental, and not, properly speaking, active. Such a spirit will never bring forth anything new, although it is highly useful, especially when applied practically.

In spite of that, every true greatness of the intelligence consists in having been acquainted with all the wealth, change, difference, and complications of things, in having multiplied and enlarged the study of their relationships, although the vulgar mind looks on these things as an immediate and plain fact. But woe to the man who has become bound up in this state, for he indeed is thereby rendered unprofitable and useless! And an ignorant man will in this case have an advantage over him in that his labour will be more sure and free, for where the ignorant man sees only a single fact the latter sees a cluster of them. The new unity, the new unique vision of the world, must be newly created by him, by his flesh and by his blood: then he may truly say that he has enlarged the world, that he has it in his power, and is of it: not a lost atom, but a lord and master.

By means of the process which we have explained above, whilst new kingdoms of art are being invaded by science, art itself is continually advancing, and it may therefore be said that artistic and creative imagination is the daring, adventurous explorer who, eager to discover new territories, runs on ahead unwearied and indefatigable, whilst scientific activity represents the multitude of colonists who will exhaust the resources of the discovered lands.

What I say is especially applicable to human truth. Psychology may even be said to be the dividing line between art and science; and thus, whilst art encroaches upon science with the novel, science encroaches upon art with moral psychology. But this harbingering and initiating function of art holds good also for other truths, not merely for human truths; but, where the former are concerned, the function I have referred to is more difficult to prove by documentary evidence and established facts, and is thus, of course, less clear. It has long ago been observed that the greatest scientists, those who invent or discover, possess a kind of artistic fantasy, and for this reason again it is said that they are poets.

For analogous reasons, especially in view of the datum that the truly essential characteristic of scientific genius is artistic and creative imagination, we may note that the greatest inventions and discoveries were made in periods of civil maturity and artistic splendour, and that, in them, science as it were assumes a warmer colouring, a character of greater vivacity. Another concordance may also be remarked, viz. that great inventors and discoverers have not a vast store of learning, and they are therefore all the more misunderstood by learned men.

All I have said must be taken in a wide sense, for I hold that every human fact may, at the first glance, be classified in a category; but when examined more closely it reveals a double or polarised nature, one part of it predominating in the fact itself, and homonymous in the category referred to; the other opposed to it. To speak in more concrete terms, it cannot be denied that in the proving of the smallest fact there is a fragment of creation, and that even the weakest investigator of empirical facts is a creator of the lowest order.

Proceeding to the study of work in its more direct aims, the production of merchandise by bodily labour, and of knowledge by intellectual labour, we shall find that these are merely secondary ends, and that a healthy and vigorous personality proposes two objects to itself: wealth and creation respectively.

These two facts, which, on account of the affinity between them, I am taking together, are both integrations, recoveries, of a personality offended and diminished by work. With the acquisition of wealth man gives the rein to his desire for mastering things—a desire which had been suppressed and hindered by society; he once more finds himself, and his own deep and uncorrupted nature. With intellectual creation man feels that he has acquired the ease of a being without cares and anxieties, the ease of a free animal, of a God who multiplies himself in his creatures.

Everything that precedes creation is accumulation of energies, tension, and power; creation is discharging, and the creative act has all the characteristics of a discharge: suddenness, violence, expressiveness, shortness of duration.

Creation, like the satisfying of the amorous instinct, is an indication of exuberance, of vigorous growth of power, of excess of humours. The instinct of love is nearly related to the instinct of dominion: and the power of creation is the third brother—the youngest and most human, but likewise the most marvellous. A few of his characteristics show him to be of the same race; but his lineaments are sweeter and gentler, and possess the attraction of deep and recondite things— a mysterious attraction caused by the reflection of the life of all beings, vital or otherwise.

Creation enchants us with the fury of a sudden squall, and makes us sublime and happy like the moment of voluptuousness of love, as the latter covers one's eyes with an unforgettable forgetfulness of the world, whilst our life concentrates within us the whole life of the universe.

Voluptuousness, love, the eternal strength of our nature, a strength perpetually concealed and perpetually reappearing in magic forms! For love is at the beginning of all the beautiful productions of man; and what greatness is there that does not spring from it! For is it not a fact that only man creates, and not woman? It is man who is the voluptuous and vigorous being, the ardent and powerful being; his organism is sharpened, incited, by the stimulation of desire, even when he believes himself to be cold and chaste. Why, again, should chastity be called the condition of creation, unless because the incitements of our instinct and the strength which they induce us to exercise are scattered in another direction and manifested as conquests of thought? It is not for nothing that man exercises in love his active, enterprising, and aggressive nature; and it is likewise man who almost invariably creates in matters of the intelligence. The sexual coldness of woman is in agreement with her greater aptitude for servile labour. And it is well known that women who bring themselves to the fore by their intellectual abilities have often masculine characteristics, whether physically or morally.

Truly great creation in science and art is reserved for a few, as is likewise the ability to be great lovers. Many arguments assume a close relationship between sexuality and creation, in the sense that both proceed from the same source, or rather that the latter is sexual power itself which, hidden and downtrodden by exhibiting itself as such, vivifies and animates the highest human faculties. It is in the sense of this equivalence or rather substitutability that we should interpret the famous Baconian dictum: *"Amare et sapere vix Deo conceditur."* [73]

The greater number of men who give themselves up to intellectual activity remain during their whole life in a state of servile and brutal work: they are the labourers of thought; only

---

[73] " Even a god finds it hard to both love and be wise"

a few reach the stage of creation, which is a directive function, synthetising and elaborating materials brought forward by others. To fulfil his function properly the creator must have a deep and extensive knowledge of what is for others the final aim of their activity, without such knowledge weighing down his personal and synthetic qualities.

But every human ability and speciality, every superior form of operation, has its particular conditions of existence; we cannot arbitrarily give our attention to the first thing that presents itself to us, and, under the intellectual differences which make us call one man a philosopher, another a poet, and a third a scientist, there are very much marked differences of tendencies, impulses, and perhaps of life. Thus the acquisition of knowledge is not possible unless by putting one's self, so to speak, within the personality of a learned man, with a kind of transitory forgetfulness of higher qualities, even with their temporary abolition. These qualities do not differ from those which, as we have already seen, belong in general to the aristocratic spirit, to a healthy and vigorous personality.

If, however, the momentary quiescence of these qualities is to be entrusted only to personal will, this latter would be liable to be very easily disturbed; *from which arises the necessity for a precious diminution of personality, or, in physiological terms, of vitality,* so that it may be adapted to the work which is implied in the acquisition of knowledge. As we have elsewhere emphasised, it may be said of a large number of men of genius, the details of whose personal lives are known to us, that they suffered from grave illnesses in infancy, or that they were very sickly. This is certain, for example, of Newton, Goethe, Voltaire, Rousseau, and Napoleon, and it is very probable that, if we had exact particulars of the lives of other geniuses, we should find them to be afflicted in like manner. Need I repeat that a diminished vitality has no result other than that of permitting the development of the intelligence of a youthful personality, of grafting mental acquisitions upon it; but that the true value of this personality comes from qualities which slumber, and await their awakening?

The creator is thus shown to be an aristocratic individuality, whose vigour is for a longer or shorter period weakened by contrary conditions (which may be ascribed to biological influences, such as illness, or to social influences, such as poverty or restricted environment). These contrary conditions, however, do not suppress the capacity for expansion and the hidden strength which, in their very nature, lie perhaps in sexual elements. These elements, as many facts show, may have a very different lot from that of the bodily elements which form the rest of the organism with its diverse systems. If, therefore, the young, little-developed personality is made to conform to the discipline of work, it is not finally conquered and impoverished by it, which happens to most people: whence, with the lapse of time and a general progressive improvement, *those qualities which were previously latent show themselves as creative and synthetic activities upon elements which the discipline of work has brought about, and of which it has enriched the personality.*

Conceived in this way, genius is liberation, an aristocratic mind's finding itself after having been held prisoner by inferior conditions.

All the qualities and peculiarities which are attributed to genius are in this way made clear: the deep and exquisite sensitiveness, the continual impatience with the things that surround it, the perennial dissatisfaction with whatever it is at the moment, the fear as of one who perceives the enormous distance which separates one's dream from reality, the spasmodic aspirations towards conditions of a superior life, "the feeling one's self born," to use the words of a poet, "with the privileges of a prince."

As well as by this special combination of physiological conditions that we have already lightly touched upon, which accompany the development of genial personality, the growth of this delicate plant is made very difficult by the circumstances of one's surroundings, which we must take into consideration, consisting of an unstable balance between difficulty and easiness, wealth and poverty, peace and war.

In other words, a certain contrast and a kind of hardness of life are necessary; but, by going too far in this direction, we run the risk of for ever destroying this latent strength, as, on the other hand, excessive leisure and a calm existence take away the stimulus to work.

Need I remind the reader that I do not pretend to explain the nature of genius with the ideas I am putting forth here? Not yet being in a position to say anything in regard to the genesis and the essential processes of the intelligence in its lowest forms, it would be quite absurd to say that I am throwing any light upon the question of genial intelligence.

It is perfectly clear to myself that my remarks merely touch the fringe of the actual problem, and they are to a certain extent useful as being based upon the datum of common and average mentality, which I accept as such.

The differences between servile work and creation are very many. While servile work is slow, methodical, and disciplined, and necessitates, at least in the beginning, continual constraint, creation is bizarre and rapid, and partakes of the nature of instinctiveness. It arises from the depths in complete oblivion of everything else, like a solid, formed entity, accompanied by a violent pleasure which intoxicates and takes possession of the entire mind.

All this happens because the genetic conditions of genial creation are extremely frail and delicate. The mind of the creator is not a quiet and orderly workshop, but a most unstable balance which it is difficult to maintain. A great but disturbing sensitiveness is at the base of every higher intelligence; but for this very reason creation runs the risk of being destroyed by the least shock; that condition, then, deep and inexpressible, which I liken to sexual power, shoots forth by irregular *poussées*,[74] like the lava of a volcano, the eruption of which cannot be foreseen.

Morasso, in the book which we have already quoted, refers to what he calls "the act of accusation of work," showing its degrading and deforming action; but he at the same time gives us an apotheosis of science, and especially of its mechanical applications, which appears to be contradictory.

This results from the fact that he could not rise to a higher principle, he could not consider the fact of creation as a main point of view and show that the subordination of knowledge sprang out of it. Creation is lordly work, and, even in science, it falls only to the lot of a few to be creators, inventors and discoverers of new paths. This characteristic is even more evident in art. We must not, however, forget that every human act, in so far as it is an instrument, a means, of progress towards higher acts, is work, and in so far as it avails itself of acts of less importance, it is creative and aristocratic; but, as we gradually ascend the hierarchical scale, the absolute value of these latter acts increases.

But, having reached the last stage, the hierarchy of creation, we may be asked: But what are the characteristics of genius? How is it distinguished from talent? We often hear both spoken of, and qualities of the one attributed to the other; but it would be difficult to find two other words which are used so arbitrarily as these.

Talent, in my opinion, is a constant and permanent state, a higher level than that of the ordinary excitability of the different spheres of the mind, and is shown by a quick perception, rapid association, perspicacity and penetration. Talent does well and quickly whatever is common and well known; it runs quickly along beaten paths; it is *routinier,* but quite incapable of finding its way in unknown ground: this even confuses it, and takes away its self-assurance, which arises

---

[74] thrusts

from instinct, for it is fixed, and not very changeable; a native quality, so to speak, not susceptible of much further development. To be more exact, it shuns and flies from the unknown, wishing to neglect it, and to disbelieve in its reality.

Genius, on the other hand, is never at ease unless when wandering in unbeaten tracks, when experimenting and investigating. Its life lies in danger, in seeking its direction and its good. That which has hitherto not been experienced by anyone tempts and seduces genius, and it would rather run the risk of being lost to sight or misunderstood than follow the example of everyone else and do what others are doing. What is common and vulgar exasperates it, and it does not think such things worthy of consideration.

This is the reason why the man of talent makes a name for himself while the genius remains in obscurity: the first does well what others do in a mediocre fashion, and he can thus be judged by them; the second does what is done by no one else, or by very few, and he must therefore be satisfied, at least at first, with the approbation of a few higher minds.

The genius discovers analogies hitherto unthought of, and comparisons which throw light upon an entire series of facts; he sees proofs and evidences where the man of talent sees only an unimportant fact; he establishes relationships which had previously been overlooked.

Talent, like all natural qualities of lightness and facility, is widespread among the southern peoples, who are therefore known to be more clever and rapid than the northerns. Genius is, on the other hand, perhaps equally distributed among different nations; it is certain that men of genius of different nations resemble one another much more closely than do mediocre men. Genius is more cosmopolitan, although possessing a special colouring which it obtains from the psychological nature of the people among whom it has arisen. Thus we may expect Italian genius to be more like talent, while German genius will partake of the motley, gigantic, and indistinct German nature. While talent is precocious, and soon assumes a fixed shape, which usually remains unvaried throughout the life of the individual, the genius is a personality brought about by long evolution and continual development; he always seems young, i.e. plastic, adaptable, and changing. So far as precocity is concerned, therefore, genius is often inferior to mediocrity.

History relates frequent instances in which men, hailed as geniuses in later years, were looked upon as almost fools in infancy. Amongst others I can recall Aquinas, surnamed by his companions the "dumb ox"; Ludovico Caracci, who had a similar nickname bestowed upon him; Claude Lorraine, Racine, Balzac.

The man of talent achieves a systematisation of his mental life at a certain age, and this systematisation is not, as a rule, changed; but, on the other hand, we often see radical changes and profound metamorphoses in the entire mentality of the man of genius. This longer plasmability and facility of transformation is regarded as a fault by the crowd of Philistines; but it is rather the unavoidable condition of every true greatness of comprehension.

The problem solved by genius in general, but more especially by artistic genius, is the problem of all human nature. The capacity for deep, great, and complex conceptions, vigour of imagination, and sincerity and nobility of feeling, are to some extent in opposition to the capacity for expression, exteriorisation, facility of forms. Such a contrast is but too often seen in all human facts, from love itself to the most daring philosophical conception. Thus, if Petrarch spoke truly:—"He who can tell how he is burning is in a small fire"—it may also be affirmed that the greatest human conceptions are perhaps often among those which are lost in clouds of dreams and fantasies.

It is hard for us Latins to understand this antinomy. For us, and especially for our women—who are even more subject to what I would call the southern prejudices—everything of which the exterior expression is not contained in a word, in a gesture, or some other manifestation (even if we are willing to forgo all elegance and beauty) either does not exist or is contemptible. Whoever has had experience of human beings must on the other hand admit that a delicate and sensitive mind is always modest and reserved in the expression of its feelings. I would even go so far as to add that every great and absolute delicacy or sensitiveness is by its very nature reserved and shy; and in the expression of its own delicacy of feeling, even if indirectly, there is a kind of charlatanism and bad taste, a kind of coarseness, which, in the case of really sensitive people, smothers sincerity of expression at its birth.

It is for this reason that silence is sometimes held to be a sign of greatness. And it is not without justification that mystics would make it an instrument of moral perfection; but ... alas for our poor human nature! . . . when they begin their propaganda they leave silence behind, and then ... we cannot be persuaded!

To come back, however, to the psychology of genius, it is agreed that there is opposition between thought and deed, feeling and will, an opposition which comes from their different real and concrete conditions of existence and development; it may even be said that the more we concentrate and perfect ourselves in the one, the more we lose our aptitude for the other.

Genius, then, is the force which overcomes this opposition, insuperable for mediocre natures, and gives a shape of reality and beauty to the deepest, widest, and most intricate thought. It is thus that ordinary men, finding their own embryonic and undefined thoughts and uncertain observations in the works of a man of genius, exclaim that he indeed sees into minds and spirits.

The positivist and democratic psychology of some twenty years ago held that in exercising its function genius merely took these ideas from a vaporous state, so to speak, in order to concrete them, and that genius was therefore, to some extent, merely the representative, the speaking-trumpet, of obscure, common thought, which follows it at a distance.

Such a way of looking at the matter is entirely wrong; on the contrary, the man of genius discovers, invents, and, even in the moral world, proceeds by himself towards the unknown. Common thought follows after as closely as possible, and avails itself of the efforts of genius, spreading and making known its discoveries.

If anything definite may be affirmed here, it would be more exact to say that genius avails itself of the discoveries of the ancients rather than of its contemporaries, but of the greatest ancients only, it must be added, whose thoughts it elaborates and advances. And indeed the neglect, not to say the contempt, shown by the genius to the world in which he lives, is often very evident.

Depth of meditation, power of thought, and the faculty of abstraction, which are northern qualities, are found in all geniuses: they are what I like to call the primary qualities of genius, no matter to what sphere of activity it may be directed, or to what country it may belong, not of northern genius only, as Madame de Staël thought. It was her opinion, for example, that Tasso did not owe his greatness and madness to power of penetration or reflection, or to the analysis of his own heart; but to the impetuosity of his passions, to his exterior qualities. This is quite an illusion, which I should call an illusion of distance. If we moderns are inclined to see only the exterior side of works of the past, it is because, as we have a greater power of interior life, which we are always endeavouring to enlarge, we cannot very well perceive what the works of ancient writers cost them. These works appear to us like Minerva who sprang armed out of the head of Jove, although they are really but an attempt and a means of expression. The incommunicability and indefiniteness of thought have perhaps been always felt, and likewise, though in a much smaller degree, by the ancients, for our interior life always precedes expression.

The gap between our interiority, our tormenting and tormented modern mind, and the mind of the ancients is certainly immense; but we need not take things *au pied de la lettre* and accept the traditional conception of the Greek mind which we have inherited from the Renaissance. Even in the case of the Greek mind itself the illusion of distance is seen in the greatest degree, and even it—although, perhaps, to the least possible extent—felt the opposition between thought and expression.

At all events, simple and clear-cut features, a grave yet expressive countenance, a perfect fusion of scattered particulars into a single unity, the harmonic correspondence of thought with speech; all things, in fact, that go to make up what we call classical taste, are natural gifts, and the privileges of the aristocratic races of the south. The ancient Greek poetry, which, by merely depicting exterior actions—almost without any mental labour — achieved an artistic result, is a primitive but eminently aristocratic poetry. Every civilisation which followed that of Greece brought with it a greater tendency to study minds and feelings, but at the same time exterior actions gradually became neglected, and a change in taste was soon apparent. This fact is on a level with the other that continually increasing masses of people began to take an active part in common life, raising themselves from ignorance and obscurity, and brought into literature—which is the knowledge of a people—their store of feelings, ideas, and aspirations. Thus the study of characters prevailed more and more, and for exterior description, for the relation of facts and occurrences, for strange and marvellous adventures, there was substituted the sight of the battle of the passions.

This kind of progress was in every age regarded as an attack against the taste of the ancients, so that in Greece itself we see the admirers of Aeschylus and of Sophocles censuring the art of Euripides, who had nevertheless enlarged the realms of tragedy to such a great extent, and we see Aristophanes making him the object of many satirical allusions.

So again in modern times, Shakespeare was long considered as a tasteless barbarian by the critics of classical France, and his unmeasured genius was recognised only after the lapse of centuries.

If human progress consists not so much in the objective conquest of things and worldly wealth, which we obtain by labour, as in the enlargement of the internal subjective world, in the complication of the mind, then literary and artistic genius is entitled to the greater share of merit, as it more and more brings to light this ever-growing inner world of ours. By the phrase "bring to light" I mean here to bring to aesthetic signification, that is to say, to make our inner world beautiful. The progress of art, entire modern art, is merely this enlargement of the confines of the beautiful, for ideas and thoughts which were beyond the pale of the classical ideal that immediately preceded have now come to be acknowledged as beautiful sentiments and fancies. For this reason every innovator is at first called a barbarian, and afterwards accepted by the common taste which he has influenced and modified. Thus in serene Hellas, as may at least be perceived from its most ancient works, the torment of thought, the whirlwind of passion, had not yet entered art, and there predominated instead a conception of pure, limpid, marble-like beauty. Grief, when it began to be represented, was prevailingly physical.

With the coming of Christianity and the increasing strength of the plebeians, a new spirit which arose from the crowd of sufferers came to maturity in the minds of thinkers, was refined in the minds of poets, and introduced new voices and anxieties into art: affliction, emotion, all the varied scale of moral grief, cover the divine, clear, motionless beauty of the

Hellenic sky. It must be recognised that there was continual decadence from absolute, ideal beauty; but that there was also an enlargement of its confines and the removal of a certain monotony. A comparison may perhaps be allowed.

Everyone knows that the progress of modern music consists in bringing together different harmonies, dissonances, and polyphonies in pleasing sounds, whilst in former times the mere successions of sounds, melody, or simple harmonies, were considered as pleasing to the ear.

It follows that an excessively musical ear, with a perfect and orthodox taste, would certainly prefer an air, a melody of Cimarosa or of Paisiello to the symphony of a German musician, even a classical one; but the greater number of moderns find the former music too simple and monotonous, and with too many repetitions, and prefer the latter because it expresses our more complicated sentiment, and our deeper modern mind.

This is certainly due to an enlargement of the sense of musical beauty, produced, and even imposed, by the great composers. In the same way the more common literary genius continually expands the limits of the human mind, and impels ever-increasing deviations of our thought to formal and aesthetic expression.

*   *   *   *   *

Whatever is natural, easy, elegant, lives in leisure. The imprescindible exigencies of existence, however, exercise upon us a power which arises from hunger, and which is therefore more active than the suggestion and seduction of idleness.

The human mind seems to oscillate continually between these two poles, these two extreme modes of being; and genial creation, whilst it draws its substance from laborious activity, takes its more formal characteristics from leisure and aristocratic idleness. It seems spontaneous, in other words, the expression of a fullness and of an exuberance, like a deep and free joy, not coming, like that of work, from a habit which has gradually become second nature, although troublesome and vexatious at first. The common form of discernible activity—knowledge—is for the genius something presupposed, a preparation, a prehistory. He unites contrary things. The suggestions of nature, the motives of the human race, our instinct, in a word, which makes us love what is frivolous, pleasing, immoral, and the incitements of society, the causes of reflection, our reason, which all impel us towards duty and morality, are harmonised and united in a higher synthesis in the mind of a genius. Hence come the philosophical serenity and indifference of superior minds, which embrace the whole world in their spirit: *and creation itself possesses this double characteristic of depth and humanity, of grace and elegance.*

The genius, being a highly plastic personality, a youth throughout his life, is on this account more liable than other individuals to moral illnesses, deviations, deformations. Besides his susceptibility to unfavourable exterior influences, he is still more in danger of losing himself by his own wealth of sentiment and inner complexity. In a previous chapter I have quoted a very suggestive remark of Nietzsche's, and the psychologist can nevertheless only confirm what he says.

There are diseases peculiar to some minds which are unknown to science, and which science investigates most unwillingly. It is true that such minds are rare, and that science deliberately studies only what is mediocre and common. If, then, we can suppose that these higher minds are more frequently to be met with than is generally believed, we cannot prove our supposition to the satisfaction of the majority, for, as such minds are ruined and dissipated, it can never be said whether they would have been able to flourish and expand to a still greater degree.

At all events, such interesting and uncommon subjects for study escape our observation. But marvellous stories of such minds have been immortalised in literature for centuries.

Hamlet, Werther, René, Obermann, Adolphe, are similar cases of diseases of mind in higher men.[75] The authors in these cases have depicted themselves, or rather the critical episode of their lives, but they brought to the task all their power of reproduction and suggestion; and the terrible agitation which we experience when reading them arises from our deep feeling of the peril which they underwent. On such occasions they must certainly have often experienced the shuddering which a man feels when walking on the brink of a precipice, they must often have given up all hope of saving themselves, and this period of their lives was always present to their minds even after the lapse of years.

For this reason these works have very different effects on their readers. To those who are strong, and who are rising above this stage, they may give a greater knowledge of, and throw more light upon, their present state, and even help them to withdraw from it; but on weak men, on the other hand, they exercise a dangerous fascination; they may provide them with such seductive suggestions that they will finally lose themselves altogether. As a proof of this we may recall the number of suicides which followed the publication of *Werther.*

I think it proper here, in conclusion, to emphasise briefly a particular aspect of thought closely connected with the problem of literary and philosophic genius, an aspect which forms a stage of the evolution of this type of genius, but which is often enlarged to such dimensions that it may almost be said to be a disease of its development. I refer to romanticism.

Romanticism indicates a passage from thought to expression, from analysis to synthesis, from diffusion to concentration, from multiplicity to unity; it is a struggle and a dispute, a quest, a vision of rapid shafts of dazzling light, followed by long darkness; it is an unsteady groping along and

---

[75] *The Sorrows of Young Werther* by Goethe; *René* by François-René de Chateaubriand. *Obermann* by Étienne Pivert de Senancour. *Adolphe* by Benjamin Constant.

recognising the right path all of a sudden; it is a confused struggle to grasp something which is but faintly perceived, the abandonment of a country that one loves and yet detests, to go to another that smiles at us from afar. Like the passage from youth to manhood, it is tempestuous, uncertain, oscillating, exuberant, and contradictory; it is not well acquainted with itself, and it loves and hates itself.

This characterises the intermediate point of the rhythm which governs so many human phenomena, and distinguishes that moment which unites a stage of preparation, accumulation, particular and limited activity, and of work to a creative and synthetic stage. And it is also the change of a democratic state of mind into an aristocratic state of mind. Romanticism is for this reason the special aspect of northern poetry and thought, as in general of an immature intellectuality, and for this reason, again, true genius overcomes it.

Romanticism and classicism are not opposed terms. I must emphasise this. The romanticist is a classicist in intention without knowing it, a classicist who seeks his path: if he sings of dim and gloomy mediaeval castles, rusty drawbridges, and love-sick pages, it does not follow that he is not an unconscious admirer of the clear contours of a Greek temple near the shore of a limpid sea and under an azure sky!

It is indeed true that the romanticist often attains a classical state of mind after many efforts have been made and difficulties surmounted, and his adoration of classicism is often expressed in a romantic style. Take, for example, Renan's "Prayer on the Acropolis"!

Perfect classicism is a momentary pause and not a stage, it is a goal, an intuition, a dazzling instantaneous light, and a short *liberation* in the widest and most Goethean sense of the word.

Goethe, who was the genius that, better than any other, incarnated this metamorphosis, this continual progress, often experienced, perhaps to a greater extent than any one else, these magnificent instants in which the mind feels a new strength flowing from every internal source, in which it feels itself created lord of all things, and endowed with an infinite amount of power. This elevation and these high views, this security and sense of power, the complete feeling of liberty, serenity, and perfection constitute the classical spirit. It is, so to speak, a perfect maturity, the summer of the mind; but if a writer goes beyond this point he will fall into decadence, rococoism, quaintness; if he does not reach it, he will be obscure, coarse, and heavy. Thus the sense of proportion, which is the most distinct gift of a classical taste, is the guide which gives our thought that particular, even unique, form which it must assume.

For the man who is truly original, the classical spirit is not innate, sure, and instinctive; but is a slow, and even a hard-fought-for acquisition. Let the example of Goethe serve for all, the man who from the most exalted and unrestrained romanticism passed to the surest and most serene classicism. Goethe, indeed, represents the finest example of genial creation, and likewise the most significative personality which could be presented to a psychologist.

CHAPTER XI

THE MEANING OF THE ARISTOCRATIC IDEAL

We have seen that the jealousy, the envy, of the working-classes and of the "have-nots" towards the rich and leisured classes is in truth the stimulus, the constant incitement, which gives rise to revolutions and to all great social movements. From the primitive struggle for a woman to the most complicated battles of classes the fundamental fact of the envy of the weaker for the stronger is always present. Progress itself, however, as a dynamic force, is essentially dependent upon this emotional state, and we should therefore regard it as an element which, generally speaking, has a good effect upon social life, although to some delicate minds its appearance is odious.

Aristocracies have in this way a function in the social aggregate which I should be inclined to call fermentative, for they arouse and stimulate energies which would otherwise remain inert. This function is, however, purely passive, for aristocracies, considered from this standpoint, serve only as examples and models for the other classes. The sight of luxury, of opulence, the frequent satisfaction of his instinct, so dear to the man of power, the example shown by the higher classes: all this serves continually to quicken the efforts of those who have not been favoured by fortune to put forth all their energies in order that their ambitions may be realised.

Besides this obvious function, however, aristocracies have yet another, which is still more worthy of the name, for it is truly active: a unitive, restraining, and directive function on the social group. This function, let us add, presupposes one of the highest of human qualities: it necessitates a virtue and a strength uncorrupted by the exhausting and diminishing discipline of work. The excellent nature of this quality, by which those who possess it succeed in fusing together, organising, and adapting those precious yet rebellious and untractable energies—human will—the exceptional nature of this quality, I repeat, is shown by the close relationship which unites it to a higher form of intelligent activity: synthesis.

For this is really a synthetic, intuitive, immediate, and natural quality, which eludes descriptive artifice of every kind, like all other natural qualities; but it nevertheless exists, and possesses a high value despite the rude denials of theorists of democracy, who would like the capacity and aptitude for command and direction to be qualities within the acquirement of every one. Indeed, would not the democrats of knowledge —the specialists, the learned men of "contributions" and "notes"—persuade us that synthetic faculties are an intellectual luxury, and that only analysis has any right to exist?

This strengthening and directing virtue of the aristocratic mind is seen to be all the more necessary and beneficial the more the growing division of functions makes the greater number of men mere "beasts of burden," simple instruments, who, taken out of their ordinary mechanical rut, are capable of nothing, and do not see a yard before their eyes: so that a people of specialists, each one capable of working wonders in his own particular sphere, would be the most incapable nation possible, if there were not men in it who, with more or less ease, could survey the exigencies of society with a single glance. Accustomed to work in their own particular grooves, most men entirely lose their sense of reciprocal relationship, the sense of the co-ordination and subordination of their labours. *"Propter vitam vivendi perdere causas"*[76] is the motto which, unfortunately, seems applicable to the specialists of modern society.

To mention a well-known and recent example of what I am affirming, that is, of the want of organising capacity

---

[76] "To destroy the reasons for living for the sake of staying alive." A line from Juvenal, *Satire* VIII.

among the lower classes and democracies generally, I may remind the reader of the ill-luck which, in Italy, at any rate, has overtaken the majority of popular economical institutions: cooperative stores, pawnshops, etc., and that, where such institutions have succeeded in obtaining a foothold in the commercial world, this has been due to the personal action of some reputable individuals who took charge of them, if not in name at least in fact.

An organising capacity, like all synthetic qualities, is an attribute of the aristocratic mind, the virtue of a strong and healthy individual who has deep inner convictions and the courage to assume responsibility, which is not exactly a virtue of the masses. The great error of the democratic principle arises from the rationalistic and theoretical conception of the average man: in the implicit presupposition of a certain ultra-modern sociology, society would merely be the juxtaposition of individuals having everywhere the same qualities: a collection of mediocre men engaged in co-operative production. Nothing could be more incorrect. The existence and preservation of a social aggregate is possible only by the restraining and directive action of certain classes (which, without bodily fatigue, draw from life all the good it has to offer, and are known as parasites) upon other classes which possess qualities of labour, analysis, and production. In other words, society—and certain metaphysicians must be made to understand this fact—must be conceived dynamically as a combination of internal actions and reactions of the different elements which compose it, and not statically as a contiguity of individuals and classes.

The oppressive and diminishing influence of aristocracies upon plebeians is certainly more apparent in states founded by conquest. In such countries, with the formation of distinct and separate classes and castes, this psychological mechanism, which is the unfailing condition of every aggregate, is rendered, so to speak, quite palpable and transparent.

A perfect limitation of classes is a material necessity, not only for the advantage of the dominating class, but also for that of the state, and all barriers and precautions are to be regarded as legitimate which, through marriage, prevent the intermingling of the classes. Aristocracies everywhere dread, and rightly, a mixing and lowering of their blood: this so-called noble prejudice has a profound justification, and is the sentimental and conscient form by which an intimately physiological necessity of nature is made manifest; for, if a *substantial* difference were not felt, the greatest support of and the strongest incitement to this dynamic action—an important element in social life—would be wanting.

What, then, is the origin of the so-called prejudices of antiquity towards high birth and nobility, prejudices which, despite modern enlightenment, are still strong and powerful, even upon those who despise aristocracy? They arose, in my opinion, from the fact that the employment of power and wealth, assuring to many generations favourable surroundings, rich diet, and opportunities for realising their personal gratifications, must have increased or preserved the primitive strength of aristocratic classes.

Too often in reality the employment of wealth and leisure is abused, and thus becomes a cause of degeneration, and even in the greater number of cases heredity of strength and vigour in aristocratic races exists merely in appearance. Even in cases like these, however, the symbolic power of the name always remains, a power that, in this instance, is not a vain and idle superstition of theorists. And we have thus come to something which it is of more importance to note.

The fascination of the spoken word *aristocratic*, the attraction it possesses, although unwillingly and sometimes not at all admitted—for it is often hidden by sentiments which assume grave and honest appearances, yet being at the same time envy pure and simple—this fascination, I repeat, comes from the real value which this word stands for. *Aristocratic* is that which is closely connected with the essential causes of the existence of the race and its continuity; it is the exaltation, the exaggeration, and accentuation of the conditions which favour it to the greatest extent: in a word, the nucleus of the conception *aristocratic* is sexuality, the central phenomenon of life. Sexual, aristocratic, beautiful, are conceptions which are closely related to one another, if not, indeed, the same thing seen from different aspects. Thus I have already said that love, dominion, and genial creation have a common root and a common soul.

It is for this reason that the aristocratic individual is shown to be almost an enemy of sociality and of morality, because he is the representative, against these, of rights of race, strength, and virtue which tend, in their greatest and most glorious manifestations, to increase and perpetuate. Thus in German the word *Geile* stands for a flourishing state of life, vital exuberance, vigorous growth, and also voluptuousness.

* * * * *

In what we call human beauty, plastic beauty, as seen in the lines, for example, of the Apollo or the Venus dei Medici, we must perceive visibly and suggestively crystallised the entire mass of the best properties of the species dedicated to love. Why this arrangement of the figure, or that form of the trunk, or those proportions of the limbs, or that special development of the muscles should represent the *optimum* of the conditions of the sexual embrace, I do not know; I merely admit the fact without being able to give a reason for it.

Some facts may, however, enable us approximately to determine its physiological value. In the well-developed breast and the slightly sloping shoulders we observe a body uncorrupted by the physical degradation of work, in the long neck we perceive the savage agility of the head; and, in the small belly, health and the subordination of the digestive functions.

In this way the strength of the most important instinct of the race is expressed in the aesthetic sensitiveness of that beautiful figure—a fact which is still true in spite of the numerous decadences of the race. The impression of human beauty is the notation, the conscient form, in which the combination of the organic qualities most favourable to love is revealed. The frequent coincidence of the type of beauty with the aristocratic type is characteristic; but this does not happen so often in the case of facial lines as in the form of the body and its proportions.

It is well known, for example, that artists regard it as an element of beauty, especially in the case of women, if the shoulder line is not horizontal—which forms the so-called "square shoulder"—but with a rather downward slope, and if, again, the back line of the neck is almost a straight continuation of the line of the back. Now, these two elements are proper to the aristocratic type. The proof of this fact struck me immediately when looking at the collection of portraits in the Uffizi gallery; and it is but natural that in portraits of women, if the neck and shoulders are not covered with any article of dress, these signs may be remarked better than in men; in whom, however, they undoubtedly exist. It seems to me quite certain that these two characteristics have a sexual signification of the first importance; they recall the healthy animal with his long, active neck and alert sensitiveness, quick at every movement. For the rest, the shape of the neck and shoulders is a most important ethnic characteristic.

Scientists and philosophers have always attached little importance to the beautiful, although this is really the most important, most mysterious, and the most significative element of our psychical life. Would this be due to the fact that scientists and philosophers are, as some writers hold, two *ugly species?*

Beauty is the spiritual form, the ideal and intellectualistic transposition of the experience of the race as regards the conditions most favourable to life; but especially to the most important act of life—love. The animals, men, and nations most devoted to love are those who are, for the most part, the most beautiful. Tropical nature, so rich, so varied, and so luxuriant; the landscapes of the south, so warm and many-coloured, make their beauty felt directly, perhaps because everything in these places seems to speak of love, and to be prepared for it. The beauty of northern nature, with its frosty winters, its leafless trees, its ice and fields of snow, is not immediate and direct, it is a fine reflex, so to speak, of the creation of man, and for this reason, to feel it, one must possess a great amount of interiority and soul. Nevertheless, no matter how much this interiority may be supposed to be developed, there is no comparison between the beauty of a winter scene in Norway and the sight which the Bay of Naples offers on a summer morning.

The close connection between beauty and sexuality is shown not only objectively but also subjectively. Thus the coldest natures, those least inclined to love, and logical, ascetic intelligences, have the smallest aesthetic sense. This, according to my view, would be a kind of discernible intuition of the highest influences favourable to love.

What I have said applies especially to natural beauty; but for the beauty created by man, the work of the artist, the conditions are complicated by other elements, although the fundamental relationship remains the same.

The aesthetic sense is therefore the best agent for the perfection and amelioration of the race, and aims at maintaining its vigour, which is based especially upon sexuality. Only extraneous and superimposed reasons have made man so much afraid of love, and he has been frightened in this way only to further the ends of society. Art, therefore, with its amorous suggestiveness, which really exists, and is proved by the antipathy of all anti-amorous religions towards it, exercises a beneficent action. The sense of beauty remains in us men as an infallible indication of our highest good.

In the presence of good aesthetic taste, which is the highest intellectual phenomenon, every other intellectual fact takes second place; as likewise if we were confronted with a work which expresses a clear and exact sensation of beauty, we should feel as reverent as if we were in the presence of a revelation that throws a sudden light upon whatever interests us most: the conditions of our strength and expansion, which we often seem to forget, oppressed as we are by the necessity of existence. And we should be grateful to those who reveal these conditions to us, to those who, by a Titanic effort, recover these lost tracks and point them out to us: we should reverence artists, in other words.

To sum up in a few words the arguments which I have alluded to rather than developed in this chapter, I will say that the aristocratic ideal, in its triple aspiration towards leisure, power, and love, is manifested to us as *a perpetual struggle towards natural conditions of life; a healthy, strong, and vigorous nature; pure animalness*. The existence of this ideal is seen to be antagonistic to sociality and morality, which both make for the impoverishment, the organic degradation, of the species man.

Every healthy individual development tends to the realisation of this ideal, even if it be hidden under the most diverse disguises and reached by a longer or shorter route; so that we may deduce a conclusion which is less paradoxical than it seems: "The ultimate aim of every form of social activity is animal leisure."

CHAPTER XII

A CONCEPTION OF CIVILISATION

So far as sentiment and ideas, political institutions, and advantages acquired by or bestowed upon individuals are concerned, humanity seems to proceed continually forward, oscillating, however, between two opposite poles: barbarism and decadence. In primitive peoples, coarseness of habits, cruelty, and ignorance are not unaccompanied with a certain aspect of beauty which arises from their strong animal healthiness: among civilised peoples, on the other hand, culture, mildness of customs, and widespread wealth are often merely the disguise, the deceitful aspect, of a fatal decadence, the indication of the weakening of the race.

In the path of a progressively increasing sociality, different human aggregations, nations, peoples, and races find only their historical death: but the sound progress of a nation's life is, on the other hand, in the direction of a sense of individualisation which takes place within a solid and collective spirit.

The first act, and, I would add, the essential momentum of the civilising process, is a vital diminution, a loss. Only by means of such mechanism is it possible to acquire new elements, and especially to develop thought; for civil progress, every *humanisation*, makes itself felt in the individual and in society by a withdrawal from manifestations of life, and especially from love and action. "To think," said Bain,[77] "is to stop speaking and acting." If this psychological axiom is true and evident in its more concrete signification, in its conscient and voluntary form as applied to modern man, it is even more

---

[77] Alexander Bain (1818-1903) was a Scottish philosopher who wrote widely on psychology, education and the philosophy of science.

true when applied to the origin of thought and intelligence, which border upon the subconscious.

The great necessity for production, as incarnated in the historical shape of social work, leads to this diminution of energies, which, however, for the advantage of work itself, must not go beyond certain limits. But the adaptations caused by the exigencies of work pass beyond the limits indicated by the conditions which we have called the *optimum* of existence; that is to say, they lead not only to that degree of vital diminution which permits of this adaptation; but, through social struggles, competition, misery, and the hindrances in the way of sexual intercourse, they give rise to all those phenomena of exhaustion and incapacity that give the finishing touch to degeneration.

It should almost seem that civilisation is a barbarous and cruel deity who requires an immense and perpetual sacrifice of human victims, for the work of civilisation consumes successive individuals and groups who gradually suffer from the deteriorating influence of work, until finally, after they have passed through every degree of the social scale, all traces of their lineage are lost. Civilisation is therefore biologically harmful to the greater number of individuals considered as such. Only of few of them can it be said that they receive the benefits of the work and blood of others, and it is these who transmit the race sexually: the strong men with sexual inclinations, the masters, the rulers.

Progress is a rhythm perpetually renewed in ever-extending and comprehensive double phases; human nature is on that account continually becoming wider and deeper. The first step in this direction is invariably an increase in inferiority, and, from the emotive and sentimental point of view, must be regarded as a diminutive, depressing, and painful phase (democratisation); upon this follows an augmentative, exaltative, eccentric phase (aristocratisation); but in this latter phase true acquisitions are not made; those already made, however, are perfected, refined, and formed.

Although in the social group itself, taking into consideration the period of its development, it may generally be said that every individual participates more or less in both phases, nevertheless the different functions which each phase presupposes are always distinct and separate in individuals. Thus the deepest, strongest, and most animal-like qualities of the race (those which essentially maintain it continually capable of branching out in new directions in spite of contrary influences of the most varied description), the qualities which enable it to last, despite all impoverishments, alienations, and mutilations, are not common to all men, but only to some individuals, those whom I call aristocrats, whose most prominent psychological characteristic is egoism, and whose most prominent physiological characteristic is strong sexuality and organic vigour.

The succession of generations which are intermingled in a thousand ways, fusing together among themselves the most dissimilar elements, does not proceed in a direct line, that is to say, the continuance of the race, by the very force of circumstances, is not entrusted to all persons who, in point of age, are capable of propagating it, but to a group—a stock— which gives out collateral branches doomed to death after the complete impoverishment of their energies, and which gives out also one direct, apical branch, the richest, most succulent, and, in a certain sense, the most parasitical branch, which will propagate the species.

In society all different human characteristics, produced by a kind of division of psychological work, have given birth to the great variety and the wide scale of human sentiments; but these developments, often exaggerated and morbid in their extremes, have been achieved to the detriment of organic and fundamental qualities, and especially sexuality.

Sexuality is the great matrix of every social activity, and it almost seems that by a kind of transformation this power is manifested in the different forms of our complex life. In this way, if ethnic groups in any primitive society whatever be put in the position of servants, or economical groups of workmen in a modern aggregate, or in the position of more restricted groups in the same class, they expand and dissipate all their energies in fulfilling a function which is beneficial to the group considered as a whole; but, with the sacrifice of their own entire strength, they lose at the same time all the vitality which they possessed, and die out, being no longer able to generate further plastic material.

All social development is achieved by the vital and sexual sacrifice of entire groups, and all progress is a series of sacrifices of this nature.

Subordinate, anonymous, and collective work is performed by the throng of weak and downtrodden men, those who no longer take part in the work of propagating the race; whilst directive work, especially final victory, is reserved for those who remain uncorrupted and pure. It is the task of the weak, the conquered, and the humble to make new conquests in the kingdom of the human mind; and all our modern ideal and sentimental complication, all the modern *humanity* of thought, arises from the ever-increasing participation in knowledge and feeling of a multitude of suffering men. This condition of things is reflected in literature. Compare the aristocratic and golden simplicity of the Greek tragedy with the complication, the density, the entanglement of the tragedy of Shakespeare.

But the discoveries in interiority made by suffering plebeians, like the physiological complications which we find in subjected groups, are instilled by the virtue of love in the primitive and aristocratic section of an ethnic group. Aristocracies passively suffer the movement, to which, however, considering their conservative and indolent character, they may be said continually to offer resistance; but, no matter how stubborn they may be, they always end by enduring what they cannot withstand, although their moderating power is of the greatest utility. Through contagion and imitation their habits become gentler and their customs milder, and they lose their characteristics of rudeness and barbarism which we find in every force of warlike origin. Thus mediaeval noblemen, coming into touch with minstrels of popular origin, formed their courts of love, and, through the influence of artists, made themselves patrons of the learned.

This balance, with a thousand different blendings, which we find between the excessively innovating tendencies of the lower classes, urged on by the stimulant of grief to whatever is new, and the conservative tendencies of happy and powerful rulers, constitutes the normal state of the average man in every age, a state which takes its special colouring from different conditions of classes, professions, and surroundings.

It may therefore be said that the humble, the weak, the incapable, the erring, and the morbid—the so-called degenerates produced by innumerable social actions and reactions—are the factitive and creative elements of progress. In saying that, we are still far from the ridiculous simplicity of certain Darwinians who, impugning the two formulae of the struggle for existence and the survival of the fittest, affirm that the suppression of the weak is the means for securing the future prosperity of society.

It follows from what has been said that we often find in the *healthy, normal* man of a given epoch what constituted the disease, the morbidness, of the preceding epoch, for every new conquest is made by extremists; and everything new today was realised by the morbid, aberrant, and fantastic men of yesterday.

In speaking of progress and acquisitions, I mean purely inner mental and moral facts, that is to say, progress of intelligence in the abstract, and of morality; but to these, in their turn, are due those benefits which increase the power of man over matter, from the smallest invention to the most important mechanical application of a theoretical discovery. Every invention springs from a weakness, from the humility of a knowledge which feels itself inferior to things and men, and necessity is the mother of invention. But whatever is discovered by the activity of workers is diffused, and influences others; all discoveries have even been utilised better and to a greater extent by those who were at first most unwilling to accept them: the rich and powerful, who, by means of these discoveries, become even richer and more powerful.

Sexual degeneration as far as impotence, sterility, madness and death, following upon a diminished resistance to illnesses, is the extreme limit of the descending curve of those branches of the race which are little by little becoming exhausted under the heavy yoke of social necessity.

It is very difficult for a family group to preserve its vitality for a long time, and this proves that the continuity of the race is reserved for a *phylum* and not for a multitude.

The much-discussed degenerative morbid heredity is probably merely the more prominent accentuation of the physiological fact which I have established to be at the base of the phenomenon of *sociality* which is its true primary and secondary cause. Indeed, a large number of these causes which are assumed by science to explain degeneration spring from social necessity, and have the value of proximate causes.

Some of these causes stand in an accidental and contiguous relationship to it, like epidemic diseases, for example, which there would be, perhaps, even if society did not exist, but which, at all events, are increased in intensity owing to the fact that people in a society must live close together: the other causes are directly related to sociality, like the exhaustion brought about by work, and the misery of great masses of people, considered not as a fortuitous effect, but as a condition really favourable to production. Thus chronic madness should be interpreted as the consequence of an excess of social action on the individual, who gradually loses his store of energy. In other words, the same causes which engender the development of the intelligence and favour the development of knowledge, gradually increasing in intensity, occasion the bankruptcy of the mind through madness. Chronic insanity would thus probably be even the most manifest form in which the deleterious influence of sociality on individual personality would be revealed.

For all that, the human race, with the great sacrifice which it accomplished and is accomplishing by means of work for the benefit of society, would in time die out if the sexual energy of refractory, parasitical, and healthy individuals did not reinforce the thinning ranks of humanity.

Conformably to what has been said, the course of civilisation should not be conceived as a progression in a direct line, but as an oblique, sidelong march. The progressive elements would even tend to draw the social body after them laterally; but, if these elements gave way to this excessive tendency, the social body would soon die out, where it was not sustained by strong, healthy, and aristocratic elements.

In short, however, *the human race*, whatever resistance may be offered by some individuals, *is slowly and with fatal progress withdrawing itself from the direct line of pure animalness, and from conditions of balance, to assume a position of relative non-balance.*

The proposition which I have just enunciated I value as a true law, and I hasten to translate it into more concrete terms, elucidating by its light some aspects of social life and some phenomena which the events of civilisation present to us.

Thinkers have hitherto done little or nothing to interpret the value of art, and the special significance of some facts of its history, for forming a judgment as to the course of humanity and the development of thought. The development of different arts in the same civilisation is not contemporaneous, but successive, and perhaps corresponds to the psychological differentiation in the individual of different mental and elementary faculties and activities. It is difficult, and perhaps hazardous, in the present state of science and criticism, to construct a genealogy of arts; but it may perhaps be said that, however much they may spring from a common source, considered as single forms they have for the most part a successive development.

It is true we may affirm that all that is most certain in this order of things can be deduced from the Italian Renaissance; but these deductions are in harmony with psychological views which may be established *a priori.* In other words, by means of numerous inductions on the psychology and physiology of language, sight, and writing, the following series should perhaps be admitted—music, painting, sculpture, architecture.

Now, it is noteworthy that this psychical order is not the order in which this series developed historically, or better, it does not correspond to the order in which each had its greatest development in the course of time. It is well known that architecture and sculpture made themselves felt in Greece with a sureness and a splendour which has never since fallen to their lot, much less been surpassed, or even equalled. On the other hand, painting, in Greece, so far as can be ascertained from the few remaining examples we have of it, did not attain a very high degree of excellence, and the same, or still worse, may be said of music. Greek genius was plastic, creative, visual, and likewise sensual: it possessed in an extraordinary degree the gift of form, with the art which implies the greatest power of expression. On the other hand, the apogee of painting was at the time of the Italian Renaissance. Sculpture, although honoured by the names of Michelangelo, Donatello, Verrocchio, and Ghiberti, and architecture by the names of Michelangelo, Leonardo da Vinci, Palladio, and Brunelleschi, not to mention others of less importance, never attained the grandeur and strength created by Hellenic masters.

Those nations which, after the Renaissance, successively bore the torch of civilisation, and had even periods of political splendour and social expansion, did not possess this creative power in the plastic arts. With the exception of the names of a few really great painters in Spain and Holland, other countries were almost sterile. Thus architecture became one of the useful arts rather than the expression of artistic power; sculpture is represented by mediocre names and nothing more. On the other hand, however, the development of literature in some of these countries was magnificent; in France, for example, which possesses the glory of having what is perhaps the richest and most significative literature of modern, if not of all, nations. I have already briefly referred to contemporary German music, with its eminently fantastic and vague character.

The careful student will perceive that all these facts have a single signification—*the ever-increasing disproportion between the inner element of meditation and feeling and the outer element of expression and action in the dual unity of life,* a dual unity which art exaggerates, multiplies, and exhibits most clearly. It is important to note that the southern nations of Europe, those who are organically the strongest, should have attained *d'emblée*[78] the greatest perfection in the plastic arts; this indicates the deep and intimate relationship which exists between organic strength and artistic and creative tendencies.

We have still other elements of judgment, however. Why is modern science so much wider in scope, and more perfect, than ancient science, while we are so much inferior to the ancients in arts? Some easygoing and simple popularising thinkers, starting from this datum, and from the opinion that our epoch is a period of progress and enlightenment, have come to the conclusion that art is inferior, that its value was confined to periods of barbarism, and that it was destined to disappear.

The chronological series of the greatest development of particular arts would seem to show that these thinkers are

---

[78] from the beginning

right; but we shall see that it would be better to interpret it differently.

Science, art, and philosophy are closely and reciprocally connected through every historical period, or, to express this thought in words that will be better understood after what I have said in chapter IX., through every double phase of the perennial rhythm which regulates historical phenomena; but, granted that it is hazardous to discuss the pre-eminence of one or other, since these two forms of thought are connected by relationships of exchange and reciprocal utility, I should nevertheless be inclined to say that art was of the greatest value.

If modern thought has a prevailingly scientific characteristic, this arises from the fact that *civilisation has a tendency to stop in the first phase of the rhythm, as we have seen happen to northern personality in the sphere of individual psychology.* Or again, making a perfectly legitimate comparison, influenced by the expansion of science modern civilisation has tended to become broader rather than higher.

There are, however, still other considerations to oppose to the too easy affirmations of the kind I have mentioned above. We live in an epoch which represents a point in a particular rhythm; but we are induced, by our desire for generalisation, so natural to man, to believe in the continuity and perpetuity of certain aspects which are merely transitory. We live amidst a number of extraordinary phenomena which are subject to certain laws; but the curves which mathematically represent their lapse are intermingled and confused, and influence one another to such a degree that it requires great critical acumen to discriminate between them and to recognise them. As we are near them, so to speak, even within them, we cannot apprise them exactly, to do which it is necessary to be outside of them; one must see them from a very small visual angle.

Although every civilisation on earth has one phase of growth and another of decline, an obscure phase and a luminous phase, it nevertheless comprehensively represents a period of youth and of immaturity in respect to the phase that follows. It must, however, be remarked that the words youth and immaturity are not by any means the right words to use. Even in early civilisations we may note a prevalence of the formal element over the inner element in proportion to their distance from the south. (It is in this way, for example, that we can explain the wealth of detail, of friezes, the abundance and liveliness of colours in Indian, Assyrian, or Egyptian architecture.)

Hellenic civilisation signified perhaps the culminating point of the history of civilisation on earth, as it showed a perfect balance between interiority and exteriority, between form and substance. This correspondence and harmony between real and ideal, between thought and execution, between the beautiful and the true, glittered perhaps like a transient meteor in the Greek sky. We at least with our Renaissance saw only a very much diminished light derived from it.

After Hellenic civilisation the world may be said to have proceeded towards a want of equilibrium in the inverse sense of the two fundamental elements of our life. We find evidence of this fact in the civilisations which followed one another as groups emigrated from the south to the north, and in the ever-increasing deficiency in form, in objectivation, so that perhaps the extreme part of the descending curve will in this case be shown by the future society of the farthest north: perhaps life will there reach the maximum of its divergence from natural conditions of existence, from animalness, in the immense development of thought, in the disease of the incommunicable, in the enormous disproportion between desire and the power of acting.

Up to this point we have proceeded in our assertions with a firm and sure step, supported by deduction and by the observation of facts. It may now be permitted us to give more rein to our fantasy. All that follows may be considered only as a gratuitous hypothesis; but it often happens that a future truth is hidden in similar ambiguity.

It may be that all civilisation will touch upon the borders of madness (remember the extraordinarily morbid character of mentality in the extreme north, which we have seen represented by and intensified in its literature), and that life, as a balance between its two aspects, will be near dissolution; but who knows? perhaps a radical change in production, an unexpected progress in technology, will once more lead it into the path of health and strength.

Perhaps the course of civilisation will retrace its steps and descend once more towards the south, and all past history will be manifested as the first phase of a wider and more universal rhythm which will have prepared an almost immeasurable greatness for man.

What forms will be assumed by human activity, then grown to such a gigantic size; what summits will be reached by action at whatever points the daring and hardihood of men may impel them; men whom an enormous knowledge will have made capable of almost infinite power? Our imagination is confounded at this point, and is lost in the bizarre phantasmagoria of dreams!

EPILOGUE

At the highest point of our thought, in the elevated regions where all the antinomies of empirical observation are fused together, one final conjecture occurs to us, robed in the candid, purple vestment of a higher truth.

Who knows whether all our sociality with its low necessities, and the diminution and degradation it imposes on human beings, is not merely a simple episode, a circuit, a small instrument used by Nature with the ultimate aim of giving back their original values to all men?

Nature, who clasps and overpowers our trifling inventions, who takes all the more from us, as Goethe says, when we think we have succeeded in rising from her arms; Nature, indifferent, immoral, for whom every means is fair, certain as she is of her final victory: has she not even pleased herself by pretending to be overcome and mastered?

Why speak of opposition between society and nature, sociality and love? These are perhaps merely relative and inferior truths, good enough for us who have given all our attention to what happens in our own little moment!

Nature is too great to have no post without making claims to a new extraneous reality—our society. This may have been imposed by her upon men only to give back to them, when she is overcome, the liberty and beauty of all living creatures: thus Nature will have borne down and mutilated primitive individuality, integrate and complete in itself, but small, and acting in a restricted sphere, only to prepare for *human* individuality an almost unlimited greatness, and an almost divine power.

APPENDIX: A Reply to Critics

The few, not to say the very few, readers who have followed the vicissitudes of my book *On the Tracks of Life*, published early in 1907, may perhaps be surprised (if this be not too strong a word) that I have not until now replied to the criticisms passed upon it, especially to the first, which were undoubtedly the best. I will not disguise the fact that my silence was partly due to the unrealised hope that some further critics would come forward and deal with the subject more thoroughly; but it was due still more to the fact that I did not wish to write polemics merely for the sake of *autoréclame;*[79] but only to reply to those criticisms which were worthy of being answered, not to deal in detail with the comments of every minor critic who interested himself in my book.

However, as criticisms became poorer and poorer, and at last, as often happens, even the minor reviewers began to think that my silence was due to lack of grounds for objecting to their criticisms, and raised their perky little heads like young cocks, with crests not yet full-grown, which nevertheless imagine themselves to be kings of their coops, I decided that the moment had come when matters should be put right.

And as *à tout seigneur tout honneur,*[80] let us speak in the first place of what was written by my good friend Amendola,[81] who has certainly made the most thoughtful observations of any that have been written in regard to my book.

He begins by praising my sincerity. I am satisfied with this up to a certain point; but, my dear friend, I cannot get rid of

---

[79] "self-promotion"

[80] "honor where honor is due"

[81] Giovanni Amendola (1882-1926) was an Italian journalist, professor and politician. An opponent of Mussolini and Italian Fascism, he was attacked by Blackshirts in 1925 and later died from his injuries. His wife, Eva Kuhn, was associated with the Futurist movement and wrote under the pen name Magamal.

the notion that the praise of sincerity resembles the expedient of those who, not being able to say of a man that he is handsome, hasten to exclaim emphatically: "he is so lovable and sympathetic." I esteem sincerity; but it is to some extent foreign to my work and to its appreciation, which is determined by the value and the abundance of the ideas contained in it.

Besides, Amendola has made an observation which shows that he himself is not too certain of this sincerity. I refer to the words: "It is in my opinion a form of programmism and of attitudinising, which goes to show Mr. Séra's sincerity, and is highly valuable in itself, but which in general contains a falsification...." I must confess it is difficult for me to understand how programmism and attitudinising can be sincerity, unless we are dealing with the sincerity of the actor who ends by believing himself to be the actual character he is representing ... which does not of course satisfy me, and which I hence deny.

For the rest the praise of sincerity, even if sincerely attributed to me, does not concern me, and neither does that of insincerity. For, in writing of such a subject, what signifies one or other? Only that certain *intellectual formulae* are, or are not, more or less completely impregnated with *sentiment*. This, however, would not necessarily be explained even if these formula were *by themselves and in themselves* right or not, and even less if they were good or otherwise for a certain person, or several persons. And these would be the first truly interesting problems. The ulterior problem which would then remain quite unsolved would be that of the hierarchical value of these different formulae, that is to say, the question of the superiority in respect to life in the widest sense of the word, from one point of view or another.

I do not put much faith in the criticism that speaks of attitudinising as with the conviction of having attained definite truth. Attitudinising, which may be a rigidity, a veneer, would merely show that, as for certain points (mysticism) which Amendola has alluded to rather vaguely—that is, just enough not to see the contradiction into which he has fallen—there is a need, really and sincerely felt; and, in short, accepting this conception, we should examine into this need when we discuss a work that could, by a formal necessity, have availed itself of certain traditional means and formulae more by an instinctive polemical expedient than by perfectly true and proper mental agreement with it.

But there is more than this in pressing logic to extremes. If a man had succeeded in expressing in words a state of mind which could not be felt for long, that is not something which we could reproach him with; much less could it be utilised to demonstrate the erroneousness or the unacceptableness of this state. If the word attitudinising means anything, it means that the habitual life, customs, and manners of a person are contrary to those presupposed by such attitudinising. No one, however, could legitimately deny that whoever would write in this way did not did not realise this state, even approximately, and for a short time.

For analogous reasons I by no means feel the abnegation of taking to myself the accusation of a theorist of egotism. Amendola is mistaken in this regard, for I only endeavour to describe the genesis of egotism, or, to be still more exact, of some egotists; but I have not hesitated to pass a somewhat severe judgment upon some manifestations of egotism. I shall have to be even more explicit in a detailed study of egotism, in which I shall throw some light upon the frail, unacceptable, I might almost say morbid, elements, which take part in its formation.

For the rest, if I felt the strictly logical necessity for intellectually justifying egotism, I should show not only the "man who thinks," but also the "man who lives," for I know that, if we wish to come into immediate touch with life, we must remember that the *present-day* man thinks more intensely about life (even without necessarily being a philosopher) than did the man of former times.

I admit that this may, for some individuals, reach the limits of a real disproportion between thought and action, and hence of weakness; but this would not necessarily occur in all cases, and not, of course, in mine ... of which, however, a demonstration cannot be given immediately.

My book was not, nor was it intended to be, "an attempt to live intellectually what had already been lived artistically." A book, in my opinion, should always be a means and an instrument, not an end in itself, not even for the writer of it; and I even think that the value of a work is determined among other things by this relationship between itself and its author; but this relationship of my book ... to its author Amendola could not and cannot affirm, because he does not know me; or at least he knows me only imperfectly.

If I had had, I do not say the intention, but the disposition that Amendola attributes to me, I should have kept my thoughts to myself and not printed them at all: that would have been sufficient: it was only the thought that they would have some influence on others that impelled me to write them down. Moreover, to such hybrid and solipsistic hedonism I should prefer that of the *bonne chère* with the rest.

As for the dorsal spine of Nietzschean thought, I think it already exists, and others will in future be able to demonstrate it better than I, for the influence of Nietzsche is hardly, in my opinion, in its period of ascension; but I frankly cannot accept what Amendola attributes to me of having sought to add the famous dorsal spine to the "doctrine of the master."

In spite of my ... medical studies, I do not feel myself to be capable of so much, and I freely confess it. I modestly think that, if Nietzsche were studied as he really ought to be, this dorsal spine could be added to a great many people who are at present in want of it; and I may say this without malice, for I highly value those whom I call my friends.

"The scientist," says Amendola, "must look upon the world with an eye free from preoccupations; the moralist must, on the other hand, determine the essence and the basis of moral life without taking too much notice of the natural life by which he is surrounded."

As if it had not been the chief purpose of my book to criticise contemporary science!

It was moral and social preoccupations, and the influence of motives of conservation, not of knowledge, that I tried to combat, and upon this point I have been very explicit. In regard to the second statement, my dear Amendola, I believe for my part that the moralist merely verifies, protocols, and conserves; if he does not then take note of the natural life by which he is surrounded, what must be meant is that besides being the keeper of a museum he is short-sighted as well!

I do not, however, think that Amendola seriously believes that the moralist has any great influence in establishing morals. Moral science is a *cul-de-sac*, a kind of museum where the objects, the customs of a people, are collected; moral life springs from very different conditions, although I will not deny that moralists contribute to it in part. But this part is so small as to be almost nothing in comparison with the remainder.

In respect to his distinction between science and literature, and the mixture that I would make of them, I think that Amendola has made these observations only because he was acquainted with the nature of my early education; but, even if it be granted that he made them without thinking of this, I will say that I cannot well understand this profound distinction of species, and especially its opportunism.

I am endeavouring to throw as much light as possible on my questions. What does it matter if I speak of biology or literature? All is in all and for all. Try to judge whether what I say be true, if my comparisons be sound, and not whether I take some arguments from biology and others from literature. However, I foresaw this objection, and put the reader on his guard not to let himself be taken in by it too easily. But there is more to follow.

Literature should not be decried to such an extent, for, in the end, it is the genuine form in which the first knowledge of a people is manifested. We must not forget that the first formulation of truth, and especially of human truth, is literary, and that all other forms are merely transpositions and points of view reflected from the same substance of facts and experience invented by writers.

If this is true in general it is even more true in my own special case, where the subject under discussion was psychological and physiological knowledge.

The difference between biology and literature is rather a traditional difference, a difference of convenience and of perspective, than a real difference.

What, for example, have novelists done but treat of man in the widest sense of the word, and describe and review life in its complexity, in the variety of its types and of characteristic individualities?

The true difference is that in literature we employ introspection to a greater extent, and thus what we can say of men in general is more conscious, partakes to a greater extent of our own feelings, and, in particular, is but we must yet admit that a writer, speaking of types of men very unlike himself, relies largely upon analogy and inference.

The same process, however, is certainly used more conspicuously by the man who studies the remaining part of the living world. It seems to me, on the other hand, that Amendola has seen more biology in my book than there really is in it.

We try to ignore what does not please us, and official psychologists and philosophers dealing with the science of man show an unwillingness to recognise certain facts, which is most instructive when compared with their claims to universal knowledge.

Now, Life says to such thinkers: "Observe men as they are, and in all their varieties: do not exclude one particular variety because it is repugnant to your nature. The humblest novelist, when delineating some unamiable character, displays more of the objective science of man than you who lay claim to so much; and you, who think you understand all, understand none, *because you hate.*"

Literature, then, may teach you many things, and may enable you to see life better than you do now, for you have not as yet learnt how to raise yourselves from the grade of an actor, from the position of an organ of life, and you have all the prejudices of classes, groups, and arts.

Every class, profession, or state has a particular atmosphere of feelings, ideas, and prejudices in respect to itself and to other classes, professions, and states. It would perhaps be saying too much to affirm that the object of such an atmosphere is to hold every individual fixed and enchained in his own particular state; but it may certainly be said that in those who are well anchored in their position, and who are perfectly capable of carrying out their duties, this atmosphere is more adherent and immutable than in others. From this we may draw the conclusion that, *up a certain pointy* the more a man is capable in a restricted sphere—in a profession, for example, the less he is capable of quietly judging different men and different capabilities.

The man who would know the human heart, and who asserts that he tells the truth about society, must not therefore be bound down to any particular state, but must nevertheless *feel* them all.

This is the *apparent* antithesis that contrasts being and knowing, which, in my opinion, can be explained with only one hypothesis: that there is a hierarchy of intelligences corresponding to every state or condition, and that the most *vastly* comprehensive intelligences, those which can embrace the greatest number of human characteristics, are necessarily to be found in the higher ranks of society, or at least, under deceitful appearances, they always tend to reach these higher ranks.

Replying now to the objection of confusion between science and literature, I will say that wherever something new is affirmed, one returns, to a certain extent, to a state of indifference, where diverse distinctions established by tradition are confused in apparent disorder.

All true and fecund progress in a restricted field of knowledge, as in the doctrines and knowledge of any one epoch, comes from having called in question the very *principles* of the branch of knowledge, or the entire range of knowledge, which is always characteristic—that is to say more or less individual—of every historical period.

It should almost seem that every period of life, for every single science, as likewise for the entire range of knowledge, is the development of certain principles, certain assertions, which, in the knowledge of the preceding period, had not a definitely ascertained value, but merely represented either a state of relative truth, or an approximation of it.

True progress, even in the region of the particular, of discovery, of invention, is always due to a revision of principles, and nothing is more false than to say that the development of knowledge is *continuous*, in the sense that certain routes are indefinite, or at least very long and hard. On the contrary, the varied knowledge of different epochs may be represented as divergent branches belonging to a short and partly underground trunk, and, as new branches appear and old ones die out, the fresh ones grow more *in the direction* of the trunk that bears them, without perhaps ever being able to develop in exactly the same direction.

The position I have taken up is not therefore that of Aristotelianism, nor yet of Platonism. The genius of Aristotle gave conceptions to thought, and formed future ideas which have been utilised by humanity ever since, being especially helpful in the development of the sciences during the eighteenth and nineteenth centuries. It is to Aristotle that we owe the separation of mechanics, physics, biology, and psychology, and also the theoretical preformation of a great part of contemporary scientific knowledge. And yet it has been thought possible to take back thought, *for its own good,* to a pre-Aristotelian period.[82]

Every strong and original thought, if it is a means, an open door for the majority, is a difficulty and an obstacle to be overcome by the strongest men, and it is really curious that one of the historical fatalities of progress is that of going back to appearances at a point far removed from, its development, which appear at first sight to be already overcome. Certain points of view which are at present in evidence, being now at the fullness of their ultra-modern development, may nevertheless trace their essential nucleus to very far-off periods.

All modernity has *apparently* acknowledged that Aristotle was right in his systematic development of the sciences, the principles and general trend of which were established by his genius.

We have, however, during recent times, heard more and more affirmed a discernible principle of a higher order which *appears* to us an end in itself, and which is certainly above and beyond all sciences, for it may consider them from a high standpoint in their historical development (the history of sciences), that is to say, in the very reasons of their development in view of the general ends of society, through which only they arose; and this principle is not therefore in the *spirit of science*, but in a higher order of things, as any man who is *able* to judge another is of a higher order. This principle,

---

[82] I'm not sure to what this refers since it was written in 1909, but it brings to mind the work of Martin Heidegger, who would publish *Being and Time* some twenty years later. [Ed.]

however, as a *power*, must certainly have existed previously to the historical development of sciences.

If I have dwelt at some length on this point, it is because I wished to make manifest how unjust was the specific accusation of the confusion of kinds, as I desired my work to be a radical criticism, putting aside the question whether I had attained my object, which may not have been the case.

If I have afterwards spoken of Aristotelianism and Platonism, it is only because the example of the history of sciences seemed to me not to be very common, and very probative. For the rest, I humbly sue for forgiveness from Aristotle and Plato for having (in the opinion of my critic) brought them into my own case, even indirectly, and I faithfully promise not to disturb them again for like reasons.

The study I have made of science and literature was not then, according to Amendola, examined and corrected by a philosophical valuation.

Either this philosophical valuation is something that alters the appearance of and transforms science and literature, like the patent of nobility that makes the ragamuffin of one day the peer of the next—a conclusion that I cannot admit; or science and literature have a value of themselves, without receiving another from a philosophical valuation. The problem is different, in my opinion: is what I have stated true or untrue, right or wrong? Are my science and my literature good or not?

Philosophy, in the opinion of Amendola himself, has nothing to do with sciences, and still less with literature: why, then, should we wish to review them both to see whether they have their coats properly buttoned and their sabres well polished, as a sergeant would do with a troop of soldiers?

Knowledge is knowledge, whether true or false, and a wave of a magic wand will not transform it into philosophy.

The truth is, it seems to me, that every scientist, like every literary man, artist, or practical man, has an unconscious philosophy. It is only in a few special individuals that we find the clear intellectual elaboration of these rudimentary elements; and, I would add, there are some men of letters, artists, and scientists who are better philosophers, intuitively of course, than professional philosophers themselves.

At a certain point Amendola asks me: "But why has Séra not perceived that, by letting his own personality and tastes appear too prominently, he has lessened the force and efficacy of his demonstrations?"

This question would imply that Amendola cannot have entered at all into the spirit of my exposition. From this it follows that only one man in the world is right, or right to the greatest extent—I do not mean by that that I am he; but it seems to me that from all this it follows that truth is on one side only, and this establishes hierarchies, and the why and wherefore of hierarchies. It would have been strange if, on the other hand, I had not brought personality prominently into view, and had plunged myself into an amorphous and diffuse world of equal intelligence, which is the tendency at the back of certain contemporary movements (syndicalism), that seem almost to wish for the disappearance of intelligence, as a natural necessity, from the brains of all mankind. The reaction of man against nature never found a more acute expression than this; but one at the same time more unacceptable. And, my dear Amendola, I have the differences only too clearly in mind, and I feel myself to be only too well provided with natural experience to let myself be moved by hypotheses, not, indeed, well expressed, and crude in themselves; but which, when closely examined, mean nothing but this: the inconceivable absurdity of natural equality.

In regard to what Amendola calls my principal thesis—the identification of aristocracy, physical superiority, and repugnance to work—I must draw his attention to the fact that the necessity for a concise exposition has made him present the matter to his readers rather summarily, in a manner that does not perfectly correspond to my thought. I cannot, however, blame him much for this, in view of the real difficulty of making the subject clear in a review. This hypothesis, however, that the first workmen were the weaker individuals, is not admitted, as he states, by all socialists.

Amendola asks me: "What can the truth of this thesis regarding the social origin of work tell us for or against work as a moral fact?" and he answers: "Nothing, absolutely nothing."

Well, he would be right if the moral fact constituted a *category*, an irreducible and originary conception; but if the psychogenesis which he despises so much *demonstrates* the recent and subordinate origin of the moral fact, if, on reflection, we see its mental composition from other antecedent elements of intellectual and physical life, *then* it is quite another thing, my friend, and this social origin must really be taken into account.

Does it seem to Amendola that "physical force was of service to a group of men only in a determined historical or prehistorical period"? Nonsense! This is voluntary blindness towards what is most evident, out of respect to far-off theoretical finalities, which are exchanged for immediate and present realities.

It is very kind of Amendola to apply the word *aristocracy* to those who work; but let him nevertheless recollect that some people flatter the populace merely to get themselves placed on a pedestal, and that the populace was hailed as sovereign by the bloodthirsty leaders of the revolution, who, whilst they slaughtered members of the nobility with some show of reason, sent away honest citizens to be slaughtered by the allies.

I have nevertheless laid some stress upon the conception of the form and the quality of activity which establishes classes and ranks, and I must finally conclude that Amendola has not attentively read the chapters relating to this point: "Social Rhythms," and "The Meaning of the Aristocratic Ideal." I am sorry, I must add, to be obliged to say this.

"Séra's aristocratic ideal appears to me a return to a most remote past, that is to say the contrary of an 'ideal.' " There is no reason to limit the meaning of the word *ideal* to possibilities not yet realised; but I have no desire to raise useless questions of vocabulary or conception. Now, I am convinced, like Amendola, that nothing returns identically; but at certain times it may be found necessary to go in one direction rather than in another, and this should not be called a retrogression.

If we desire a patient, just recovering from a disease brought about by sedentary habits, to walk about and take exercise, this is not a retrogression; it is only recognising and putting into practice what is most opportune for the individual, it is a wise repentance that will permit him, never again putting his active life entirely on one side, to turn once more with increased vigour and greater results to his intellectual activity.

And would you call it a retrogression to return to that wisdom which should never have been abandoned?

Then call progress the bestial obstinacy that will lead this individual to his death!

Let Amendola note that the comparison is something more than a comparison, it corresponds perfectly to the state of certain societies in the modern world.

I cannot understand, then, how the aristocratic form could have been made an "ideal" through ethical treatment. Another wave of the magic wand? But what is worse is that I have never perceived, nor do I even now perceive, this transformation.

The difference between us is therefore greatest where Amendola says that "the philosopher does not rely upon sociological and biological unreality, but draws directly from within himself his conceptions and his values." Often as I have read this phrase it has yet been impossible for me not to think of the philosopher as a conjurer who draws all kinds of things out of a hat: flowers for the ladies, ribbons and decorations for the men, sweetmeats for the children, and who at last, by way of a final surprise, lets off some fireworks from the miraculous hat. Frankly, I envy the philosopher who can draw such a splendid assortment from … nothing at all.

It is then said that I have confused the *origin* with the *value* of a thing. Well, I do not accept the method of objection, common to many philosophers, of hypnotising the superficial reader with a word on which a certain emphasis is laid, and especially of taking him out of his latitude with distinctions which are in their own nature by no means definite, and which have even been left in an almost voluntary obscurity!

But which particular value is referred to? There are so many kinds! And may it then be granted that the origin of a thing has no influence on its value? If I know of a certain man that he was born in the country, I have ninety probabilities out of a hundred to support me in thinking that he will be of under-developed mentality and of restricted morals. What Amendola affirms will perhaps be true as regards philosophical reality; but not for sociological and biological unreality, in which, however, I should prefer to remain! *Patria est ubi bene*, and I am modestly content with my unreality, although I am not secure, just as the Neapolitans live willingly on their territory although visited now and then by lava and earthquakes!

I am not displeased with the advice Amendola gives me, for I know he speaks with conviction; but … it does not suit me, as some advice I could give him would not suit him either. If he were a democrat, however, which I do not think he is, I should certainly not advise him to kill this personality of his. It is a convenient habit at the present time, a time which is somewhat dangerous for those who do not agree with it, just as the Carnival is dangerous for the man with a tall hat.

But the Carnival passes away, and everything else may pass away too. And I hope it will!

I myself think it very interesting to penetrate into the essence of morals; but ... have moralistic philosophers so far succeeded? If something has been begun, it is not in the field of philosophers pure and simple, who have always more or less limited themselves to the duties of catechisers ... without catechumens, and have taken over the functions of theologians without possessing their efficacy; but it is in other directions that more progress has been made.

Amendola may believe me when I say that I have no desire whatever to be a bad philosopher, however much I may fail of being a good scientist, which he admits I might become.[83]

I wish to limit myself to the much less apparent function of fighting for some ideas, some truths, which it may be useful to uphold, and in some field; but more especially for ideas and truths which bring with them a usefulness that is near and concrete, and certainly not far removed, abstract, and hypothetical.

I have a strong belief—I may, perhaps, be deceiving myself, but I do not think so—that more than one reader has attributed to me academico-philosophical intentions. Aspirants to chairs of philosophy may reassure themselves. Philosophy is not my aim, I solemnly declare, because I do not like philosophy to live for, but to live for philosophy, that is, for truth, which, it is well known, does not in general lead to the professorial chair.

I understand professors of science, indeed; but I do not understand professors of philosophy, as I likewise do not understand either those who say they can teach one how to become an artist, or professors of strategy. Someone may remark that there are a great many things that I do not understand! It may be so; but I at least admit that I do not, and ... it seems to me that this is some little merit. But I admit that what I have said is subject to a few exceptions ... and

---

[83] Séra did in fact become a good scientist, which is his primary legacy today. [Ed.]

every reader is at liberty to think himself one of the exceptions. And if I am desired to speak more seriously, I must not forget that Kant was a professor; but ... I cannot forget what Kant was in addition!

There remain many problems which are neither strictly philosophical nor scientific, nor yet actually practical, and they are most important at the present time. My attention shall forthwith be turned to these, even if great utilitarian advantages do not result therefrom; if, indeed, anyone is interested in knowing what I am going to do! It will be seen from this that I am more of an idealist than I show myself to be in books. These things will happen! I know a socialistic professor who, in a volume strictly scientific in character, declaims against the glaring inequality of fortune, while he possesses a magnificent house, furnished most luxuriously. I do not know whether his sincerity has been praised; but certainly he has not been accused of programmism and attitudinising.

In fact, he has had no adverse criticisms at all; because every one agrees in describing his work as one of the best productions of contemporary Italian science!

*   *   *   *   *

I take the liberty of somewhat immodestly putting forward the opinion that some of the ideas expounded by Amendola in his article "The Impotence of Thought" are not completely foreign to my work, and this appears to me even more certain as regards his other article "Choses connues, Choses mortes."

Unless Amendola, in these articles, whilst going some little distance beyond certain former ideas of his, has stopped at a point which cannot be upheld by his uncertainty and ambiguity, it would without doubt be more convenient to adopt even Croce's thesis rather than his. It is therefore with some reason that Prezzolini[84] should put forward some

---

[84] Giuseppe Prezzolini (1882–1982) was an Italian literary critic.

objection to his views, in regard to which objections, however, as I shall show later on, there is something to be noted.

If philosophy were always and in all its forms a *function* of life, Croce[85] would be right in strengthening this function, and making it autonomous, by proclaiming the omnipotence of thought, in the same way that in the State certain institutions cultivate antagonistic views, illusory in essence, to strengthen their own particular work; and in the same way that the spirit of rank, false when taken in an absolute sense, is a means of preservation for the army, and hence a vital expedient, and therefore of relative truth. But the conception of philosophy as a function is a practical, state conception of social origin, one, moreover, at which many great minds were forced to pause, and which, again, is a thousand times superior to that conception of rank in which thought, whatever substance it may contain, is held to be the most noble attribute of humanity.

This state conception of philosophy comes, in my opinion, based on a close examination of the problem, from the usual democratic view of the theoretical equality of all men.

The dualism, which even Amendola himself cannot avoid, comes therefore from his logicism which cannot perceive the error upon which he takes his stand, the untruthfulness of his premises, and from a defect of his mind; a defect, I hasten to add, that may be remedied, for I think I know Amendola. He is, in a word, in the sphere of rationalism, which, while reasoning in the best possible manner, does not observe equally well.

Amendola's mistake is shown in a phrase which he uses in reference to Croce: "the thinker," he says, "who in philosophy has endeavoured to make the abstract subordinate to the concrete." No! This is not really so. At the most it may be said

---

[85] Benedetto Croce (1866-1952) was one of the most influential Italian philosophers of the time.

that Croce has endeavoured to subordinate life to philosophy as a formation in itself, autonomous, and his error lies perhaps in this; an error in regard to life, truth, and sense of opportuneness, in view of the considerations I have given above, in regard to philosophy, of which he well represents the general interests.

Amendola vaguely puts forward a solution of the problem in these words: "There is unity between these two things; but it is in life, and it is a unity that may leave only a slight trace of itself upon thought, since to grasp it concretely one must feel it and live it."

How, even formally, can Amendola hope to invest two things with unity when he gives a greater value to one of them? Well, then, can you guess what Amendola lacks that he cannot come to a just conclusion? Something very simple and banal in the eyes of an unprejudiced observer: the conception of the hierarchy of individualities.

Objecting to some statements of Amendola, Prezzolini says: "Life is in essence something very restricted," "we can live only one life," "we must at every moment *choose* from among a thousand probabilities, and *kill* nine hundred and ninety-nine of them." This last statement considerably lessens the weight of the others.

If you grant the faculty of choice and elimination, you grant also a certain breadth in life, at least up to the point at which successive choices have gradually limited the infinite possibilities, which, on the other hand, make life less restricted.

Dilettantism, then, in my opinion, indicates a partly beneficial tendency, because it acts contrarily to a crystallising tendency which modern life brings only too much into evidence with all its might, and which is particularly prominent in the specialism and formalism of degrees and diplomas: this tendency of dilettantism, then, shows the necessity for at least prolonging a period of uncertainty, by means of which an individual may find the path that is most suitable for him. I agree that dilettantism is in a great measure an evil; but we must not forget that it contains a certain amount of good. I cannot thus tell to what extent "decisions for eternity" are suitable for higher men.

History shows that often, very often, great thinkers, writers, artists, and politicians, have begun their careers as courtiers, lawyers, and clerks.

The men whose lives can be traced from their early youth, who have begun, for example, by being pork-butchers, and who have ended as pork-butchers, have very rarely made a figure in the world, even if they became millionaires, with the exception of F. T. Graindorge,[86] who, however, when he began to philosophise, and went to Paris to see life, had given up the actual control of his business affairs, at least according to the narrative of his dear and amiable biographer!

I will not therefore say with Prezzolini that thought is broader than life, for, considered at least in its perfect and conscient form, this is very doubtful. And my own statement, which may, by logical subtlety, be taken as an argument to the contrary, is merely an approximate supposition, an intuition, that is to say, a newly-rising thought. I will only say that in some men the strongest thought coincides with the most intense life, and that these men are, or should be, at the top of the tree. It is quite possible that a vigorous thought may not be in or may never arrive at the position it is entitled to occupy; but then either this thought is in some way defective or lacking, which is most frequently the case, or the most extraordinarily difficult circumstances impede its progress, which is not uncommon.

A man may be very courageous; but if, to save some one's life, he has to run through a fire which cannot immediately be put out, he will either give up the thought of saving him, in

---

[86] A fictional character from the novel *Vie et Opinions de M. Frédéric-Thomas Graindorge* by Hippolyte Taine (1828-1893).

which case he will not attain his object, or he will be burnt alive if he rushes through the flames.

Thought, in my opinion, is only formally impersonal and abstract; but substantially it is most personal and concrete: in short, it is the only certain thing we can know of an individual, while all his physiology may remain unknown to us in spite of our greatest efforts to understand it.

Prezzolini speaks of the superiority of life over thought, and his remarks are on the whole just; but the question, I repeat, is one of hierarchy: in the highest stages life *coincides* with thought, and it is only when going down from the two parts of the hierarchical curve that we find either the predominance of life in its lower and more brutal functions, or thought more or less morbid with its abstractions and abstrusenesses. I maintain, however, that for the highest interest of life, its preservation, I incline to the first defect rather than to the second.

In a word, the fact is that the greater number of men are only, properly speaking, half-men ... if not even smaller fractions. The complete man is a being not often met with, a development attained by very few individuals of the race. This is why it is incomplete to speak of the superiority or the inferiority of life over thought. "As regards whom?" we must at once inquire in such a case.

On the other hand, if you admit this power of the choice of possibilities, *which is without doubt an attribute of thought,* you implicitly give greater value to thought, even if you maintain the contrary.

Thus, when you call this employment of choice "noble and sacred," you give it those adjectives which have up to the present always been used with the word thought.

There is an intelligence that acts as a light, as a guide to wider and stronger action, and which is superior to science itself, and to philosophy, considered as functions. In fact, the sciences and the philosophies of a given epoch are *culs-de-sac,* trunks that decay without putting forth new branches, crystallisations no longer permeated with life. The intelligence I am speaking of is rather uncertain, but it is at the same time nearer to truth, which, being rich in so many possibilities, has not merely one single formula.

These sciences, and this philosophy, although necessary, are finite expressions, approximations, half-truths; this morality is a formulation without any influence on life. Those who *make life* have a sane and healthy intelligence, for they *perceive* what are the exigencies of society, point them out to their equals, and adapt themselves to them.

I do not wish myself to be understood as drawing the conclusion that Alexander the Great was the greatest philosopher of antiquity; it is one thing to philosophise and another to reign; but I think that, generally speaking, there would be more harm done to life if philosophers reigned than if kings philosophised.

I think, then, that all will agree to the statement that more injury would be done to the state if philosophers reigned than to philosophy if kings philosophised!

The undeniable fact is that, in every stage of social life, the function of thinking is subordinated to other functions. and is merely the aim of a few groups who have not, and cannot have, the first place in society.

Whether this is just or unjust is another question, of which, in confidence, I answer the first part in the affirmative; but it is another question, it must clearly be understood, because we must take our stand on facts, and as we wish to establish a doctrine of society we must observe society as it is, and those factors which have formed part of it from the commencement of our historical knowledge; and we must entirely forget what, in the opinion of some writers, society ought to be.

Let us remember that the first qualification of the impartial thinker is to rise out of himself and to neglect the reasonings of his own special group; in my opinion, this is even the sign of a modifying virtue, of the virtue of self-improvement as a quality of vigorous thought; in other words, *true knowledge makes one abandon* successive limited points of view: first of all of individuals, then of classes, and then of nations, to make one's self reach a truth of universal value, or one at least widely applicable.

Only one consequence, however, comes from all this, a consequence that I do not evade, which is that, as I pride myself upon thinking about these things, and … I am perhaps weak enough to think myself fairly perspicacious, and as I, too, had a scientific training, I may fall into the incongruity and contradiction referred to above.

Well, in my opinion, there are only two ways out of this difficulty. One may either remain in a subordinate position and consent to be used as a passive instrument by the hands of others—limiting one's self to be, as it were, an eye that sees as sharply as possible—and give up the notion of being the hand that acts, and continue to exercise this function, really or … illusorily useful, while having had a glimpse of a higher truth, do, in short, what our Galiani[87] did, who typified this attitude, frankly aware of and consistent in his own qualities; or put himself on the level where thought and action coincide.

This latter is the greater work; but it may be long and dangerous, and subjected to alternatives, to partial returns, in short, to all the changes of fortune of great works, to carry out which one must possess genius, but more especially *primary aptitudes*, which can neither be improvised nor obtained by the greatest efforts, without reckoning upon the fact that circumstances may be absolutely hostile. For this second work,

---

[87] Ferdinando Galiani (1728-1787) was an Italian economist and writer. He was often cited by Nietzsche, who in *Beyond Good & Evil* called him "the profoundest, most clear-sighted, and perhaps also filthiest man of his century." (sec. 26) Elsewhere in that book he says, "There are free, insolent spirits who would like to conceal and deny that they are broken, proud, incurable hearts (the cynicism of Hamlet—the case of Galiani); and occasionally even foolishness is the mask for an unblessed all-too-certain knowledge." (sec. 270) [Kaufmann translation]

therefore, a transient and momentary artistic intuition does not suffice, as in the first case, an intuition which may even be forgotten without much danger, that is to say, it may not have that strength of inner persuasion which is certainly in a great measure the gift of temperament.

And when a man does not possess this temperament, he must summon up as much dignity as possible to choose the first position I have outlined.

As to this there is no possible doubt, at least for the man who has any sense of reality.

I must admit that, considering the views I put forward, Amendola's words have astonished me not a little: "Beyond philosophy, there remains only art—which we have already passed beyond, or else life, without a programme and without voice." As I am quite sure that the second hypothesis does not concern me in any way, I will deal with the first, which greatly interests me.

We have passed beyond art? But in what sense?

Like a mountain which we have climbed; but of which we can still perceive the clear-cut glacier peaks above our heads?

Art is eternal, like the mountain that every courageous man has longed to climb, and which for a moment he believes himself to possess for ever, but of which he afterwards finds he must go down the other side.

No! you must not use the plural, my dear Amendola; I for my part have not yet climbed half-way up the mountain; I should like to become an expert at it, but alas! I do not know whether this is merely a pious wish; I should certainly think myself lucky if I could one day say that I had accomplished the feat; or that I had even come near the summit. At all events, I shall certainly not act the part of the fox when he could not reach the grapes.

I do not want my words to be taken in a wrong sense. By art I do not mean formal poetry, painting, or any form distinguished by tradition in intuitive activity.

I mean that the function of art is perennial, that some particular forms of intelligence have a prevailingly harbingering, intuitive, and germinative function, while others have a verifying, methodical, and distinctive function.

As, however, the material of knowledge is infinite, these different distinctions will always exist, that is to say, *the man who sees and verifies* will always exist. The progress of thought is nothing but a continual passage from intuition to cognition; but the very necessity of this progress will always render necessary these two mental forms.

There remains the question of the hierarchy between these forms, which is differently answered by different persons, and in different epochs; but I observe this, that when social sanction protects the verifying and classifying function to too great an extent—protects science, in a word—and represses intuition, then begins the academising, or rather the very decadence, of knowledge. You require logs of wood to build a house with, do you? Very well, then, cultivate forests where the trees will grow and reproduce themselves, and do not merely heap up piles of wood!

Woe to the nations that heap up piles of wood and do not cultivate the forests! But this is just what is happening in modern times under the influence of democracy and rationalism!

Moreover, while intuition, although uncertain and obscure, is complete, cognition is always necessarily lacking in something. This is the reason why it is said that great men of action can see better than the greatest learned men. It is, in short, the practical man who gives us the first indications of a new truth, but he is a generous giver, and does not stand up for his own rights ... for the reason that even he himself often fails to perceive that he is on the threshold of truth.

The essential part of the process of scientific mentality is not so much the invention of ideas as their verification, the making them go through all those stages of passage, and at the same time those transformations, which will render them acceptable to the common sense of the majority. For this reason scientific tendencies are in their nature democratic. The other characteristic of science, the development of all the practical and utilitarian consequences of a given truth, is essentially democratic.

For the professed scientist, the *Fachmann*, the expert, a germ of truth is not so important as its demonstration, and especially its experiment. Which, for the rest, is all very well, considering its nature as an instrument, a functionary, of knowledge, which will accomplish its function the better the more severe it is.

From this, however, spring the defects of science. What does not exist is knowledge of dead things, as Amendola affirms; but scientific knowledge is something truncated from reality, an approximation. The planes of the world, comprehension and action, have become separated, but only for the greater number of men; for almost all men, but not, however, for everyone: I know very well, I may add, that this is something most men will never come to understand, and that it is useless to keep on telling them of it. What would the public do with a truth that hurt its self-love, and which would not be of use to it in any way?

It is not the case that comprehension is in touch with the past and action with the future, as Amendola says; but that the first is necessarily imperfect, and it is only in great men that the second implies a knowledge of an order superior to that of specialists and dabblers in knowledge.

It is not that the effort to adapt reality with its movement, its change, to logical forms, is in vain; but that it has merely an instrumental value for most people.

Your words, your knowledge, your symbols, although merely fragmentary objects, yet suffice for all men to call up the inexpressible image of the world, will constitute the sacred fire of humanity, and will be, *for some,* the means of enabling them to comprehend other fragments of reality.

I do not, however, consider this knowledge as of more than didactic and practical value, for perfect knowledge is to be found elsewhere. Moreover, as for this science of ours, of which the empty heads of socialists and positivists are so proud, does it not change every twenty years, or even less? It is asserted that the principles of science are securely established. Nothing, however, is so much subject to successive oscillations and integrations as the theoretical bases of sciences. And this is the best proof of my statement.

Again, how often has not the science of one period been the greatest obstacle to that of the succeeding period?

The tendency to give an *absolute value* to knowledge, instead of a didactic and practical value, constitutes rationalism, which is of course dangerous to true knowledge, as it protects the science of the present time to the detriment of that of the future.

I am not, however, so blind as to fail to perceive the great and immense advantages which may be brought about by rationalism in certain particular conditions of historical development and surroundings. I firmly maintain, for example, that it may be useful to Italians at the present time, and especially to southern Italians.

We are by nature too much inclined to be easy-going, to admiration of talent; we are all intelligent and artistic ... and this is known to everyone; so that under the appearance of intuition and a happy instinct of the intelligence, we are in great danger of falling into gesticulation, charlatanism, stereotypedness, and intellectual indolence.

I frankly declare, then, that I have more sympathy for the Hegelian logicist rationalism than for the *petit-fatalisme* of positivism, to use Nietzsche's expression. I am pleased to declare publicly to how great an extent I am indebted to Croce's work, who, I well know, has no need of my esteem to be what he is; but to whom I do not feel myself the less indebted on that account.

My sincerity, however, makes me add that, if I think a method, a discipline, and especially a *respect* necessary for most people, in order that true culture may be restored amongst us, I hope that the above-mentioned reasons for such an opportunity may be only transient, that is to say, dependent upon the present phase of development of Italy, and not upon permanent and irreducible qualities. In any case I repeat that, in general, the process of higher knowledge is creation, intuition.

We must not forget, gentlemen, that there is the king to be reckoned with, and if the king comes along we hear the shouts: "Hats off, make way for the King!" A contrary attitude would be rather discourteous, or the irreverent pose of a village Jacobin!

In a word, I am under the impression that in this respect Amendola has in his criticism been even more Crocian than Croce himself, for if Croce, in the domain of aesthetics and elsewhere, has made many affirmations which, in my opinion, cannot be accepted—e.g., that of the identity of taste and genius, it is nevertheless indubitable that there are in him, as in Faust, two men, or at least two thinkers, one of whom is in more immediate contact with reality, and it is from the latter, if the great critic will permit me to express my opinion, from whom I have learnt much, and from whom I have still more to learn. Amendola has, on the other hand, been more *singular;* but, even to a greater extent, more confined.

Must I now come to a declaration of faith? I do not evade it; but neither do I require it. I am certainly neither a materialist nor a positivist in the customary sense of the words, perhaps not even a realist; but neither do I feel myself to be an idealist. I am sure of that, and I will not tell a lie in this regard.

It may be that I shall one day reach idealism; but this "may be" does not imply the slightest germinal foresight or preoccupation; it is a simple formula of mathematical probability.

It is certain that I do not care for anticipations, that is, the acquiescence in certain systems, so to speak, for they have on their part a fashion, a renewed novelty, an eccentricity; philosophical snobbishness is, so far as I am concerned, the worst form of snobbishness.

And there are snobbish philosophers in Italy, even occupying high positions. It may be that the acceptance of the formulae of certain philosophies and ideologies is a case of pragmatism, and pragmatism still enjoys a certain reputation, although at present in a decadent state; but I have never had any sympathy for pragmatism, which I think I was the first to define as the theory of the non-theory. It may be that some people instinctively accept some formulae in the hope that they will one day possess the spirit of them. And spiritualism is discussed elsewhere by others.

For my part, however, these are examples that I will not follow. If I must accept some ideas, I will do so as clearly and as conscientiously as possible. If philosophy is the clearest knowledge of life, I will reach it by a slow but loyal, courageous, and sincere effort, and in my own presence. I wish the subconscious to have the smallest possible share, if it must have a share at all.

I do not therefore wish to follow one path more than another. The uncertainty of a shrewd, cautious person may be more certain than the certainty of a thousand easygoing, self-sufficient men, and of ten thousand credulous and hysterical women.

*   *   *   *   *

I will now deal shortly with the other criticisms.

The anonymous writer in the *Revue de Métaphysique et de Morale* attributes to me the intention of raising a scandal. If such had been my intention, I should have taken care not to send my work to this review, on the staff of which, as everyone knows, are to be found the most correct, the most moral, and the most Jansenist persons in all France!

The writer in question must remember that where scandals are concerned his own country generally takes the lead, a lead which I frankly did not and do not wish to follow.

It may perhaps be that I was wrong in sending my book to this review, and that it would have been better for me to have sent it to some other publication of the kind in which France excels, publications which are in general perhaps to be preferred to some writings that may be found in the *Revue*, for in them I should certainly have found someone to read my book more attentively and intelligently than this anonymous critic.

He also finds that my essays lack continuity, just the contrary of what all the other critics, even the most hostile, have remarked; but then, of course, when one writes a criticism one must say something out of the common. And then the desire to "se distinguer" is so very French!

The antithesis between the notion of race and that of society, which the reviewer fathers upon me, is unfortunately not mine. I thought it out, it is true, on my own account; but I must admit it was only in July, 1907, that, with my little erudition, I found it had already been expressed in an essay worthy of special consideration, but now almost forgotten, by ... a Frenchman ... a Frenchman of genius, however (there are some, it is well known; and there are many of them, perhaps more than in any other country, I will add). And this

Frenchman was none other than Broca,[88] the great anthropologist, who, so far back as 1872, was even more explicit than our own Venturi, who in his excellent but little-known book expressed almost the same opinion in 1892.[89]

I have therefore had some ... precursors, and Frenchmen into the bargain, to whom we fortunately owe some other great ideas.

If this idea has until now been neglected, I have no doubt that this has not been due to anything that could be said against it; it simply means that great interests have been opposed to its development.

The task has been waiting for others to carry out, and the honest reviewer may be sure that these others will not forget who put forth the idea for the first time.

I will not even refer to another Frenchman, one Vacher de Lapouge,[90] who took up this idea (it was through him that I came to know its original author); I am therefore sufficiently well-informed to know that certain bestialities have been thought out in France, and not only among Neapolitans or negroes.

Speaking of negroes and of certain ways of criticising books, I might say in my turn, adopting the manner of this anonymous reviewer, that he must be either a Laplander or an Eskimo. The Eskimo, it is said, see the sun only during one half of the year, and the Laplanders happen to see the sun at midnight. I think something like this must have happened to my reviewer. Let him console himself, however; the Laplanders

---

[88] Paul Broca (1824-1880) was a French anthropologist and physician. He was an advocate of polygenism, the idea that different human races have different origins rather than one common ancestor. He is the author of *On the Phenomena of Hybridity in the Genus Homo* (1864), a scientific study of race mixing.

[89] See note 20.

[90] Count Georges Vacher de Lapouge (1854-1936) was a French anthropologist and advocate of eugenics and scientific racism.

have elementary school-teachers, and good clergymen who take care of their souls, things that should be pleasing to this dear man. Oh, pedagogy and Sunday functions are certainly great consolations even to Lapland! And then the Laplanders are such sympathetic people, so amiable and hearty!

Mr. X., let us call him so, accuses me of "beaucoup d'ignorance." What seems to be ignorance today, my dear sir, may be (I say may be, not is) the science of tomorrow. In regard to the observations upon which I have based my theories, I have only to say that they have been approved by two of our greatest anthropologists, Morselli and Mantegazza,[91] the first of whom has already expressed himself in this regard, and the second will shortly do so.

Finally, Mr. X. advises me to re-read Plato's Gorgias. Either Mr. X. knows that there is something more substantial in it which will show me where I have gone astray, and he is therefore wrong in not enlightening my ignorance— although I had not forgotten to read Plato—or he wishes to tell me euphemistically that I have not understood Plato: and then I will frankly tell him that he has either not read or not understood my book. Hence a want of philosophical honesty or of intelligence. As an *honest man* I incline to the second hypothesis.

I should now speak of the reviews of Messrs. R. Schoener, Oscar Levy, Assagioli, and Picardi; but these good friends will permit me to say that I value more highly the kindness and sympathy with which they have written. And in these days of

---

91 Enrico Morselli (1852-1929) and Paolo Mantegazza (1831-1910). Morselli was an Italian physician and psychologist who wrote on mental health and also on eugenics. He wrote the Preface to Pio Viazzi's *Sui Reati Sessuali* (see note 20).

Paolo Mantegazza was an anthropologist and physiologist who defended the ideas of Darwin, with whom he maintained a correspondence. Mantegazza, like many of the other scientists favored by Séra, believed in polygenism and a hierarchy of human races. In addition to his physiological writings, which included a now-famous paper on the effects of cocaine, he also wrote a science fiction novel called *The Year 3000* which correctly predicted air conditioning, credit cards, and virtual reality.

treacherous or browbeating criticism this opinion is very significant.

I will now mention only the reviews of Chieco, Palmarocchi, and Calo. Whether they give unconsidered and random blame or praise, they are hardly worth the trouble of replying to, especially, of course, as regards the blame; for the writer who praises my book, after having read it superficially, shows that he must have some scruples or preoccupations. For the benefit of Palmarocchi, whose review has some merit, I can only quote the words of the Marquis of Colombi: "Things are either done or not done." That is to say, let him either speak of my book, or speak of his own ideas.

Finally, I will mention the opinion expressed by I know not whom in Marchesini's *Revista:* that my essays have the stamp of popular readings rather than the value of scientific criticism.

If there was one thing that absolutely could not be said of my book, it was this. I do not know where and how the writer fished up this opinion. Can this wonderful result have been due to the positivist method? Everything warrants my thinking so, and I congratulate myself upon it with its inventor.

And with this I will stop.

GIOACCHINO L. SÉRA.

www.ingramcontent.com/pod-product-compliance
Lightning Source LLC
Chambersburg PA
CBHW061555120626
46550CB00004B/1495